Early Latino Ballplayers
in the United States

Early Latino Ballplayers in the United States

Major, Minor and Negro Leagues, 1901–1949

NICK C. WILSON

McFarland & Company, Inc., Publishers
Jefferson, North Carolina, and London

LIBRARY OF CONGRESS CATALOGUING-IN-PUBLICATION DATA

Wilson, Nick C., 1947–
Early Latino ballplayers in the United States : major, minor and
Negro leagues, 1901–1949 / Nick C. Wilson.
p.   cm.
Includes bibliographical references and index.

ISBN 0-7864-2012-X (illustrated case binding : 50# alkaline paper)∞

1. Baseball players— United States— Biography.
2. Hispanic American baseball players— Biography.
3. Baseball players— Latin America — Biography.
I. Title.
GV865.A1.W545   2005   796.357'092'368073 — dc22   2005004471

British Library cataloguing data are available

Cover photograph: Rafael Almeida (*National Baseball Hall of Fame Library*)

Manufactured in the United States of America

*McFarland & Company, Inc., Publishers
Box 611, Jefferson, North Carolina 28640
www.mcfarlandpub.com*

To my mother, Rose Maloof Wilson,
who gave me the passion to write.
Every word is dedicated to her.

Acknowledgments

I wish to thank Tim Wyles at the National Baseball Hall of Fame Library and Museum, and Steve Steinberg, Jay Sanford, Eduardo Valero and the staff of The Society for American Baseball Research, for their contributions.

I am grateful to the people who helped me edit this work, including Joe Culinane, cousin Nancy Reed and Spanish-language expert Charlotte Ronning.

As I have noted in the introduction, this book would not have been possible without the research conducted by Peter C. Bjarkmann, Roberto González Echevarría, John Holway and Brent Kelley.

Special thanks to my good friends Tom Kimball and Victor King, who set up my irascible computer to handle this lengthy project.

Additionally I want to acknowledge Ralph Maya, Michael Bolton, Wayne Stivers and Jeff Brophy, chief executive at the Boxing Hall of Fame for helping me contact many of the Latin athletes.

This book would not have been possible without the encouragement and access given to me by B.T. Galloway and Wanda Padilla of *La Voz Hispana de Colorado*.

The coaches, managers, writers, broadcasters and former players who offered me their time and shared their personal stories must also be recognized.

I know that Hall of Famer Rafael Felo Ramírez must have cringed when he saw me racing towards him each time the Marlins came to Denver to play. He was barraged by my many questions and yet his kindness and patience always shone through.

Finally, the source of inspiration for the style of writing that I employed in this project was the legendary Roger Kahn. No one can take an everyday story about a common man and turn it into a spellbinding account the way he can.

Contents

Introduction

Within the forty-five days after the close of the 2003 season, the annual ritual of bestowing MVP honors began. Barry Bonds won the National League title in a run away sweep for the third consecutive year. The honor roll of eligible candidates who followed Bonds on the balloting revealed an interesting fact.

Of the top 17 players in the NL, seven were natives of a Spanish-speaking country. In the American League, New York born Alex Rodríguez won the honors, followed by Carlos Delgado in second place and Jorge Posada in third. In fact, of the top eleven players in the AL, eight were either from Spanish-speaking countries or were first-generation Americans of Latin descent.

Today, an average major league roster includes at least 25 percent Hispanic or Latin-born players. In 1900 there were none; by 1911 there were two. After World War II, American GI's returned to the playing fields, and there was, for a brief period of time, only one Latino in the major leagues. The men who cleared the barrier-cluttered road for A-Rod, Manny Ramírez and Pedro Martínez are largely forgotten. From 1900 through the 1940s they suffered discrimination, poor accommodations, low pay and home sickness to play the game they loved. The early Latin players who were light-skinned enough to make it to the majors were mocked for their foreignness, and the players in the black leagues were segregated and ignored.

This project should shed some light on the personal lives of these pioneers. Bland statistics do not tell us about their struggles. Rather, it is the backdrop of their personal lives which adds luster to their public careers.

Rodolfo Fernández, a black pitcher from rural Cuba, started his career in the late 1920s and continued in the game until 1973. But little is known about his life and accomplishments. In 1998 he told me, "The younger generation in Cuba doesn't know that we existed." Later he confessed, "You know, when we played (in the United States) we did not have a record of our achievements."[1] When Harold Rosenthal was writing for New York newspapers in the thirties, as he sadly acknowledged, "There was a tacit agreement among the papers that they wouldn't print anything on Negro baseball."[2]

Many influences led me to take on this project. The interviews with Fernández sparked the original flame. Then subsequent meetings with former stars like Minnie Miñoso and Orlando Cepeda, plus revealing conversations with historians like Felo Ramírez, made me realize one important fact: The men who knew about the secret lives of the obscure Latin heroes were themselves aging.

Historians are born every day, but the men who lived during these pivotal times are dying quickly. The stories they held in their memories had to be set down on paper. It is my good fortune to be the baseball columnist for one of this country's best Hispanic newspapers, *La Voz Hispana de Colorado*, through which I have gained access to the men who were at the epicenter of the great Latin invasion from its earliest days.

It wasn't just the Latin American or Caribbean players who could tell me their stories. Former major league and Negro League players from the 1920s I had interviewed for my first book, *Voices from the Pastime*, left me with a gold mine of information. Fifty-six men were interviewed for this book, and nearly 160 magazines and newspaper editions were studied. As I noted in my acknowledgments, this work would not have been possible without the exhaustive research conducted by historians before I began.

I did not want this work to evolve into a clinical study of racism in twentieth-century America or an in-depth review of our country's sentiments towards foreigners and African Americans—although both issues are an integral part of these biographies. The fact is that the United States offered these men opportunities, and they yearned for a chance to display their talents here. In his autobiography, *Just Call Me Minnie*, Orestes "Minnie" Miñoso stated, "I knew things weren't perfect here, but this was the United States of America, and for me a dream come true."[3]

There were American-born heroes who tried to lift the barriers of segregation in the United States while the villains refused to see the rationality of interracial play. And there were heroes and villains among the Latin players who came here, as well.

This project would have been too ponderous to read, and too overwhelming to write, if I had attempted to include the biographies of every known player who came to the United States during the first five decades of the twentieth century. I apologize in advance if any notable players were excluded or given abbreviated recognition.

Three men are featured in separate chapters because of their historical importance. The first Latin superstar, the mercurial Dolf Luque, takes the lion's share of this project, while the first Latin-born players in the "modern era" major leagues, Rafael Almeida and Armando Marsans, deserve a great deal of attention.

On the other hand, two men who, I believe, began the Latin Revolution of the 1950s are not included. Although Minnie Miñoso and Roberto Avila made their major league debuts in a handful of games during the 1949 season, their impact was not felt until the next decade.

I hope that this book will be a contribution to the vast puzzle that baseball historians are trying to assemble about those long-forgotten heroes.

1

The 1900s

J.D. Whelpley is not a name that you will easily find in baseball's archives. But his research at the turn of the century helped buttress the fears that would haunt the owners of professional franchises for the next forty-seven years. Whelpley told the nation that one-third of all Cubans were very likely bred from the mixing of races.

Harper's Weekly published Whelpley's findings on May 19, 1900, in a remote corner of their back pages, innocently titled "The Cuban Census." Whelpley wrote: "It is a surprise to the people of the United States to learn that, including those of mixed blood, only 33 percent of the (Cuban people) are negroes." He was actually challenging earlier claims that 50 percent of all Cubans had "negro blood in their veins." He did reveal that the mixing of races occurred more often in Santiago, where "…45 percent of the population is of negro or mixed blood."[1]

At about the same time, the United States Supreme Court was grappling with the issue of declaring citizenship for all natives of Puerto Rico, black and white. This was not idle trivia for the baseball establishment of that time as more Caribbean athletes displayed their talents to visiting major league teams, the question of their heritage became a primary concern. As the biographies in this book show, race and assimilation were always major issues, and race always trumped talent.

Prior to 1900 and the flowering of what we now know as the modern era of baseball there is very little evidence of Latinos playing professional ball in the United States. The first Latin-born athlete to play at the highest level of professional baseball was Esteban Bellán, a Cuban who played with the Troy Haymakers in the National Association beginning in 1871.

It would take another forty years before another player from a Spanish-speaking country would be welcomed to a major league team. (There was a California-born athlete of Cuban heritage named Sandy Nava who caught in the American Association in the 1880s, but the impact he had on baseball is of little consequence.)

Records from the early days of segregated barnstorming teams reveal that an outfielder calling himself Miguel González played briefly in 1890 for the first professional black club, the Cuban Giants. González could have been Cuban, but most likely the name was a pseudonym for an African American who wanted to give the roster a Latin flavor. But as the new century began and the modern era of baseball took shape, an initial wave of Latin athletes started to experiment with the opportunities of making a living in the United States.

As early as 1904, clever promoters in Havana, and ambitious scouts from black teams in America, sought out the most talented players in Cuba. Despite the environment of segregation that existed in 1900, America held the hopes and dreams for a new generation of Latinos who embraced this national pastime. A few minor league and semipro circuits in the Northern states added men of dark hue to their rosters, including the team from New Britain in the Connecticut League.

By 1909 there were 246 white minor league clubs representing 35 authorized leagues. Cubans of black African decent and those of light complexion started their careers in the United States with clubs like the Havana-based All-Cubans barnstorming team (beginning in 1901); the Brooklyn Royal Giants (beginning in 1905); the Cuban Stars of Santiago (1905); and the Cuban Stars (West) of Cincinnati (beginning in 1907). As talented Cubans began to swell the ranks of black ball clubs in America, respected personalities such as John McGraw and Christy Mathewson openly, and favorably, compared them to the best white players.

Fearful and reluctant, however, the major league owners still refused to mine the rich deposits of eager talent that just a signature away. The Latin firestorm began with a spark.

Julián Castillo and Luís Bustamante

The first to receive acclaim outside of Cuba

They may not have been the first Latin-born players to earn a salary playing in the United States, but Julián Castillo and Luís Bustamante were certainly the first to receive acclaim outside of Cuba. Castillo made a living at first base while Bustamante was an exquisite shortstop. They initially toured the eastern shores of the United States in 1904 and 1905 for the All-Cubans of Havana, engaging independent black ball clubs in exhibition play. The All-Cubans were so successful during their brief existence that they are now considered to have been an integral part of black baseball in turn-of-the-century America.

Among his contemporaries in Cuba and the United States, the diminutive Luís "Anguila" Bustamante was considered to be one of the greatest defensemen on the diamond. John McGraw saw him in Cuba and called him a "perfect shortstop." Similar acclaim was documented by black ball managers. Although he was an average hitter, his sure hands and accurate arm kept him in professional baseball in the United States for nine years. His career and his life were cut short because of a drinking problem, but he was nonetheless revered by many of his contemporaries. When the Cuban Hall of Fame was created in 1939 Bustamante was one of the first men inducted.

Julián Castillo was the exact opposite of Bustamente in many ways. He was a giant of a man, standing 6'2" and weighing 240 pounds. While he was considered only average with the glove, he set numerous hitting records in Cuba. He is tied with three other players for winning the most batting titles (four) in the 73-year history of the Cuban League. He also won the home-run crown three times. Men who knew Castillo in that period described him as having "legs like tree trunks, a barrel chest and broad shoulders."[2]

His career in America covered five seasons between 1904 and 1912, but he began shattering batting records in Cuba as early as 1901. Castillo was inducted into his country's hall of fame four years after his teammate Bustamante.

It would be of great historical value to know what inspired both men to leave their country and what obstacles they had to overcome to set the pace for future Latin players in the Negro Leagues. But those intimate biographies are lost to time.

José de la Caridad Méndez

It seemed that a good Caribbean wind might knock the slender
right-hander off the mound.

The average temperatures in Cuba fluctuate between a balmy 75 and 80 degrees during the month of November. So it wasn't just the allure of an extra payday that brought the congregation from Cincinnati to the sun-drenched shores of the Caribbean in the second week of November, 1908. The frigid climes of the Midwest would soon be a distant memory as they prepared to spend the next two weeks hunting, fishing and tasting the forbidden pleasures of this tropical paradise. They were the athletes of the Cincinnati Redlegs and they would be the first major league team to play *their game* in Cuba. Upon arrival at the Port of Havana they displayed an air of confidence, expecting to roll easily over the island natives in a series of 11 exhibition games.

The Reds were a veteran team whose starting lineup included a collection of players well past 30 years of age. Their third baseman, Hans Lobert, had batted .293 that season and finished among the top five hitters in the National League for total bases, slugging percentage, stolen bases and triples. For sheer physical intimidation their catcher, Larry McLean, stood 6'5" and weighed 230 pounds. Their pitching staff had posted a 2.37 ERA and their infield was anchored by that year's best defensive first baseman, John Henry Ganzel. He was also their manager. Although they were a fifth-place team in the National League how could they lose against a group of unsophisticated players who had probably never faced the wrath of elite major leaguers?

The exhibition schedule included games against the Almandares Blues and the Havana Reds, plus one contest against a team of African Americans named the Brooklyn Royal Giants.

The exhibition schedule included games against the Almandares Blues and the Havana Reds, plus one contest against a team of African Americans named the Brooklyn Royal Giants. Redlegs won their first contest on November 12 against the Havana club by a score of 3–1; hardly the rout that they had envisioned. Three days later they met the Almadares club in front of 12,000 jubilant fans at Almandares Stadium.

What raced through the minds of the Cincinnati players when they realized that they would inaugurate their tour by facing an unimpressive-looking 21-year-old black pitcher who was a rookie among his own teammates? It seemed that a good Caribbean wind might knock the slender right-hander off the mound. Although José Méndez had distinguished himself early in the season, the other Almandares players had devised a questionable nickname for their young pitcher — "Congo."

The Reds were featuring a rookie pitcher of their own on that day: twenty-year-old Jean Dubuc. The Vermont native had earned a starting role by pitching 15 games in the National League and recording a 2.74 ERA.

In the first inning Méndez retired the side in order. His rising fastball and swooping curve were impressive, but certainly, they thought, not unhittable for major leaguers. The Cubans scored in their half of the first inning on a hit by the club's veteran catcher "Strike" González. (The runner who scored on the González single was Armando Marsans, who would make a historical impact three years later.)

The score of 1–0 held for the next few innings as both Dubuc and Méndez pitched brilliantly. Méndez seemed to glide off the mound with the same effortless movement, whether the ball was floating or exploding.

As the fifth and sixth innings ended the overflow crowd began to rustle, because Méndez had not allowed a hit. Six Redlegs were retired in the seventh and eighth innings; still, no hits. In the final inning the American players must have been desperate. Their tour seemed doomed to commence with an embarrassing no-hitter at the hands of a black-skinned rookie.

It was an unlikely hero who delivered them from humiliation in the ninth inning. At 5'6" and 140 pounds, Miller Huggins, their weak-hitting second baseman (.239), caught a piece of a Méndez fastball and softly bounced it into a no-man's land just shy of second base. He reached first, but would be stranded. The game's final out concluded a 1–0 masterpiece while a new national celebrity was born.

As towering as this one-hit victory was, it proved to be only the beginning. Méndez then set out to establish a standard that has been nearly impossible to approach. On November 28 Méndez was called from the bullpen in the third inning with the Redlegs ahead 3–0 and he retired the side in order. He continued to dominate in the fourth, fifth, sixth, seventh, eighth and ninth with shutout innings.

Almandares lost, but Méndez was creating a frenzy, because the statistics reflected that he had pitched sixteen innings of shutout ball against big leaguers. On December 3 the frail looking fire-baller again started against the Cincinnati squad. They squeezed out their best performance against Méndez, but there was little pride to carry away. Five hits were all that the Redlegs could muster, and again, no runs.

The big leaguers limped away from Havana, having won only four games out of eleven, as the Cuban was preparing to pitch against other professional teams from the United States. On December 13 Méndez faced a professional club from Key West, Florida, and shut them out. On December 17 he sailed to Florida and pitched his most impressive game yet: In a rematch of the game on the 13th, Méndez pitched his first no-hitter.

On December 24 he faced the Havana Reds and held them scoreless for two innings. When his opponents pushed across a run in the third the young Cuban's scoreless streak was stopped at 45 innings. Soon, the American press would be asking about the enigmatic Cuban with super natural skills.

Historians have been divided on Méndez background, with some maintaining that he was signed to a professional contract by Almandares straight out of the sugar cane fields, while others state that he was a trained carpenter and accomplished musician (clarinet and guitar).

Men who knew Méndez during his prime have passed down bits and scraps on his personal life, but do not give us enough to complete the historical puzzle. In general he was characterized as a decent man who carried himself with great dignity.

"He was quiet and unassuming," said George Sweatt, a Negro Leaguer who played with Méndez in the twenties.[3]

Born on March 19, 1887, in Cárdenas, Cuba, Méndez began pitching at the age of sixteen. He was a capable fielder, hitter and pitcher when he was discovered by one of Cuba's greatest pitchers at that time, Bebé Royer.[4] Méndez was signed by the Almandares team and played his first professional season in the late fall and winter of 1908, racking up a 9–0 record.

José Méndez poses in 1924 in Havana wearing the uniform of the Santa Clara Leopardos. Méndez began his career in 1908 by holding the Cincinnati Reds scoreless for 25 consecutive innings in exhibition play. (Source: Jay Sanford Collection.)

During the summer of 1908 the Brooklyn Royal Giants signed him for a short barnstorming tour in America where he recorded a 3–0 record.[5] The Giants were one of the most solid of the Eastern black-owned teams, in terms of circuit victories and financial stability. John Conners was the African American entrepreneur who started the Royal Giants in 1905, naming the team after his restaurant, The Brooklyn Royal Café.

When word spread that Méndez had vanquished the Redlegs in Havana he received an offer from the Cincinnati-based Cuban Stars (West), for the 1909 season. Continuing his near-mythical display of talent, Méndez won an astonishing 44 games for the Stars while suffering defeat only twice. On July 24 he turned in his best performance, a 10-inning perfect game.

When major league teams returned to Cuba for the 1909 winter season Méndez finally proved that he was a mere mortal. He was battered by the Detroit Tigers in their first matchup, but acquitted himself well in two subsequent games. Later he beat a team of big-league all-stars. When he beat the world champion Philadelphia A's twice in the winter of 1910, the American press started to invest ink in his story. Ira Thomas, the veteran catcher for the A's, admitted, "It is not alone my opinion but the opinion of many others who have seen Méndez pitch that he ranks with the best in the game." Thomas compared him favorably to Walter Johnson and used the phrase "phenomenal" when describing the Cuban.[6]

In the 1911 winter season Méndez was matched against the great Christy Mathewson and the New York Giants in an exhibition game on Thanksgiving Day. Méndez held the Giants to five hits, but lost the game when Mathewson allowed only three.

Impressed by what he had seen, John McGraw, the manager of the New York Giants, made a series of exceptional pronouncements. Summoning any reporter who had a ready pencil, he exclaimed, "Jose Méndez is better than any pitcher except Mordecai Brown and Christy Mathewson — and sometimes I think he is better than Matty."[7] Possibly stung by that comment, Mathewson came back and defeated the Almandares Blues in a rematch — although Méndez pitched four innings in relief and allowed the Giants only one hit.

Once again McGraw held court and declared that he would pay $50,000 each for Méndez and his batterymate Gervacio "Strike" González if only they were white. Larry Doyle, the Giants' second baseman acknowledged, "I've never seen a pitcher with better control."[8]

According to legend, a nickname emerged from the Giants' admiration. They would now refer to Méndez as the *Black Diamond*, because the derisive appellation *Congo* was no longer fitting for a national celebrity.

Despite the verbal bouquets that McGraw and company were offering Méndez, the Thanksgiving Day contest was marred by controversy and retaliation. Many of the Cuban fans thought that the American players had been rude to Méndez, and when McGraw had a confrontation with catcher Miguel González they became angry. Several unpopular calls by umpire Charles Rigler, who was part of the McGraw party, didn't help calm the situation.

After the game McGraw and his friends retired to a Havana restaurant where they indulged themselves until three o'clock in the morning. Suddenly they realized that their table was surrounded by a group of Cubans who were intent on defending the honor of Méndez. One of them brandished a knife and Rigler, who was a giant of a man, responded by seizing the assailant's arm. A struggle ensued and soon the restaurant was filled with policía and curious citizens. The next day McGraw and Rigler were fined $20 each by a judge and the Giants' skipper was encouraged to pen a letter of apology, to be published in the *Havana Post*.[9]

The message was clear: You can beat the Cuban team, but do not show disrespect to José Méndez.

In addition to his other extraordinary feats, in 1911 Méndez beat the New York Lincoln Giants and future Hall of Fame pitcher Smokey Joe Williams in a game that was billed as the "Colored Championship of the World."[10] He also beat the Philadelphia Phillies twice that year, including a three-hit shutout.

Further accolades were now emerging in the (white) American press.

> Many of the black players have been as good as their white rivals, but credit never been given them for their skill. One mighty black, Jose Mendez, did manage to force himself into recognition. Major leaguers who batted against Mendez in Cuba acknowledged that he was in the [Christy] Mathewson and [Grover Cleveland] Alexander class for pitching ability and have also indorsed [*sic*] many other Cuban blacks as grand hitters, fielders, and base runners.[11]

In 1913 a rumor surfaced that Méndez had become embroiled in a civil disturbance in Cuba and was nearly killed for his association with the rebels. An observer gave this account:

> One of the recent stories from Cuba, where good baseball narratives crop out all the time: During the recent negro [*sic*] insurrection, Mendez, the famous black pitcher,

took a large gun — which he didn't know how to shoot — and went out in the hills a-revolting. One Colonel Amiel, a Cuban commander, cast a drag-net, capturing great numbers of dusky fighters, and among them, the valiant Mendez. "Stand them up against the wall and shoot them down!" thundered the ferocious Colonel. As the firing squad took its position, several of the soldiers, dropping their guns, set up a clamor: "Colonel!" they cried; "this man is Mendez the pitcher — Mendez, The Black Diamond!" Colonel Amiel turned pale. "What?" he shrieked. "Mendez? Heavens, man, what a narrow escape! If I had shot him, who would be left to pitch against the Athletics next week? Take this man to Havana under guard; protect him like a price-less jewel, and see that he doesn't get into trouble again!"[12]

Through his well-publicized victories the Cuban press had eagerly polished their new national hero to a lustrous shine. Hall of Fame broadcaster Felo Ramírez remembers that during his childhood in Cuba he constantly heard the adults speaking about Méndez. " Not only my father spoke about him, but everyone in Cuba had a lot of respect for him and loved him.

"There was a joke in Cuba," continued Ramírez. "People said that if they painted Méndez with white paint he would finally be good enough to be a superstar in the United States. That was the only talent he was missing."[13]

Méndez was a once-in-a-lifetime phenomenon during his first eight years as a professional, but the wear and tear of pitching eventually caught up with him. Already in 1913 Ira Thomas reported that Méndez was beginning to lose his once-won-derous talents: "it seemed to me on my last visit, that he had slowed up a little...." Thomas added, "He has seen years of service, has worked uncommonly hard and no doubt the effect of it all has begun to tell."[14]

According to historian Peter Bjarkman, "Almost over-night in 1915 his arm mysteri-ously went dead."[15] But a yellowed newspaper clipping dated November 6, 1915, may add another dimension to the story of Méndez's decline.

This poster from 1914 heralded the arrival of the Cuban Stars in Cleveland. Note that it promotes Mén-dez as "the best pitcher in the world." (Source: Jay Sanford collection.)

Méndez had taken the mound on October 22 to pitch batting practice for his Cuban teammates when the accident occurred. His pitching-mate Jose Figarola took his turn in the batter's box and was struck in the chest by a Méndez fastball. The coroner later claimed that Figarola died "instantaneously" from the blow, which landed just above his heart. The American newspaper report sensationalized the incident, calling Méndez "the Cuban Demon."[16]

It would be pure conjecture to state why Méndez did not pitch in the Cuban Leagues between 1916 through 1920, but the death of Figarola may have had a jarring impact on his confidence. Although Méndez did continue to play in the United States, he no longer enjoyed the reputation of an indomitable pitcher. Bowing to his increasing physical limitations, he spent 1912 through 1919 playing summer ball as an infielder and fill-in pitcher for three barnstorming ball clubs in the United States.

According to everyone who knew James Leslie Wilkinson, the frustrated minor league hurler from a middle-class white family didn't have a prejudiced bone in his body. He was the son of a Des Moines, Iowa, college president and grew up nursing a deep love for the national pastime. In 1912, at the age of 35, J.L. Wilkinson abandoned his lifelong dream of pitching in the major leagues and, with his partner J.E. Gall, organized his own professional team.

Wilkinson's strategy was unique, because he sought athletes of all skin colors and ethnic backgrounds to play. He mustered a squad of Orientals, Hispanics, American Indians, blacks and whites, and traveled throughout the Midwest giving exhibitions. The name of his organization would be the All Nations and everyone would be treated regally.

Wilkinson purchased a custom-made railroad car for $25,000 so his players could sleep and eat in their own Pullman coach. They would never again be expelled from segregated restaurants and hotels. He commissioned builders to construct portable bleachers with a canvas awning so that fans would not have to sit unprotected in the sun.

Just in case baseball wasn't enough to entertain the throngs he engaged novelty acts such as wrestlers and musicians to accompany them. In 1912 he added a woman to the squad, naming her after the eccentric temperance leader Carrie Nation. Local sporting goods stores took turns sponsoring the team to help defray the cost of uniforms and equipment.[17]

To attract talented players Wilkinson relied on his many contacts in major league baseball. Casey Stengel, then an outfielder with the Brooklyn Dodgers, would endorse black players he had seen in exhibition play. John McGraw may have been the advocate who recommended José Méndez to Wilkinson prior to the 1912 season.

The cultural gulf between the well-educated, financially secure Wilkinson and the nomadic black man from a poor island nation could not have been wider. But their relationship thrived on mutual respect and was destined to last a lifetime. Méndez joined the All Nations team in 1912, enduring an aggressive schedule that took them to Missouri, Kansas, Iowa, Nebraska, Minnesota, Wyoming and Wisconsin.

If the crowd demanded music for an impromptu dance Wilkinson's family and a few players would oblige them by taking positions on the bandstand. Méndez would join the party, seizing a clarinet from his equipment bag.

Within a few years Méndez was relegated to infield work and did very little pitching, but he could still run and hit like a young man. He also did a little managing. Another player whom McGraw once coveted had joined the team in 1913. Cristóbal Torriente, a hard-hitting black outfielder from Cuba, added power and speed to the All Nations roster for three scattered seasons.

By 1917 the war in Europe was taking a significant toll on the All Nations team. Manpower shortages and the "Fight or Work" rule forced Wilkinson to disband the club and abandon his glorious cause. Méndez was still a big box office draw, however, and his unemployment did not last long. He was quickly recruited for the 1918 season by Rube Foster to pitch and play shortstop for his Chicago American Giants. After registering a 1–1 pitching record and hitting only .189 he migrated to the Detroit Stars for the 1919 campaign.[18] In Detroit, Méndez joined a black pitcher named Frank "The Red Ant" Wickware, who had achieved national fame by outdueling Walter Johnson in a 1913 exhibition game. The team's two catchers were Cuban-born José Rodríguez and Tennessee native Bruce Petway, who threw out Ty Cobb three times— in three attempts— during an exhibition game in Cuba in 1910.

The team barnstormed throughout the Midwest, eventually gaining a berth in the Michigan Semi-Pro Tournament, which they won. Méndez again found himself relegated to the back burner while three younger pitchers saw the majority of duty. There seemed to be little time left in his brilliant career. He was nearly 33, his arm was tired and he would soon require surgery. But neither he nor J.L. Wilkinson was finished with baseball just yet.

In Chicago, Rube Foster's dream of creating an organized league for black players was taking shape and by 1919 he was beating a loud drum to get everyone's attention. Wilkinson responded to Foster's pleas and applied for a franchise, paying a $500 fee in late January of 1920 under the name of the Kansas City Monarchs. His trump card was the lease that he held on the American Association Park in Kansas City, one of the finest minor league ball fields in the Midwest.

In order to solidify his relationship with the black owners of the five other applicant-teams, Wilkinson assumed the title of league treasurer and then sponsored a ten-course banquet at the De Luxe Café in Kansas City. The dinner and a late-night boxing exhibition occurred on February 21, one week after the final constitution was drawn up for the new Negro National League.[19]

Méndez, who was thought to be working in a Havana cigar factory rolling tobacco, would be the cornerstone of Wilkinson's new team. By February 21 Wilkinson had submitted his list of players to the Negro National League offices and "Joe Mendez" was listed as one of the twelve men who had agreed to a contract.[20]

The team included future Hall of Fame pitcher "Bullet Joe" Rogan, knuckleballer Sam Crawford and two other Cubans: catcher José Rodríguez and former All Nations third baseman Bartolo Portuondo. By the time spring training had commenced in early April, Méndez was posted on the roster as a manager-player. Wilkinson would consider no one other than the *Black Diamond* to run his new team.

In appraising the qualities of each team in the new league, the *Chicago Defender* noted, "Kansas City is the only club in which the [analyst] cannot put his hand right on the one department and point out exceptional strength. But Kansas City is working under a strange manager, whose methods are not generally known…"[21]

On Friday, May 14, 1920, the Monarchs faced the hometown St. Louis Giants in their first game of the regular season. Burdened by poor attendance, the two major league franchises in St. Louis, the Cardinals and Browns, were awed by the enthusiasm — and the turn-out — of the Giants' fans. Méndez and his team participated in pre-game ceremonies that were "augmented by a parade extending several blocks in length and jazzed on by two or three highly spirited bands."[22]

Six thousand St. Louis residents jammed Giants Park while another two thousand fans were forced to listen to the cheers from street level. Although Méndez did not play, he skippered his team to a 2–1 victory behind the brilliant pitching of Sam Crawford. Holding a 2–0 lead in the eighth inning, Crawford gave up a double to the St. Louis leadoff hitter, Johnson Hill. Mendez walked onto the field and pulled his ace hurler for reliever Rube Currie, who gave up an RBI hit but finished the game for the victory.

With a record of 2–1 the Monarchs played their home opener on June 6. Hoping to replicate the pageantry they had witnessed at home openers in other cities, Wilkinson and his partners, Q.J. Gilmore and Harry St. Claire, planned for a massive celebration. It was reported that Gilmore and St. Claire "nudged the affairs to a height that will stand for many a moon as a high water mark for the debut day tooters to shoot at." In wild anticipation, the fans of Kansas City started the festivities two hours before the first pitch.

Local writer David Wyatt exclaimed, "The long line of parade hopped off promptly at 1 p.m. and besides one of the very best bands ever heard in an event of this kind, there were exactly 150 gas, electric and otherwise propelled carts [automobiles] in the line, every one owned by a Race [black] man. Fully fifty more were picked up en route." He added that, "The blare of the band dragged fully several thousand wildly enthused baseball bugs along with it."[23]

The game that followed this extravaganza was an exciting contest, although Méndez's Monarchs lost in eleven innings to the Indianapolis ABCs despite holding a three-run lead going into the sixth frame.

The season proved to be a great success overall with Kansas City holding down second place behind Foster's Giants. Filling in as an emergency starter and reliever, Méndez recorded an 8–2 pitching record, but resigned his position as manager at the end of the season. Because of arm problems he could not replicate his success when he returned home for the 1920–1921 Cuban winter league campaign.

In 1921 Méndez was replaced as manager by the knuckleball pitcher Sam Crawford, and again the Monarchs finished in second place. In 1922 Crawford's Monarchs finished in fourth place, and in 1923 the team seemed destined for another mediocre campaign — barely able to hold on to a fourth-place position late in the season.[24] On September 15 Méndez took control of the Monarchs again and led them to an incredible, come-from-behind pennant championship with a 57–33 record. Crawford left the team after the season ended.

During that two-year period Méndez had again proved himself capable as a reliever and emergency starter, recording a combined 6–0 record.[25]

One of the highlights of the 1922 season came on October 22 when the Monarchs beat a major league all-star team, led by Babe Ruth and his Yankee teammate Bob Meusel, in both games of a doubleheader.

Back in Cuba, Méndez missed the 1922 writer season entirely. The rumors persisted that the *Black Diamond* was forced to work in a cigar factory to earn money while he rehabilitated.

In October of 1923 the Cuban people had a new hero to welcome. Havana-born Dolf Luque had been a successful pitcher for the Cincinnati Reds for several years, but this season he was the best hurler in the National League. Beating out future Hall of Famers Burleigh Grimes, Grover Cleveland Alexander and Dazzy Vance, the fiery right-hander won league honors in victories (27), ERA (1.93), winning percentage (.771) and shutouts (8). From Cincinnati to Havana Luque was proclaimed the greatest pitcher in baseball. His arrival at Havana Harbor was followed by a parade and theatrical productions replicating his finest moments in the major leagues. When an extravagant public celebration was planned at Gran Stadium, Méndez was invited to attend.

Ushered to a front-row seat, the ailing hero of earlier days watched as Luque was given a new automobile and lavished with laudatory speeches. After the festivities had concluded Luque walked over to Méndez's box and acknowledged the sad truth. "You're a better pitcher than I am." Luque exclaimed. "You should have gotten this car. This parade should have been for you."[26]

The reasons for the injustice were apparent. Luque was light complected and had blue eyes. Mendez could not hide his ancestry under the cloak of Spanish parentage.

In 1924 Méndez returned to Kansas City, but he had a strict admonition from his doctor. During the winter he had undergone surgery and he was told to sit out the entire season.[27] Despite the possible consequences, he pitched occasionally and eventually led the Monarchs to a world championship in the first Negro League World Series.

The historic contest pitted the best teams from the Negro National League and the rebellious Eastern Colored League in a nine-game series. The Monarchs captured the pennant with a 55–22 record while their opponents, the Hilldale Club (sometimes known as the Daisies), had earned a record of 47–22. Foster had arranged for the series to be played in minor league and major league stadiums in Philadelphia, Baltimore, Kansas City and Chicago.

Going into the seventh game the Monarchs were down two games to three, (one game ended in a tie) with the *Black Diamond* working sporadically out of the bullpen. The game was hard-fought and extended into extra innings with the score tied at 3–3. Méndez inserted himself as a relief pitcher and held the Daisies in check while his team scored the winning run in the thirteenth inning. After rebounding to another victory in game eight the Monarchs lost the next contest, thereby forcing a final showdown in game 10 at Chicago.[28]

At the age of 37 Méndez was facing one of the most important games of his career. Having been described as "gray, gaunt and grim," he took control of a weary pitching staff and named himself as the starter in the deciding match of the series.[29] When the final out was made he had recorded a two-hit shutout, beating the Hilldale team 5–0. The Monarchs were the first "World's Colored Champions" of organized baseball.

During the ten-game series Méndez pitched in four contests, going 2–0 with an ERA of 1.42.[30] That evening he joined his ball club for an all-night celebration in the famous Sunset Inn in Chicago. The party included a musical concert performed by three of the biggest names in Chicago-area jazz. Each player had received a portion of the winners' purse amounting to $308 — about a month-and-one-half's salary. Wilkinson pocketed $4,900.[31]

Under Méndez's direction the Monarchs made it to the Negro League World Series again in 1925. Although he suffered one loss with no victories on the mound, and his team lost to the Daisies in six games, Méndez had proven his worth as a manager. But he was still a relative unknown to the majority of sports fans in the United States. His career was winding down and, despite sporadic accolades from the American press, he had never received the attention outside of Cuba that he deserved.

In 1926 Méndez signed with the Monarchs for one more season. Wilkinson had scrapped the railroad car and purchased a furnished bus for $9,000 — an extravagant expense at that time. Their expanding schedule of league games and exhibition contests required the team to travel into areas which were inaccessible by train. On these rural exhibition treks the players had to pitch tents on the outskirts of a town. Their cooking was done over an open campfire, frying fish they had just caught in a nearby river or stream.

Coincidentally or not, this was the last year that Méndez stayed with the Monarchs. Despite his tired arm, he had amassed an amazing record of 20–4 with seven saves during the seven seasons he played for Wilkinson.[32]

During the 1927–1928 winter league season in Cuba he valiantly struggled through ten games, surrendering slowly to an illness that was taking his life. When he left professional baseball after that season he had accumulated a resume that would lead to his induction in to the halls of fame in Cuba and the United States. In the Cuban League he pitched for thirteen years, ending with a 74–25 record.[33] In four consecutive seasons (1908–1911) he led that league in victories and winning percentage.[34] Pitching against major leaguers he had a record of 8–7, although in the beginning of his career (1908 through 1909) he beat them four times in six encounters.[35] Sadly, his Negro League and barnstorming records in the United States are not complete.

Fighting the effects of tuberculosis, José Méndez finally succumbed to broncopneumonia in Havana just as the 1928 winter league season was beginning. The gasps that were heard during the first years of his career were echoed again when the greatest pitcher ever to come out of Cuba died on October 31 at the age of 41.

Others on the First Wave

John García "dropped dead" during a ball game in the United States while chasing a foul ball.

The majority of Latin players who came to the United States during the years 1904 and 1905 were catchers and outfielders. All were from Cuba. Those early pioneers included José Muñoz, who started as a pitcher in 1904 and survived seven years playing for independent black teams on the East Coast.

José Figarola played for four black teams between 1904 and 1918 and is considered to be one of the best defensive catchers ever to come out of Cuba in the early years. Emilio Palomino (OF), S. García (OF) and John García (C) also came in 1904 but had relatively short careers in the United States. According to famed writer Bob Considine, John Garcia "dropped dead" during a ball game in the United States while chasing a foul ball.[36]

In 1905 two catchers, Pedro Medina and Regino García, each had a cup of coffee, but outfielder Rogelio Valdés lasted two years. Regino García won the Cuban League batting title four consecutive times between 1904 and 1907, but had problems adjusting to pitchers in the United States. Another superb Cuban hitter who could not adapt was Antonio García, who joined the All Cubans in 1905. Although his stateside career lasted only five seasons he had distinguished himself in Cuba by winning three batting titles in the 1890s.[32]

Luís Castro

Castro's historical role is in serious doubt.

If you search through any statistical handbook you will find that the first Latin-born player in the major leagues during the modern era was Luís Castro, born in 1877 in Colombia. Castro played 42 games at second base, shortstop and outfield for the 1902 Philadelphia A's and then vanished. Based on incomplete records for the past 100 years, historians have believed that Castro had paved the way for all Hispanic players. This legend is now dismissed by some sleuthing researchers as simple myth.

In 2001 Richard Beverage, the secretary/treasurer of the Association for Professional Ballplayers of America and president of The Society for American Baseball Research (SABR), challenged the presumption. An investigation conducted by Beverage and the SABR group concludes that Castro was born in the New York area and attended Manhattan College. Beverage explained, "What he might have been was a son of some sort of Latin diplomat."[38]

The discovery of Castro's exact heritage was made by accident. "In our office we have player cards and databases on virtually every professional ballplayer from 1925," said Beverage. "A friend of mine was doing some research and he found Castro's card. The card had a death year which was never shown in the encyclopedia. So we cross-checked in another old file and we came up with an exact death date, September 24, 1941."

At that point additional people joined the investigation. Beverage noted, "Eventually a death certificate from New York was obtained. He lived in Flushing and died in New York. There was some suspicion about Castro for many years but no one could pin this down."

After he left the Athletics' organization in 1903 Castro may have had a brief career with a minor league club in Seattle. Then he disappeared and resurfaced in the Southeast. Beverage conjectured, "We believe that a beer distributorship that he owned in the early teens in Atlanta would have gone out of business during prohibition. We believe that he lived in Queens for most of his life except for the period he lived in Atlanta. Where the Colombia connection came from we have no idea."

Although the importance of Luís Castro's historical role is in serious doubt, his personal life is sadly clear. "He applied for (financial) relief from our office in July of 1941," said Beverage, "And we paid him some money until he died. We sent him about three monthly payments of about $40."[39]

Why is all of this research into the life of such a obscure individual so important? To historians, the determination of the lineage of each historical figure becomes a crusade. In this case confirming the identity of the first Latin ballplayer in the big leagues has major significance. If Castro was not the first modern-age major leaguer the title then goes to a man named Rafael Almeida (1887–1968; 1911, Cincinnati Reds). Many believe that Almeida may also have been the first man of African descent to play major league ball in the twentieth century. The suppositions are rich with controversy, but add another intriguing dimension to the history of the game.

Armando Cabañas

An undesirable alien.

One of the strangest reports of discrimination against Latin ballplayers occurred in 1909, when Armando Cabañas, a fine defensive infielder in the Cuban League, was denied entry into the United States. A port officer in Key West declared him an undesirable alien. No, it wasn't his olive skin or Spanish accent, but rather his high cheekbones and slight build that caused the official to refuse him entrance: Cabañas was judged to be of Chinese descent. After his immigration problems were resolved the fleet footed infielder returned to the United States to spend the 1910 season playing for the Stars of Cuba. Perhaps it was just his weak hitting, but Cabañas never returned to the states to play organized baseball again.

Americans Visit the Island of Cuba

The great cross-trading of baseball talent between Cuba and the black ball clubs of North America had begun.

As the black barnstorming teams grew in numbers from 1890 through 1910, they started to cast their net across the eastern United States in search of gifted ballplayers. There were a few black-owned clubs that recruited players out of Cuba by employing local scouts or launching exhibition tours to the island. In the spring of 1900 a team of American blacks calling themselves the Cuban X Giants traveled to Havana to play ten games against a handful of Havana clubs. The Cubans stunned the Americans by winning several important contests.[40]

As early as the 1870s all-star teams comprising white professional players from the United States had begun to organize games on the island. During the Spanish-American War in 1898, and immediately following Cuba's declaration of independence in 1902, however, major league clubs were afraid of traveling to the island because of the uneasy political situation.

Refusing to let bullets and upheaval deprive them of gainful opportunities, a few entrepreneurial American promoters considered bringing the Cubans north. The first all-star Cuban team successfully toured the United States in 1901, inspiring booking agents to promote more exhibition games along the East Coast.

By 1907 American blacks began to journey to Cuba with different intentions. They were now being recruited to play for Cuban clubs.[41] The great cross-trading of baseball talent between Cuba and the black ball clubs of North America had begun.

The first time that a full-roster major league team played a game in Cuba was in 1908 when the Cincinnati Reds were paralyzed by José Méndez. That matchup was the brainchild of José Massaguer of the Havana daily *El Mundo*. Now the major league teams were starting to take notice, and one by one they began to engage in exhibition tours of the island.

In 1906 the Chicago White Sox journeyed into Mexico to play a fledgling ball club called El Record.[42]

By the end of the next decade Cuba had become a baseball mecca for many black players seeking equal footing. A writer for *Baseball Magazine* explained the phenomenon with a cruel pen: "A [typical] negro [sic] team started round April 1, played till October 31, and then, as a rule, sailed to Cuba. In the tropical isle, the agile coons kept on capering till March, when they picked up and returned to start things all over at home."[43]

Eustaquio "Bombín" Pedroso

Clinging to some shred of dignity, Detroit managed to score
one run — unearned.

When Cuban entrepreneur Abel Linares and his assistant Agustín "Tinti" Molina heard the news, they must have been stunned. The previous year they had signed José Méndez to their ball club, the Cuban Stars, after he held the Cincinnati Reds scoreless over the span of three games. Now they had heard of another phenomenal pitching performance, by a young Cuban named Eustaquio Pedroso.

On November 18, 1909, Pedroso, pitching for the Almandares team, had beaten the Detroit Tigers. But it was more than just a routine victory. It was more than just an eleven-inning complete game. It was a no-hitter against the winners of the American League pennant.

Despite the fact that Detroit star Ty Cobb did not join the tour, it was essentially the same Tiger team that had played in the World Series. Clinging to some shred of dignity, Detroit managed to score one run — unearned — on an error in the seventh inning. Further humiliation followed as the Tigers lost the series four games to two.

The Philadelphia As' veteran catcher, Ira Thomas, called Pedroso a "great pitcher" and declared, "He would find a place in the Majors without much trouble if he had the same chance that the ordinary American has."[44]

After his no-hitter against the Tigers, Pedroso received nearly $300 for his efforts and, according to historian John Holway, "Pedroso was feted and wined so much that he never pitched another game that winter."[45]

Salivating at the thought of combining Pedroso with Méndez in the same rotation, Linares was eager to have him join the Cuban Stars for the next summer season in the United States. In 1910 Pedroso joined Méndez and began an uninterrupted twenty-one-year career playing summer ball for three black teams.

His pitching record in the Negro Leagues is incomplete, but the right-hander did steal local headlines when he continued to do well against major league hitters in winter ball. In 1910 he went 1–1 against the Detroit Tigers. In his winning effort he pitched another 11-inning masterpiece, this time yielding five hits and holding the Tigers to one run. After he won two of three games from John McGraw's Giants, baseball scribe Robert Ripley quipped, "And didn't [the Giants] strike a few mines around Havana Harbor and come back slightly shattered and shot up?"[46]

Fans on the Negro League circuit loved Pedroso because of his humorous antics on the field, which included gyrating his large frame around the diamond while speaking rapid-fire Spanish.

Born in the small town of Quivican, Cuba in the 1890s, Pedroso mastered four defensive positions besides pitcher. In the Cuban Leagues he was considered a very

Eustaquio Pedroso (top, second from left) is pictured with José Méndez (middle at left) in this 1922 team photo of the Santa Clara club. Méndez and Pedroso were paired in the same rotation as early as 1909 with the Cuban Stars (West). (Source: Jay Sanford collection.)

powerful hitter, but in the United States his batting average was not exceptional. Like many of his contemporaries he played well past his chronological prime, pitching a no-hitter against a semipro team in Cuba in his forties.

African American Clubs Take on a Cuban Identity
Ulysses F. Grant was listed as a "Spaniard."

The first black ball club whose players received a salary may have been the Cuban Giants of Long Island, New York, in 1885. Despite the foreign-sounding name the roster was make up entirely of African Americans who worked at local resort hotels. When they made road trips to intolerant areas of the South they were protected to some degree because fans thought they were visitors from an exotic island, thanks to the name. The players would chatter in incomprehensible jibberish in the hopes that fans would think they were of foreign descent.[47] Infielder Ulysses F. Grant was listed as a "Spaniard" on the team's roster.

The practice of using Spanish pseudonyms continued for many decades. For example, Barney Brown, an African American pitcher for the Cuban Stars (West) in the 1930s, was occasionally listed on the roster as "Brownez." An unattributed editorial, perhaps originating from the black-owned *New York Age* newspaper, encouraged African American ballplayers to continue the ruse. It urged, "Until the public get accustomed to seeing native Negroes on big league [teams], the colored players should keep their mouths shut and pass for Cubans."[48]

Historian Peter Bjarkman noted the sad truth when he explained that Latin blacks were seen in a more favorable light than native-born blacks. "Since they were not African American," he said, "they were passed off as being foreigners, which did not tip the racial scales among hard-liners."[49]

A revealing insight into the profiling of African Americans versus blacks from other countries was illustrated by sportswriter Fred Dartnell in 1924. Dartnell referred to World Flyweight champion Francisco "Pancho Villa" Guilledo as being a "coloured man" from the Philippines, and then stated that since he was a foreigner, "[This] removes him from the 'nigger' class.[50]

Luís Padrón
At the ripe old age of 50, he defeated the pennant-winning teams from both leagues.

The "Mule" was so dangerous at the plate that rival teams in the Connecticut League threatened to expose him as a mulatto if he played against them. Luís "El Mulo" Padrón spread fear and earned his acclaim. He was one of the first Latinos to receive a tryout with a big-league ball club, and he was one of the few players to begin a career with a white minor league club and end it on a Negro League team. Because he excelled on the mound, in the outfield, and at second and third base, Padrón was valuable in any league. Padrón exploded on the Cuban scene during his rookie year in 1900, leading the league in both base hits (31) and pitching (13–4). He electrified the Cuban fans two years later when he led the league with a .463 batting average.[51] From the time that official records were first kept in 1884 to the final dissolution of professional baseball in Cuba in 1961, no one ever matched that phenomenal average. For some inexplicable reason Padrón was never offered — or perhaps he would not accept — a contract to play in the United States until he was into his sixth season of professional ball.

He came to the United States in 1906 to play for Poughkeepsie in the Hudson League and went to Brooklyn in the Atlantic League the following season. In 1908 he joined future big-league pioneers Rafael Almeida and Armando Marsans on the New Britain team, where they were all threatened with banishment because of accusations regarding their ancestry.

In describing the Cuban players on the New Britain team one newspaper affirmed, "All the men are said to be genuine Cubans except Padrón, who is part [sic] negro."[52] At one low point several league owners agreed to drop their investigation into his heritage if the New Britain team would not bring Padrón along on road trips. Since he was one of the top hitters in the league, the demand by team owners clearly was self-serving.

Possibly owing to the controversy over his ethnicity, Padrón was not offered a minor league contract for the 1909 season, but, strangely enough, the left-hander managed to get a tryout with the Chicago White Sox. The audition was a failure and he was subjected to ridicule by the veteran big leaguers in camp.

Padrón must have realized that playing in the white leagues was an exercise in futility, because he headed west and joined an all-black barnstorming team, the Cuban Stars of Cincinnati, in 1909. For fifteen years he played summer ball in Florida, Chicago, New York, Birmingham and Indianapolis. He retired from the Negro Leagues in 1926 but continued to pitch and manage various semipro teams.

During a series of exhibition games in 1931 he was able to show the major league moguls what they had missed. Despite the fact that he was approaching the ripe old age of 50, he defeated the pennant-winning teams from both leagues. He beat the American League champion Philadelphia A's 4–3 and the St. Louis Cardinals 2–1.

Padrón left baseball for good at the end of the 1938 season but decided to stay in the United States, working at a Ford plant in Flint, Michigan. Within one year he was dead, probably no older than 56 years old. He was elected to the Cuban Hall of Fame in 1943.

Alfredo Cabrera

"Canned back to the bush"

He was from the Canary Islands — a Spaniard by heritage, and a man destined to be on the "first list" in two categories of baseball history. By all accounts he looked twenty years older than his age. He was a prolific husband who enjoyed counting his children's shoes (eleven pairs in all) and yelling at his bat. He could also field a grounder as well as anyone in the minor leagues.

Alfredo Cabrera, born in 1883, was first signed to play in the United States in 1905 with the All Cubans barnstorming team.[54] In December of 1906 he was signed by an American promoter named Hank Ramsey, but did not report for spring training in 1907.

Cabrera had discovered that Ramsey was going to assign him to an outlaw league team, rather than an accredited minor league circuit. He eventually ended up with the New Britain Mountaineers in the Connecticut league in 1908, along with Rafael Almeida, Armando Marsans and Luís Padrón.

Within three years Almeida and Marsans would be playing major league baseball for the Cincinnati Reds. During the same period Cabrera was scouted by the Philadelphia Athletics, St Louis Cardinals and Boston Nationals. Although he initially signed with Boston he made his first major league appearance with the Cardinals. The fact that so many big-league teams were scouting this weak-hitting infielder proves that Latinos were being viewed in an increasingly positive light.

In 1909 Cabrera led the Mountaineers in stolen bases (28) and hit a solid .288.[55] Perhaps sensing a chance to make some money, the owner of the New Britain team contacted his friend, Cincinnati Reds President Garry Herrmann, with an offer to sell off his Cuban players in 1911. One reporter claimed that it was Cabrera, not Almeida and Marsans, who captured the interest of the Reds' front office. He explained, "It was said at the time that Cincinnati wanted Cabrera in preference to the other Cubans, as he was a first-class shortstop."[56] Even Herrmann's trusted scout Louis Heilbroner urged the Reds to sign Cabrera.[57] Eventually, however, the Reds demurred and O'Neil was forced to sell him to a team in Springfield.

In an unidentified newspaper clipping of the era, Cabrera is depicted as "the father of 11 children and known as a poor man ... he has a pair of shoes in his room for each one of his children, and that is how he keeps an accurate count of them." In addition he harbored other interesting eccentricities. It was written, "[He] talks to his bat during a game. If he makes a hit, he fondles the stick and talks baby talk to it, and if he strikes out he curses the bat and says papa will whip."

In 1913 Cabrera finally made the major league grade when he joined the last-place St. Louis Cardinals. The Cardinals led by manager/second baseman Miller Huggins, had the worst batting average in the National League (.247) and two hurlers who lost more than 20 games, but they excelled at defense. Cabrera was probably seen as a reliable backup to aging veteran Charley O'Leary at shortstop. Huggins played the Cuban on May 16, 1913, allowing him to bat twice. Cabrera failed to get a hit and was soon released.

In 1914 he returned to spring training camp with the Cardinals but was "canned back to the bush after less than half a trial."[58] Cabrera's enduring claim to fame are that he was the first Latin to ever play in a St. Louis Cardinals uniform, the first major leaguer from the Canary Islands, and only the third player to make a major league roster after spending time with a black ball club. In Cuba, he became a celebrated head groundskeeper at Gran Stadium.[59]

The Final Wave of 1900–1909

Pelayo Chacón spent 21 years playing and managing for independent and Negro League teams.

There was another surge of players from Cuba around 1909 that included several men who would eventually be superstars in the Negro Leagues.

Pelayo Chacón spent 21 years playing and managing for independent and Negro League teams. Chacón passed down his love for the game to his son Elio, who played three years in the National League in the 1960s. Others included Antonio García (C), Ricardo Hernández (3B) and Heliodoro Hidalgo (OF), all of whom lasted five years.

At least a dozen other Cubans played in the United States during the first decade of the twentieth century, but surviving records are incomplete. Either they show only the player's last name or the players assumed Americanized names for personal reasons.

One player of note was an ineffectual infielder named Agustín "Tinti" Molina, who played a variety of positions in the United States in 1907. The 6'4" 185-pound veteran of the Spanish-American War eventually saw his future in managing and promoting Cuban ballplayers. In 1911 he retired from active play to manage and in 1921 he purchased a Negro National League franchise, Cuban Stars (West) of Cincinnati. Molina's entrepreneurial efforts played a big part in bringing many Cuban ballplayers to the United States for several decades.

2

Armando Marsans
and Rafael Almeida

The first Latin-born men to play in the "modern era" major leagues.

Clark Griffith and Garry Herrmann wanted cheap talent and a chance to draw the growing Latin community. That's all. When they signed two Cuban men to play on their Cincinnati ball club in 1911, their intentions were not socially motivated, nor did they deliberately set out to add a new dimension to the national pastime by allowing Spanish-speaking foreigners to compete. They did not conspire to test the color line by bringing in men with dark complexions.

In contrast, John McGraw of the New York Giants wanted to field the best team he could, regardless of race or nationality. He schemed to elevate men of color and he failed. Griffith and Herrmann wanted to save money and they succeeded.

On July 4, 1911, Rafael Almeida and Armando Marsans became the first Latin-born men to play in the modern-era major leagues. And if you believe the random evidence, rampant conjecture and unsolicited testimony, they were also the first major leaguers of black African ancestry.

Regardless of the "firsts," the decision taken by Cincinnati Reds owner, president August "Garry" Herrmann and field manager Clark Griffith to sign Almeida and Marsans changed the direction of baseball forever.

The story of these two unwitting pioneers from Havana is rich with complexity and intrigue. Newspapers reported that Almeida was a scion of Portuguese royalty and that Marsans, at the innocent age of eleven, plotted against the Spanish occupation of Cuba. The two were sanitized to appear as harmless foreigners who had earned their opportunity to compete with white ballplayers through family title, education and a willingness to submit to the authority of organized baseball.

But in the end they proved to be courageous, independent and self sufficient. Almeida stubbornly held out on his Connecticut-based minor league team in 1910 for more pay. Marsans refused an opportunity to make his professional debut in the United States in 1907, sensing he could be the subject of a bidding war the next season. In 1914 he attempted to challenge the reserve clause by jumping to the outlaw Federal League, risking banishment from baseball.

Despite the public relations barrage that stressed their European heritage, both men endured racial taunts and personal threats while pursuing their careers in the United States.

Before the two young Cubans could be introduced to the American public there had to be an extraordinary public relations campaign to ease the fears of major league owners and color-conscious fans. One of the first copyrighted stories emerged in the summer of 1911 and spread to such noteworthy publications as the *Detroit News Tribune* and the *Philadelphia Inquirer*. An article printed in the Detroit paper in 1912 hints that the source of some of these biographies was none other than Frank C. Bancroft, the secretary of the Reds.[1]

In concert, the stories revealed that Rafael Almeida was "not actually of Cuban ancestry." The *Inquirer* announced that his father was Portuguese, a direct descendent of a titled Marquis named D'Almeida. His mother was Cuban, but born of Spanish parentage. One of his uncles was a wealthy governor of a Cuban province while the entire Almeida family were known to be affluent landowners.[2]

The story also insisted that Armando Marsan's father was a Spanish merchant — an aristocrat by birth. His mother was also Cuban but, like Almeida's mother, of pure Spanish descent. The paper kept emphasizing that both Marsans and Almeida were not only born of the best, and whitest, families in Cuba, they were also "raised in the lap of luxury."

One writer effused about "these two Cuban 'aristocrats' of the diamond."[3]

Soon, other newspapers were joining in. Additional articles disclosed that both families had fled Cuba during the civil war of 1894–1898 and relocated in the United States.[4] Both Armando and Rafael reportedly learned the game of baseball during their exile, with Marsans honing his skills in New York's Central Park.[5]

Readers were told that Marsans attended an unnamed American college while Almeida graduated from Havana University. Both families reportedly returned to Cuba immediately after the Spanish-American War.

But the most compelling story offered to the press was a drama in which Marsans played the lead role, bravely challenging the Spanish colonial authorities. The hated Spaniards ruled his country with an iron fist and, besides committing the routine colonialist atrocities, they had prohibited the playing of baseball on the island from 1869 to 1878. Determined to strike back, Marsans, at age eleven, became an accomplice in a plot to help arm the rebels. Boldly entering the Spanish barracks, Marsans and his young co-conspirators presented themselves to the soldiers, proposing a barter. The boys' rationed cigarettes would be exchanged for something that soldiers have in abundance: ammunition! The courageous adolescents then smuggled the bullets across town to the waiting revolutionaries.

This ruse was successful until one day the Spanish authorities caught Marsans in the act. The newspaper account failed to describe what happened next, but skipped forward to report that Armando and his family immediately fled Havana to New York.[6] (Luckily the writer had the good sense not to place Marsans with Roosevelt at San Juan Hill.)

The contrived story of the two Cubans was fed to the American public with a silver spoon, and covered in enough honey to hide the exotic spices. The *Inquirer* went to embarrassing extremes when it claimed, "it has been mainly through the expert coaching and the enthusiasm put in the game down there by these two intelligent lads that our national game has made such progress in Cuba. It has been Marsans and Almeida who have brought baseball in Cuba up to that class of efficiency, where the National Commission felt it necessary for them to pass a ruling forbidding our championship teams to play in Cuba."[7] The *Detroit News Tribune* stated flatly, "Marsans and Almeida have been the base ball brains of Cuba."[8]

Unfortunately the fabrications and misinterpretations are so thoroughly blended with the truth that we may never know the real story of the first Latinos in the major leagues. While the newspapers of 1912 connect the two Cubans to white parentage, there are respected sources which challenge that assertion.

Further, Marsans could not have attended a university in the United States before moving back to Havana after the Spanish-American War. He was born in 1887 and the war ended in 1898. And, if he had been well educated in an American University why was he continuously lampooned by the press for his fractured — and limited — English?

Although documents confirm that Marsans came from a wealthy family, there are questions surrounding the ethnic heritage of the two men. The epic biographical reference *The Ballplayers* describes Armando Marsans as "Half-black, [but] light-skinned enough to cross baseball's rigid color line…. Could be considered the first black in 20th-century major league ball."[9] Senior ranking baseball historian Peter Bjarkmann concluded that "Almeida and Marsans clearly had some Afro-Cuban blood. They were hassled by the fans as being black and taunted around the league."[10] Baseball great Felipe Alou remarked in his autobiography, "Rafael Almeida and Armando Marsans, who played for the Cincinnati Reds 36 years before Jackie Robinson came along, should be credited with crashing the color barrier."[11]

A memorandum dated December 30, 1910, from the Cincinnati scout Louis Heilbroner to Reds president Garry Herrmann mentioned a player named Alameida [sic]. In it Heilbroner noted, "He is a mulatto [sic], speaks fair English." Five days later he wrote, "Were he a white man, he might be good for the big show."[12]

In April of 1914 the legendary entrepreneur of black baseball, Rube Foster, referred to the addition of Almeida and Marsans to the Reds ball club with cautious optimism for African Americans. At the conclusion of that interview he exclaimed, with a bit of jabbing humor, "There were more Negroes on the (Reds) team than there were Cubans."[13]

When Almeida and Marsans played for a minor league team in Connecticut they were threatened with banishment on several occasions because they were thought to be of black African descent.

The debate over their heritage may seem to us a minor, if not an insignificant, controversy when men are now signed to major league contracts on ability alone. But in 1911 it was *the* most important issue. The questions of racial purity and subsequent accusations would hang over the heads of Latin players for the next four decades.

The questionable details regarding Almeida's and Marsans' boyhood exiles in New York are easily discarded, but the similarity in their physical features and the parallel path they took to the major leagues are remarkable. Almeida was 5'9" while his partner was a mere one inch taller. Both men filled out at nearly 160 pounds with Almeida having a slightly heavier frame. Their birth dates were within three months of each other in the year 1887, and both men played a variety of infield and outfield positions.

According to Marsans, he was a newsboy at the *Havana Post* when he approached the sports editor, a Mr. Banchini, expressing an interest in playing baseball in the United States.[14] Marsans credits the editor with eventually arranging his first venture abroad, which occurred in 1905 when he signed with the Havana-based All Cubans as an outfielder.[15]

One newspaper biography claimed that Marsans was plucked off the sandlots and installed as an outfielder for the professional Cuban team, Almandares, in 1904, but there is no proof of that. Records compiled in *The Biographical Encyclopedia of the Negro Baseball Leagues*, and a 1911 newspaper feature, state that Marsans did not begin his career with Almandares until 1907.

It was Banchini's influence which also enabled Almeida to join the All Cubans barnstorming team, touring the eastern United States in 1904–1905 as a third baseman.[16]

Both Almeida and Marsans possibly played on a semipro team in the U.S. in 1906, but records are not available. (Since both men played for black teams in the United States they are also recognized as the first two men to enter the major leagues after playing in the black baseball circuit.)

In December of 1906 Marsans was approached by an American promoter named Hank Ramsey and offered his first full-season playing job in the United States for the 1907 season. Although they reached an agreement, Marsans refused to play for Ramsey because the promoter had allied himself with an outlaw league. Then a bidding war erupted between two legitimate minor league teams for his services. Scranton, in the New York State League, was awarded the rights by the National Commission, but Marsans was unhappy with the decision and never reported.[17] This is the first example of the independent streak which would mark the careers of both men.

In the spring of 1908 Marsans and Almeida, along with Spanish speakers Alfredo Cabrera and Luís Padrón, signed a contract to play with the New Britain Mountaineers in the Connecticut League. They were immediately met with hostile crowds, biased umpires and constant threats of being expelled from the league because of concerns about their bloodlines. Columnist Bob Considine explained, "In their relations with fellow players [Cubans] were handicapped by a rather widespread inability on the part of American ballplayers to differentiate between Cuban and Negro athletes."[18]

The New Britain franchise was created around 1906 by Charles Humphrey when an ill-fated team from New London became insolvent, and an opening in the league became available. Although Humphrey "knew more about poker than baseball" and was said to be preoccupied with "the growing of a luxuriant mustache," he was keen enough to go after four affordable Latino prospects for his new cash-strapped team.[19]

After initially losing out on the bidding war for Marsans and Almeida in 1907, he picked up the Cuban-born pitcher Luís Padrón along with Alfredo Cabrera, a shortstop born in the Canary Islands. Also coming over from the ashes of New London was an African American catcher named Ruflange, who "had such a dark complexion that he looked more like a Cuban than the visitors from Havana."[20]

At the start of the 1908 season Marsans and Almeida joined the team, playing left field and third base respectively. Two days out of three Padrón left the mound and played outfield because of his homerun prowess.

Humphrey soon declared bankruptcy and turned the team over to Billy Hanna. Shortly after the sale Hanna sold a half interest to a theater manager named Tom Lynch, who eventually became president of the National League. Although Lynch liked the Cubans and often hoisted a beer with his minions, race relations were not going well in the less tolerant towns on the circuit. A local reporter explained, "The Hartford [Conn.] fans disliked the Cubans and ragged them during the game." He noted that a pitcher for the Hartford team named Ray Fisher "took a great dislike to the Cubans.... He knocked out two with pitched balls and Cabrera was carried off the field unconscious."[21]

During that 1908 season Marsans got his first major league nibble when an official of the Boston Braves scouted him for a brief period.

In their second season with New Britain, Almeida reversed the stereotypical depiction of a sure-handed, weak hitting Latin infielder. Swinging the bat with authority he hit .311 in 106 games, while his fielding average was a dismal .889.[22]

It was Almeida's bat and Marsans' speed that kept New Britain in the heat of the Connecticut League championship race in 1909. But during the final weeks of the season Marsans was afflicted with bronchitis and was admitted to the hospital in New Britain.[23] A popular legend from that time portrays a heartless conspirator from the rival Hartford team arranging for Marsans to room next to a patient who was soon to die. The villains surmised that Marsans had a superstitious streak and the deathly wails in the neighboring bed would cause him to flee the hospital, missing the final, decisive games. Indeed, the patient died and Marsans eventually left for Cuba, not returning to the United States until the 1910 season. It is pure speculation whether the death had any thing to do with his decision.

During the winter of 1909, Billy Hanna, the New Britain owner, discovered that the other team owners were plotting to exclude blacks from their league for the next season. Hanna rushed to Cuba to protect his investment. One writer speculated that Hanna "went to Havana to see his Cuban players and get documents to show that they were genuine Cubans and not negroes [sic]."[24] During his brief stay the Cubans threw a lavish party for their beloved team owner which consumed the next 36 hours. They all felt that the proper documentation (forged or not) had been provided, and their careers would continue in Connecticut. They had no idea that the ax would fall on one of them after the season began.

The preseason program for the 1910 campaign began without Señor Almeida, who refused to return to New Britain. There is no reason to believe that Almeida's genealogical documentation, which Hanna sought in Cuba, was compromising or incomplete; rather, the logical conclusion is that Almeida was angry over the paltry $200 monthly salary he had been paid during the past two seasons.

Fortunately, he did not witness the sad spectacle that occurred after the first game of the regular season, when Hanna called his team together and made an announcement. The documents that he had obtained in Cuba had cleared Marsans and Cabrera, but not his best slugger/pitcher, Luís Padrón.

It had been discovered that Padrón was "part negro" [sic] and he would be dismissed from the team at that moment. No doubt their sole catcher, Ruflange, suffered a similar fate. The pressures of running a barely profitable ball club and accommodating the watchdogs of the Connecticut League were beginning to weigh heavy on Hanna.

Several days later the entire team checked into a New Haven resort called the Lighthouse Point. It was a dry county on Sunday, but the players managed to secure beer — and to get caught by the local constabulary. Their arrest prompted Hanna to sell the team to Dan O'Neil, a former scout for the Pittsburgh Pirates and a friend of Cincinnati Reds president Garry Herrmann.

The 1910 season continued with Marsans and Cabrera picking up the offensive slack, tearing up the base paths with their lightning speed. Almeida did not return to New Britain until his monetary demands were met in mid–July. Although he was consistent on offense, hitting .306, Almeida made 24 errors playing second and third base in the final 55 games of the season (.895 FA).[25]

During the latter days of the 1910 season the owner of the Pittsburgh Pirates, Barney Dreyfuss, came to New Britain to watch Almeida and Marsans play, but no offers were made.

Almeida and Marsans could hardly have known that they were inching closer to a major league tryout during the winter season of 1909–1910. A series of exhibition games were scheduled in Havana which pitted the Cubans against three major league clubs. In the stands was the Cincinnati Reds' secretary, Frank Bancroft, who watched their sterling performance with rapt interest.

One reporter noted that Almeida's bat was "mainly responsible" for the Cubans' victory over the world-champion Athletics in one game.[26] Coincidentally, the Cincinnati Reds' manager, Clark Griffith, also heard about Almeida from his business manager, Frank Van Croft, who may have seen him in Cuba at an earlier date. Initially Bancroft recommended that the Reds sign Almeida, but the idea faced a cool reception.

In December the Reds' president Garry Herrmann received a scouting report on Almeida from Louis Heilbroner which read in part, "[He] is very independent and worth some money. Stopped at hotel at Hartford, claiming New Britain Hotel not good enough for him. Good fielder and good arm but bad on bases. Is afraid of the base runner and does not touch them when he sees the spikes." The report added, "New Britain has three Cubans on the club; [Alfredo] Cabrera playing short is considered the best player."[27]

Based on the reports from Van Croft, Bancroft and Louis Heilbroner, Herrmann decided to take a chance on the three Cubans in 1911. After all, Marsans was willing to play for O'Neil and his club for a pittance, $200 per month; the $350 that Herrmann was willing to pay would seem like a giant step up.[28]

After arranging with the owner of the New Britain club to audition them on options for a 30-day tryout, Herrmann discovered that Almeida had never reported to spring training and Marsans had abandoned the team in mid–May.[29] Marsans had

Aramando Marsans (left) and Rafael Almeida (right) are now considered to be the first Latin-born players in the modern-era major leagues. (Source: National Baseball Hall of Fame Library, Cooperstown, N.Y.)

walked out after a heated argument with the team's manager and Almeida had decided to stay in Cuba to sort out personal business.

When word reached Marsans and Almeida that there was an offer to try out with a major league ball club they immediately booked passage back to the United States. Based on their rapid return it can be assumed that the pair knew the importance of this tryout. Arriving in Connecticut, Marsans and Almeida boarded a Cincinnati-bound train with the son of the owner of the New Britain team, Frank O'Neil: The agreement with the Reds called for a representative of the New Britain club to personally deliver the players and collect the option fee at the railway station.[30]

"Is Baseball to Lower Color Line?"

On June 23 the *Cincinnati Tribune* broke the news of the impending arrival of two "very dark skinned" ballplayers, while another paper led with this headline:

IS BASEBALL TO LOWER COLOR LINE?
REDS SIGN TWO CUBAN PLAYERS IS STEP
TOWARDS LETTING IN THE NEGRO

There has never been any legislation against the black man in baseball but it has always been understood that no Negro should play in the major leagues.... Clark Griffith has signed two Cubans who may or may not be part Negro. These particular Cubans may be of Spanish descent and they may be of African ... the peculiar social conditions of the island making it mighty hard to determine the exact standings of most of the natives regarding color.[31]

Clark Griffith (right) the president of the Cincinnati Reds, and Garry Herrmann (left) the team manager, launched a public relations campaign starting in 1911 to keep Marsans and Almeida in the big leagues. Newspapers reported the Cubans as being "Two of the purest bars of Castillian soap ever floated to these shores." (Source: Nick Wilson collection)

On June 28, 1911, Garry Herrmann went down to the train station to personally greet the two Cubans and their chaperone, who were arriving on the 7 P.M. train. Having never met the pair face-to-face, he was anxious: He knew the color line could not be broken, but he had been assured that they would pass the test. At the same moment he was told the Cubans were prepared to disembark, two black Pullman porters stepped out. According to legend, Herrmann nearly suffered heart seizure.

Despite the oppressive heat that had blanketed the eastern United States during those weeks, both Cubans emerged from the train nattily attired in coat and tie. Herrmann was quick to short-circuit any further gossip by telling reporters that "Both are perfect gentlemen." The *Philadelphia Inquirer* echoed Herrmann's evaluation that "Neither one drinks, are quiet and inoffensive players."[32]

A myth persisted that Clark Griffith had only wanted to give Rafael Almeida a tryout, but because of Almeida's limited knowledge of English, Armando Marsans was asked to accompany him as an interpreter. An article appearing in *Newsweek* thirty-three years later attempted to re-create the historic moment: "Almeida, who bowed like a bullfighter at the fans when he made a hit, brought along an interpreter. After watching the two Cubans on the field Griffith remarked: 'I like his interpreter [Marsans] better.'"[33]

Both were signed immediately, but it is thought that Marsans signed first. Recalling that day, baseball historian Lee Allen wrote, "It's almost impossible to realize what a furor the signing of two Cubans caused in 1911."[34]

Griffith now had to negotiate the purchase of the two Cubans from Dan O'Neil of the New Britain club. He knew that Pirates owner Barney Dreyfus had made an inquiry but backed off when he found the price to be too high. Griffith and O'Neil eventually settled on $6,000, with Almeida costing the most at $3,500, while Marsans' price was $2,500.

The Cincinnati club they joined was mired in mediocrity. The year before Marsans and Almeida arrived, the Reds had the second-worst fielding average in the National League and the third-worst ERA. They had not finished above fourth place since 1905 and their attendance had dropped from 424,000 in 1909 to 300,000 in 1911. (Continuing to plummet, they drew only 100,000 fans in 1914.)

On July 4, 1911, the Cincinnati Reds introduced their two new players to the National League while on a road trip in Chicago. Their historic debut was muted because both Almeida and Marsans occupied positions on the bench until late in the game. By luck, Almeida was the first Latin-born player to appear in a major league uniform when he was conscripted as a pinch hitter, and struck out, in the seventh inning with the Cubs leading 8–1. Marsans followed him later in the inning with a pinch-hit single. In the bottom of the seventh Almeida took over third base for Eddie Grant and Marsans went to right field for the team's hottest hitter, Mike Mitchell.

In that groundbreaking contest the Cubs also fielded a foreign-born contingent: German-born pitcher Emil Richter started the game and batterymate Jimmy Archer was from Ireland.

Later in the game Almeida hit a single in his second at-bat, delighting the reporter from Havana who was assigned to follow the Reds and report on the success of the pair. An American newspaper was impressed with the interest that the pair generated at home. A scribe noted, "special reports on all [Marsans'] doings on the field are wired after each game to all the leading newspapers of Havana."[35]

Under the wilting heat of near-100-degree temperatures both men completed their initiation with cool reserve, going 1 for 2. The second game, which ended in a tie after 10 innings, did not see a reappearance of the two Cubans.

By the end of the season the Reds' front office would look past another sixth-place finish while pointing to their success in acquiring their bright new rookies. Almeida had proved his worth by hitting a solid .313 while Marsans hit .261 and successfully made a steal every five times he reached base.

Suddenly the American press was allocating print-space to the young Cubans. Marsans was touted as the "Ty Cobb of Cuba" because of his speed and daring on the bases, while Almeida was hailed as a future batting champion. Hall of Fame broadcaster and historian Felo Ramírez said, "[Marsans] was a great player. In Havana he was a called the Ty Cobb of Cuba. He was very fast and he liked to make jokes about how fast he was. One day he was talking to some kids and he told them that he hit a line drive and he was so fast that when he turned at first base to go to second the ball hit him."[36]

The novelty of fielding two Cubans also had a positive financial side, since it brought out many Latin fans in the major league cities of the East. The 1912 season began with great expectations. The opening of the Reds' new stadium, Redland Field (later named Crosley Field), was meant to draw new fans without having to expend more money on quality ballplayers. Attendance grew by 16 percent but the team ended the season with a fourth-place finish and a league-worst batting average of .256. The lone bright spot on offense was Armando Marsans, the only member of the roster to hit over .300. He also stole 35 bases, second-best for the team. For his efforts, he earned $400 per month, or $2,400 for the season.[37]

Marsans' .317 batting average in 416 at-bats proved to major league recruiters that Latin-born players could hit as well as field. It was the best hitting performance by a Reds player in seven seasons and it earned him a starting position in center field for the next season.

Almeida, the player who was originally touted as being the next batting star of the league, played in only 16 games that season, hitting a dismal .220. But when he returned to Cuba for the winter league, Almeida pounded major league pitchers during a series of exhibition games. On November 14 he hit a double and two singles off the great Christy Mathewson.[38]

As the Marsans and Almeida constellation grew brighter the publicity campaign was re-launched. Respected baseball scribe Robert Ripley emphasized that Marsans was "a pure Havana feller of Castilian parentage."[39] Another writer revealed that Marsans' principal diversion was a rich white man's sport, "Shark fishing in the waters of Havana Bay."[40]

With Marsans firmly secured for $3,400 for the upcoming 1913 season, Garry Herrmann went shopping for additional talent.[41] This time he grabbed two aging but popular box-office draws from the Chicago Cubs.

Sacrificing one of their starting pitchers, Bert Humphries, and a light-hitting third baseman named Art Phelan, the Reds picked up two future hall of famers—36-year-old hurler Mordecai "Three Finger" Brown and 32-year-old shortstop Joe Tinker, who also became the team manager.

The 1913 experiment was destined to fail. Joe Tinker sounded almost despondent when he learned of the trade. He said, "It was hard for me to leave Chicago. I played on the Cubs for eleven years and no one can do that without experiencing a regret at leaving."[42] He was even more discouraged when he learned that his nemesis and former keystone mate, Johnny Evers, had been named the new skipper of his beloved Cubs.

Training for the upcoming season was a disaster, and because of constant rain and a major flood the team spent a good deal of time training in a gymnasium. Opening day saw the Reds lose to the Pirates by a score of 9–2 and by early May the Reds had lost 16 of their first 20 games.

When they arrived in New York for a series against the Giants, a freelance writer named J.R. McDermott tracked the team to the Endicott Hotel and found some of the players in the lobby "with long faces.... They were unwilling to talk of their dark series of defeats and were at a loss to explain the situation." He then cast his net over manager Tinker, who was "much depressed," but more willing to talk: "It looks as though I were awfully rotten as a manger.... I am offering no alibi."

He then became more defensive and told McDermott how "painful" it was to direct the Cincinnati club: "the infield was shaky and the pitching uncertain," he asserted. "They believed, perhaps unconsciously, but none the less certainly, that they had no chance and when men fall into that state of mind it is all but impossible for them to win."[43]

Although Tinker had the best offensive season of his career, hitting .317, and Brown won eleven games with an ERA of 2.91, the team struggled to a seventh-place finish and attendance slumped by 25 percent. Once again Marsans did well at the plate, hitting .297 (second only to Tinker), stealing 37 bases (second best on the team) and leading the league in steals for a portion of the season. But Almeida was finished.

The "shaky infield" that Tinker had made reference to included the poor-fielding Cuban third baseman. In July of 1913 Herrmann attempted to sell Almeida for $1,500 to the Nashville baseball club of the Southern League. The reply from Nashville president W.G. Hirsig came in the form of a telegram which misspelled the name "Alameida" and begged out of the purchase, citing poor attendance and a lack of funds.[44]

It was ironic that the man the big leagues wanted most, Rafael Almeida, should fade into obscurity while his partner, Marsans, would be a magnet for the press, off the field and on. Almeida played in only 50 games, making 10 errors and hitting .262. Before the season ended he would be shipped off to a southern league and would never return to the big show. He departed major league baseball after three years, with a decent career average of .270, but ruptured his reputation by committing 26 errors as a utility fielder in only 88 games. (He appeared as a pinch hitter and pinch runner in another 14 games.)

From this point forward Marsans was on his own.

Beginning with the introduction of the first Latino players and continuing for the next six decades, the American press was unmerciful in their ridicule of thick Spanish accents. One example appeared in the October 1913 issue of *Baseball Magazine*:

> Our Cuban friends don't always have the same ideas. A few days ago while Rafael Almeida was visiting his old pals someone asked Almeida and Marsans if they wouldn't like tickets to a grand opera. "Si, si," Accented Marsans, delightedly. "I love gran opera — eet ees fines of all entertainment for a gentleman!"
> "I thank you very much" negatived Almeida, "but I care not to go. To me gran' opera eet soun' like de screech of de beeg tomcat, and about so much sensible!"

Marsans lashed back by referring to the mocking journalists as being lower than " the kindergarten class."[45] The press pointed to this reaction as a sign that he was temperamental and too independent. One national magazine claimed that he "did not take authority too well" and used the phrase "go to hell" much too frequently.[46]

But his actions proved that he was a team player at that time. When he realized that he would be late for spring training in 1913, Marsans sent an apologetic letter to Herrmann: "I am marooned here [Havana] against my will. But the cigar business [in] which I placed all my savings, don't let me leave this city ... but I am in perfect shape, because I play twice a week. I request permission to sail from here to the training camp on the 20th.... I am anxious to make up for this delay."[47]

At the conclusion of the 1913 season Marsans returned to Havana to manage the Almandares Blues club. Waiting for him was an award, created for him by the Havana City Council to honor his successful year with Cincinnati. During the public tribute he was presented with a medal struck in solid gold and embossed with the phrase "Cuba's greatest player." The money used for the forging of the medal was reported to have been appropriated from the city's Emergency Fund.[48]

If there was one rule that major league baseball owners clung to with an angry passion it was the reserve clause. The dread ordinance stated simply that once a player signs a major league contract he is bound to that team for as long as the owners wished. If an individual held out for more money he could be barred from organized professional baseball for life. The only way a player could go to another team was by being traded or sold by his contractual master. It was unjust and it was slavery. Even the dictatorial commissioner of baseball, Judge Kenesaw Mountain Landis, thought that the clause could not hold up to a challenge in court. But in 1922 the U.S. Supreme Court unanimously voted to uphold it.

With this in mind it is easy to understand why the creation of a third major baseball league, the Federal League, in 1914, caused so much distress. Disenchanted players jumped to the fresh venue in droves, clutching lucrative bonuses paid by their new bosses. Rumors of defection involved every celebrity in major league baseball. The stars who embraced the new league included Edd Roush, Hal Chase, Eddie Plank, Ed Reulbach, and Chief Bender.

Baseball Magazine described the fear that was surging through major league front offices, noting the extra perks that some players were demanding lest they jump to the Federal League. Phillies pitcher Tom Seaton received "a raise and his wife's traveling expenses" and his teammate, catcher Bill Killefer, received a huge contract worth $6,667 per year for staying put. (Washington Senators owner Clark Griffith secretly asked the American League to pay for a salary increase to Walter Johnson after their star pitcher was courted by the upstart league.)

In jest, the magazine conjectured that Armando Marsans would request "A Victrola, to be set at his room in all hotels, and loaded to play "La Paloma" with phonograph attachment shouting, "Viva Cuba Libre" every hour."[49]

Indeed, the Reds were not immune to the revolutionary changes. The two cornerstones of Herrmann's revitalization program, "Three Finger" Brown and Joe Tinker, signed to play in the Federal League for the 1914 season and, in hindsight, the trade of pitcher Bert Humphries for the duo was an unmitigated disaster. Humphries had finished the 1913 season with the Cubs, leading the National League in winning percentage with a record of 17–4, while compiling an ERA of 2.69.

Marsans could not have been oblivious to the fact that he was now thrust into the position of being the team's most valuable asset. In the cast of players he was no longer a supporting actor, and as the 1914 season was approaching, the Cuban slugger demanded a larger salary. Herrmann would later claim that they reached a mutual agreement on a salary increase before the season started.

Eight weeks into the 1914 season Marsans was, once again, the top hitter on the team, accumulating a .298 batting average. But there was growing turmoil behind the scenes, and during the first week of June Marsans presented Garry Herrmann with his ten-day notice of resignation. He was heading to the outlawed Federal League.

Herrmann exploded publicly: "Last winter we sent him an offer to Cuba of $3,800 for the season. He wrote back asking for an offer of $4,400 per season for a period of two years. I have the letter now with his own signature ... agreeing to play two years for this figure. In other words we met this proposition without argument...."[50]

When Herrmann finally contacted Marsans he asked him, " What do you think your services are worth ?"

"Seven thousand dollars," the Cuban replied.

"Utterly impossible," was the answer.[51]

In the end, Marsans signed with the St. Louis Federals for $21,000 for three years. He had made less than $10,000 during the previous three with the Reds.[52]

It wasn't only the lucrative contract that made Marsans take such a dangerous step. He was having a serious personality conflict with the Reds' new manager, Buck Herzog. Baseball writer Willis Johnson reported that Herzog had said a number of things to Marsans that were "not at all to the liking of the classy outfielder." He labeled Marsans' feelings towards Herzog "bitter" and stated that money was not the main reason he split to the Federals.[53]

When he walked out of the Reds' clubhouse, Marsans asked the head groundskeeper to forward his equipment on to him in St. Louis. After several weeks and numerous telegrams Marsans sadly realized that his gloves and spikes would probably never arrive: The man he thought was his friend would not betray his employer.[54]

The Reds were not about to sit idly in the corner while their star player broke his contract. On June 8 it was reported that "Garry Herrmann had Marsans on the long distance telephone this morning for an hour, working tooth and nail to persuade the fleet footed outfielder to return to the Reds."[55] On June 14 manager Herzog officially announced that he had suspended the Cuban after he broke ranks. Then Herrmann's lawyers filed suit to thwart the defection.

Days later a newspaper article disclosed the results of the legal action: "Armando Marsans, the former Red outfielder, who jumped to the St. Louis Feds, and was prevented from playing with that team, left for his home in Cuba, saying he would wait until the courts decided where he was to play—but never again would he play in a Red uniform."[56]

Marsans played only nine games for the Federals, hitting .350. He had risked everything and seemingly lost.

Organized baseball announced that the renegade players were pariahs and they would never be allowed to return. But behind the scenes, Herrmann was attempting to orchestrate a reconciliation.

The Reds were placed in a difficult financial position, because the court allowed Marsans to continue collecting his income from the Federals while "the Reds were compelled to put up a bond of $13,000 to cover his salary, and the Reds will have to pay if he is awarded to Cincinnati."[57]

Herrmann received advice from his closest colleagues, including Ben A. Hirschler, who suggested a Machiavellian strategy to force Marsan's hand. Hirschler had spent time in Cuba and claimed he was an intimate friend of both Armando and his father. In fact, he seemed to know every nerve ending in the Marsans household.

He suggested to Herrmann :

> (1) Cable his father the circumstances ... and the matter will be settled in a day or two. He is playing a baby act and I am quite sure that his father can whip him and bring him to time.
> (2) Another suggestion is that you get in touch with Mr. Henry Straus, with whom Armando signed a contract to handle his cigars in Cincinnati. Marsans is very enthusiastic about his cigar business and holds it closest to his heart. If he can be made to realize that his actions with the Cincinnati Baseball Club will not help the sale of his cigars, I am sure that he will act differently.[58]

Herrmann, however, had a different plan. In mid-season 1914 he sat for an interview with *Baseball Magazine* and pleaded his case nationally. He not only presented himself as an impoverished owner who had been betrayed by the man he'd lifted from obscurity, but he also justified the reserve clause, by asserting that the Federal League would jeopardize the only contractual clause that protects owners from bankruptcy.[59]

During the winter league season of 1914–1915 Marsans was reported to have dispatched a friend to the United States to inform the press that he would return to major league baseball if "the Giants will give him shelter." However, "he will not sign unless he gets a bonus of $2,000."[60] In addition, a New York writer named Joe Vila reported in January of 1915 that Marsans told a friend, "I made a serious mistake when I joined the Feds and I want to come back if things can be arranged."[61]

Encouraged by the rumors, Herrmann enlisted John McGraw in February, and later the diminutive manager of the St Louis Cardinals, Miller Huggins, to go to Cuba and plead for Marsans' return. Despite Marsans' earlier suggestions of playing in New York, McGraw was rebuffed soundly. "I wouldn't play for your ball club, Señor McGraw, for $20,000. I don't like it!" shouted the Cuban, his abrupt about-face apparently ignited by the bad press he had received: Marsans added, "Least of all do I like the New York baseball writers ... they have always thought it funny to poke jokes at me."[62]

Huggins later testified to the Federal District Court of Chicago that he promised Marsans that the St. Louis Cardinals would take his contract from the Reds in exchange for catcher Mike González. He promised the Cuban that "a satisfactory trade could be arranged," but that offer fell through also.[63]

The Reds released a story in September of 1914 which intimated that Armando's brother Francisco would come to the U.S. and play in his brother's stead on the Cincinnati roster.[64] Meanwhile, during the 1914 winter league season in Cuba, Marsans was playing under the name Mendromedo to protect the owners of a Havana team. He was encouraged to hide his identity when the National Commission of major league baseball threatened to punish any Cuban ball club which hired a player from the Federal League.

But, on August 19, 1915, Marsans won a significant battle when a judge on the

Federal District Court dissolved the injunction restraining Marsans from playing in the Federal League, primarily because the Reds' contract failed to bind him for 1915 and 1916. From his chambers in St. Louis, Judge Dyer stated that Marsans "may play with any club he wishes during 1915 and 1916."[65]

Marsans, now rusty from months of inactivity, returned to the Federals for the final quarter of the season, and hit a paltry .177. His tenure was limited to 36 games because on August 26 he was "seriously spiked" in a game in Chicago and was inactive for two weeks.

With all legal avenues exhausted for the Reds, Herrmann could do nothing more than stand back and hope that the Federal League would crumble under the weight of its legal bills. Indeed, in the winter of 1915 major league baseball and officials of the Federal League signed a peace treaty. The renegade circuit would abandon its cause and big league owners would partially compensate Federal League owners for their losses.

Marsans had taken a bold step. He refused to stay bound to a team where he had contempt for his boss, Buck Herzog. Although his defiance was short-lived he proved that a player could jump from one team to another and not be banned from baseball. The Cuban stood firm against the major league owners and made them sweat for a moment.

Despite all the threats of banishment Marsans returned to the legitimate baseball world in 1916 and signed with the St. Louis Browns, where he batted a modest .254. Midway through the 1917 season Marsans (who was hitting .230) caught the eye of Yankees manager "Wild Bill" Donovan. Wanting to unload outfielder Lee Magee (who was hitting .220), the Yankees traded the once hard-hitting veteran for Marsans on July 15, 1917. They also dumped $4,300 per year in salary: Marsans was earning $4,000 per year while Magee was drawing about $8,300.

One scribe noted, "The attitude of the club owners was that neither could possibly get stung because both players were so punk that the one received in trade couldn't possibly be much worse."[66] Donovan responded that [Marsans] "believes that a change of scene may help him."[67]

Marsans reported to New York on July 16 and joined his new teammates for a road trip commencing in Cleveland. His first game in a Yankees uniform was a strong confirmation that they had gotten the best part of the swap. On July 19 Marsans was added to the lineup as a center fielder, batting sixth, directly behind Wally Pipp and Frank "Homerun" Baker.

His two hits and two stolen bases in that game helped deliver the fourth-place Yankees to a 5–0 victory. In a long-winded tribute the *New York Times* waxed ecstatic over Marsans' contribution on a key play: "[Manager] Donovan decided it was time to introduce Armando Marsans into the Yankee squeeze play club, and the Cuban delivered with a perfect bunt, scoring Peck [Roger Peckinpaugh] and leaving the bases still filled, as Marsans beat out the bunt."[68]

During his next game Marsans stole another two bases. The Tigers' catcher, Oscar Stanage, one of the best defensive backstops in the league, could not contain the fleet-footed Cuban that day.

For the next four weeks, however, it appeared that opposing pitchers and catchers were quickly learning how to tame Marsans. By early August he had only two more stolen bases and his batting average with the Yankees had dropped below .230. If it was any consolation to manager Donovan, the trade was evolving into a bust for both clubs. Magee hit a miserable .170 in 36 games for the Browns.

But suddenly the Cuban caught fire again in the second week of August. On August 9 he had two hits in a game against the Cleveland Indians, including a clutch single in the ninth inning. A New York newspaper reported, "Marsans, the Cuban perfecto, set the crowd boiling with joy when he cuffed a single to centre which pushed Peck over the plate with the run which tied the count."[69]

On August 10 the Yankees faced the Indians again at the Polo Grounds. In the first inning Marsans continued his streak with a double that drove in Yankees third baseman "Homerun" Baker. Demonstrating his speed, Marsans advanced to third on a fly-ball out and broke for the plate when Roxy Walter sent a drive to deep right field. His feet-first slide into home plate was successful as the throw was wide, but the spikes on his left foot caught in the ground and his leg snapped at the ankle.

The *Times* lamented, "Marsans has been hitting the ball and filling up a big gap among Yankee batsmen." They termed the accident "alarming" and a "setback" for the team.[70]

Fortunately for Marsans he was still young (29 years old) and determined to return. His rehabilitation in Cuba would keep him idle for the entire winter and early spring, but he managed to regain his strength from an injury that would have ended the career of many other players.

Armando Marsans wearing Yankee pinstripes in the spring of 1918. Friction between him and manager Miller Huggins in July would prematurely end Marsans' season and big-league career. (Source: Nick Wilson collection.)

During the off-season "Wild Bill" Donovan was sacked. Not only had he led the Yankees to two losing seasons during his three-year tenure, he had also raised the ire of American League President Ban Johnson. In early August of the 1917 season he had been suspended and banished from the stadium grounds by Johnson for an indefinite period for harassing umpire Bill Dineen.

Embarrassment for the Yankees reached new heights on August 8 when the *New York Times* reported that Donovan "wanders" around the stadium during games, "disguised." They revealed that he would migrate to the press box until the umpires appeared, and then hide in the stands, "as if the sheriff were after him."[71]

Rather than wait out his suspension, Donovan fanned the flames by seeking legal counsel. Eager to bring a new direction to the moribund team, the Yankees owner, Jacob Ruppert, began searching for a replacement. Ban Johnson strongly suggested the former manager of the St. Louis Cardinals, Miller Huggins.

Thus, when training camp broke in April of 1918 Marsans rejoined the Yankees, and met his new manager. Huggins was different from Donovan in every way. Marsans could stand next to the gnome-like Huggins and feel like a giant. Although the Cuban was only 5'10" he was still four inches taller, and outweighed the diminutive skipper by nearly forty pounds.

Huggins was cerebral and disciplined and expected much from his players. When Marsans began the season hitting poorly he was benched, and by mid–July he had played in only 37 games and was batting a mere .236. Whether it was frustration or simply a need to change his environment, Marsans broke his contract and returned to Cuba after a game on July 15. The *New York Times* later dubbed him "the temperamental Cuban centre fielder."[72]

The Yankees ended the 1918 season in third place. In 1919, still without Marsans, they improved with a second-place finish. Ruppert and Huggins had now launched a restoration project that would eventually create the greatest sports dynasty in history.

Following the conclusion of the 1919 season a group of veteran Yankees players traveled to Cuba to engage in a series of exhibition games. In Havana, the New York first baseman, Wally Pipp, met with the enigmatic Marsans, who had been absent for over one year.

According to Pipp, "Marsans declared that he was anxious to come back and play with the Yankees." Pipp seemed to be advocating a reconciliation between Marsans and Huggins and reckoned that the Cuban would be a positive addition to the team. "Marsans has been playing ball and is in fine shape," Pipp reportedly told the Yankee skipper.[73]

When the *New York Times* learned of the brief reunion they exclaimed, "If Marsans is in as good shape as he was a few seasons ago his hitting ability and speed on the bases will be a big help to the club…. It may solve the Yankees' outfield problem."[74]

But Manager Huggins was not about to play the role of the forgiving father in the parable of the prodigal son. Paraphrasing Huggins, the *Times* reported, "the club would make no effort to coax Marsans, the Cuban outfielder, back into the game. Marsans is under suspension and it is not likely that he will be asked to come back."[75]

And why not? The Yankees had been acquiring marquée players during the previous twelve months, and now they had an outfield consisting of veterans Ping Bodie, Duffy Lewis and a converted pitcher named George Herman Ruth.

Marsans resurfaced in the United States in July of 1923, playing for a minor

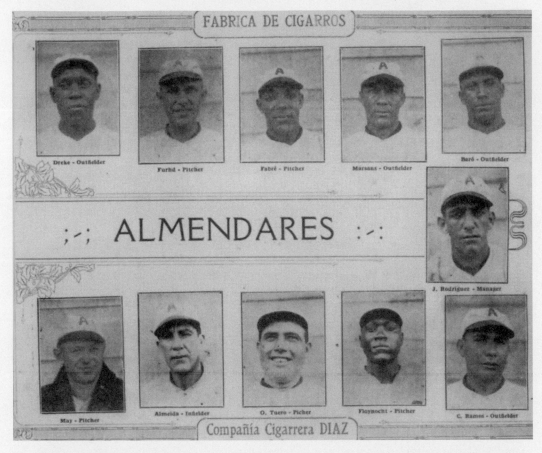

Both Almeida (bottom, second from left) and Marsans (top, second from right) were 36 years old when this team photograph of the Almandares Blues was assembled in 1923. Their teammates included Cuban-born major leaguers José Rodríguez and Oscar Tuero. (Source: Jan Sanford collection.)

league club in Kentucky. A Louisville paper welcomed the famous Cuban and proclaimed in its headline, "Don Armando, Victim of Racial Oppression, and Once Cuba's Most Famous Baseball Star, May Show Something Left as Member of Louisville Colonels." The paper claimed that many fans in Cincinnati felt that Marsans was the victim of unjust dealings in the 1914 incident with Herzog, but it stopped short of detailing what it meant in the headlines by "Racial Oppression."[76]

As the season neared its conclusion Louisville writer A.H. Tarvin admonished the Louisville fans for not appreciating the running skills of their Cuban outfielder. He wrote, "Few had ever seen anything of the sort before … there is not a more intelligent player in the game than Marsans, who seems to have an uncanny knack of knowing what to do and when to do it."[77]

Marsans also found time that year to play briefly with the Cuban Stars West in the Negro League.

In the mid to late 1920s Marsans managed a Cuban amateur team sponsored by the exclusive Vedado Tennis Club and continued to play until he was nearly 40, when a broken leg ended his playing career.[78] In the 1940s he directed the famous Marianao club in Cuba and then moved to Mexico to manage Tampico in the Mexican League.[79] In 1945 and 1946 he led Tampico to consecutive Mexican League titles.[80]

Cuban legend Minnie Miñoso has his own memories of Marsans. "I played for him when he was managing the Marianao ball club in Cuba," said Miñoso. "He was my first manager. That was in 1944 and '45, and I was with him a couple of years. I liked him [because] he used to be very funny, but when you played the game you better mind your business."[81]

As a manager in the Mexican League, in 1946 Marsans received an accolade he never would have imagined back in his playing days. One May afternoon Marsans was conducting pre-game conditioning with his ball club when he was approached by a gaunt Babe Ruth, leaning heavily on a cane. He asked Ruth if he remembered him from their playing days in the late teens. Ruth was a man who could never remember a name, but he immediately knew the face. "Sure I do," he replied. Later that day Ruth privately praised the Cuban for a managerial decision he had made during the game.[82]

Rafael Almeida returned to Cuba as well, and after his playing days ended he managed amateur clubs. Adrian Zabala, who played briefly for the New York Giants, remembers what a dashing figure Almeida projected:

> When I was thirteen years old [1939] I was on an amateur team and our manager that one year was the famous Rafael Almeida.
> *He was definitely dark skinned but that didn't stop him from getting into the big leagues though. He played third base for Cincinnati way back before I was born.*
> He was called "El Principe" [The Prince] because he was dressed really nice all the time. He dressed like he had a million dollars. He had a cigar in his mouth and always dressed in white. He wore a white Panama hat and had a big ring.
> He was a very nice man, but I was young and he didn't pay much attention to me.
> I remember one thing about him. He always tried to teach us to pull the ball to right field. He [continually] said, "When you get a man on first base try to hit the ball to right field because the first baseman has to hold the runner. You've got a big hole out there."[83]

Marsans died on September 13, 1960, in Havana, two weeks before his 73rd birthday. His eight-year major league career ended after 655 games in which he played every infield position, plus outfield. His career batting average was .269. In two big-league seasons he hit over .300, barely missing in a third with a .297 average. Eight years after Marsans died, his lifetime friend and history-making partner Rafael Almeida died at the age of 80 in Havana.

3

The 1910s

The decade of the 1910s ushered in the first group of Latinos to play major league baseball, while the creation of independent black clubs in America continued at a faster rate. Because of growing interaction between African American entrepreneurs and Havana-based promoters, the opportunities for both white and black Cuban players increased steadily.

In 1912 the All Nations team was formed, welcoming all races—and genders—to its roster. The team survived until 1918 and was the forerunner of the famous Kansas City Monarchs, which flourished from 1920 through 1950. In 1912 a barnstorming team called the Cuban Stars of Havana was formed by Dr. Hernández Henríquez. The following season he created the Long Branch (New Jersey) Cubans. Although the team was short-lived it launched the careers of many Latino players.

In 1916 the Bacharach Giants were created, with headquarters in Atlantic City, New Jersey. That organization survived for 19 seasons. The Stars of Cuba was another team which offered employment to men of all shades, touring primarily in the Midwest in 1910.

An organization of brief tenure called the National Association of Colored Baseball Clubs of the United States and Cuba was meant to bridge the final gaps between players and teams in the two countries. Its president was Walter Schlichter, the white owner of the black ball club called the Philadelphia Giants.

The most successful venue for Latinos was the Cuban Stars (East), based in Harlem, which was operated for most of its existence by the towering figure Alejandro (Alex) Pompez. The club began operations in 1916 and lasted for 14 years.

Cristóbal Torriente

Baseball historian Bill James named him
the 67th greatest player of all time.

He could have been mistaken for just another drunk, seeking shelter in one of Chicago's many flophouses. The man who spent the frigid winter of 1928–1929 subsisting on bootlegged liquor was not just any transient, however. He was, in the words of Felo Ramírez, "The most powerful hitter in Cuba"—Cristóbal Torriente.[1] His close friend Rogelio Crespo could not understand why Torriente had decided not to return to the warmth of Havana after playing so well in the 1928 season for the Detroit Stars, of the Negro National League.

By February of 1929 his body was wracked by the ravages of alcohol and inactivity. His face was swollen out of proportion, hiding his sharp features under a mask of puffy flesh. Torriente's once rock-hard physique was now a gelatinous apparition, and at the age of 31 he had run out of options.

When the time came to pull himself out of his dark, dank apartment and report to spring training it was evident that he could not play. In the batter's box he was unable to stand up straight without losing his balance. One fellow Cuban player, sickened by what he saw, commented that Torriente's only friend was the bottle.[2] Except for one season of semipro ball in 1930 and brief appearances in 1934 for the Cleveland Cubs and Atlanta Black Crackers, his career was finished.

It must be assumed that Torriente had led a pretty lonely life. Barnstorming with black teams for seven years and laboring in the Negro League for another nine was tough duty. His life in the United States consisted of struggling with a new language, living out of a bus for 14 summers and dealing with racial restrictions. Either the loneliness or his own biological failings eventually took over.

No one can pinpoint when Torriente started abusing his marvelously talented body with alcohol, but America's experiment with prohibition did not stop him from consuming unsanitary distillates or traveling back home to Havana where taverns were wide open.

If there was ever a man who was born with a storm cloud over his head it was Cristóbal Torriente. Here was a man who possessed so many natural skills that he was elected to the consensus First Team in the All-Time, All-Stars of Black Baseball. To put that honor in perspective, consider that thousands of men played on black teams between 1900 through the 1950s and Cristóbal was voted one of the three best outfielders. It wasn't only that he could dismember a man with his vicious line-drive shots. He could also run like a deer, field as well as anyone and occasionally take the mound to pitch. He was a six-tool man.

Baseball historian Bill James named him the 67th greatest player of all time, ahead of Hank Greenberg, Roberto Clemente, Ernie Banks, Ken Griffey Jr. and Christy Mathewson.

The Los Angeles Times called him the *Babe Ruth of Cuba*, and although we have dissected practically every moment of the Bambino's life, we know but little about Cristóbal. The unanswered questions about his sad existence leave us to glean only a few silver threads of truth.

We know he was born in 1895. Although official baseball records do not show his exact place of birth in Cuba, baseball historian Roberto González Echevarría claims he was a mulatto born in the town of Cienfuegos.

He is such an enigmatic figure that there have been at least a half-dozen different spellings for his full name. In 1917 *Baseball Magazine* called him José Torrente, while others nicknamed him Carlos. When he joined the Chicago American Giants in the Negro National League he was listed on the roster as Christopher Torrenti.

Very little is certain about his personal life, either. Was he ever married? Did he have children? We know he died alone and penniless but what triggered all the sorrow and misery this giant suffered in his short forty-three years?

Little is known about his family, although there were several prominent families in Cuba who shared that name. One of the more famous individuals was Dr. Cosme de La Torriente, who was appointed the Cuban Ambassador to the United States on September 3, 1923. As suggested by Echevarría, many of the black Cuban players we honor today, such as José Méndez and Martín Dihigo, were probably born with slave names. Torriente may be no different.

There are also contradictory descriptions of his physical appearance. Although Babe Ruth called him "Black as a ton and a half of coal in a dark cellar," others referred to him as "light skinned Spanish" or "Indian color."[3] Several accounts have pointed to his kinky hair as the one factor that made major league owners back off.

He batted and threw from the left side and, despite his stocky proportions could run very fast indeed. The noted historian of black baseball, John Holway, tells us that Torriente joined the Cuban army at the age of 17, but there seems to be no record of his education, the background of his parents or whether he had siblings. He came into the army as a husky lad and was assigned to hoist artillery pieces onto mules.[4] Because of his natural athletic ability he probably played on the army team during his entire military duty. One story tells that, during a pickup game with a group of his fellow soldiers, Torriente fouled off a pitch that hit the catcher, Alejandro Crespo, in the forehead, nearly killing him.[5]

Documents list Torriente at 5'9" and 190 pounds and photographs taken in the 1920s show a muscular, fireplug build with strongly carved facial features. His teammates from the Negro Leagues described him as "a fine fellow to get along with," who had "a good disposition." But they all used the same superlatives to describe him physically: "Powerful" and "Big and strong." His physical dimensions were alternately compared to Muhammed Ali (in the shoulders) and Babe Ruth (In the upper torso). One ancient pitcher described his batting stance as like that of Roberto Clemente when he stood deep in the batter's box. Another teammate said he wore a red handkerchief around his neck, while a Negro League fan remembered that he wore bracelets on his wrists and shook them before he swung for the fences.[6]

In 1913 entrepreneur Agustín "Tinti" Molina plucked Torriente away from the Cuban army and stuck him under his wing. Molina probably saw him play during one of the army's frequent games, scheduled throughout the country. The promoter arranged for the young slugger to join his Cuban Stars, which barnstormed throughout the Eastern and Midwestern United States. That was the same team which had launched the careers of Rafael Almeida and Armando Marsans, eight years earlier. While Almeida and Marsans were of lighter complexion and made it into the majors, Torriente's road to the big leagues was blocked by a white gate.

After starting the 1913 barnstorming season in the United States with the Cuban Stars, Torriente left the club and joined José Méndez on the All Nations team. He returned to the Cuban Stars (West) of Cincinnati for six full and partial seasons, from 1914 through 1918. He also jumped back to the All Nations team for a part of the 1916 and 1917 seasons.[7] The Cuban strongman began playing winter ball in 1913 for Havana, then moved to the Almandares team from 1913 through 1916.[8] For some unexplained reason he did not return to Cuba to play for two years, in 1917 and 1918. Disappearances such as these seemed to mark his entire life. The gaps in his baseball record reflect the uneven, mysterious route that his personal life took.

In 1918 Molina recommended Torriente to Rube Foster, the Negro League pioneer and owner of the Chicago American Giants. Because of the nationwide call to arms in 1917, Foster's team had lost some of its most valuable players to conscription. In fact, the Giants had lost an inordinate number of men compared to the other black league teams. Owing to his versatility, Torriente was seen as an everyday utility player, filling in for draftees Leroy Grant, first baseman; James Lyons, outfielder; and pitchers Bill Dismukes and Tom Johnson.[9]

Had Rube Foster foreseen the turbulent relationship he would have with his Caribbean fireplug, he probably would have not taken the chance. Records are not available for his 1918 season, but Torriente played only four confirmed games for Foster's Giants in 1919. The beginning of the 1920 campaign was particularly important for Foster. In February of that year he had engineered the creation of the Negro National League and he was under a considerable amount of pressure to make it a success.

When his players reported for preseason conditioning on April 4, Torriente was absent. When spring training contests began

Cristóbal Torriente in 1920. He had his most productive seasons from 1920–1925 with the Chicago American Giants of the Negro National League. By 1929 he had drunk himself out of baseball. (Source: Jay Sanford collection.)

on April 11 the Chicago American Giants were lacking offensive firepower and dropped their first game to a white semipro team 4–2. The *Chicago Defender*, a weekly black-owned newspaper, bannered a headline, "FOSTER'S CREW ARE TROUNCED."

The details of the game included the observation that "Rube worked a patched up outfield Sunday, that is only a temporary circumstance, as Torrentti [sic] will get in soon."[10] When the final week of preseason games were played, beginning on April 25, Torriente was still in Cuba. On April 30 Foster cut short a business trip and returned to Chicago to inspire his team to their first victory of the season against a semipro team called the Romeos.[11]

On May 1 the *Chicago Defender* headline read, "HELD UP."

The report went on, "Torrentti [sic], star outfielder of the American Giants, has been held up in Tampa, Fla., by immigration officers pending a hearing from

Chicago."[12] Hurriedly, Foster contacted the authorities at Tampa through the immigration office in Chicago.

By the evening of Saturday May 8 Torriente had arrived by train and settled in at the Franklin Hotel on Indiana Avenue. The next day he set the Negro League on fire. With the regular season already one week old Torriente made up for lost time by hitting a double, scoring twice and leading his team to an 8–3 victory over the Chicago Giants.[13]

News reports continued to praise him during the season for his "fine exhibition of fielding, hitting and all around play."[14] He finished the 1920 campaign with a batting average of .396 and didn't slow down for another four years. Torriente hit .337 in 1921 and followed with averages of .350, .389 and .331.[15]

In those early twenties Torriente also developed a reputation as a playboy who couldn't resist the nightclubs. Foster attempted to quell his nightlife activities with fines and suspensions, but they didn't seem to work. The slugger reportedly angered his teammates with his nocturnal meanderings and in 1926 he was traded to the Kansas City Monarchs, rejoining José Méndez.

Seemingly rehabilitated, Torriente was leading the Monarchs with a .339 average when he sabotaged his career again. In mid–August of 1926 he had lost a valuable diamond ring, but when the owner of the Monarchs refused to reimburse him he quit the team.[16]

In 1927 Torriente was either summoned by, or exiled to, the Detroit Stars, who were struggling to shed their "mediocre" reputation earned over the past six seasons.

He filled a gaping hole in the Stars' offense by hitting .320 (third best on the team) and started three games as a pitcher, winning two.[17] Unfortunately, Detroit still ended the season in the middle of the eight-team league.[18]

The following season the Stars' manager Bingo DeMoss employed Torriente as a pitcher and an outfielder in 37 games. (They played 91 league games that season.) The Cuban ended the season with stellar numbers, compiling a 7–3 pitching record and a .336 batting average.[19]

That winter he surrendered completely to his demons.

To Rodolfo Fernandez and the other players who once saw him in his prime, it was all terribly sad: There was so much that he had squandered.

In Cuba he had built a reputation as most feared hitter in the game. His career batting average in the Cuban League was a staggering .351.[20] He led the island league in batting average twice, hits three times and home runs once. In 1916 he finished with a batting average of .402.[21] In 1916, 1919 and 1922 he led his countrymen in stolen bases. Batting against major league pitchers he had an average of .311.[22]

Two men who played with him in Cuba were not hesitant with praise. Armando Marsans told an American reporter, "That boy has them all beaten a mile," while one of Cuba's best hitters, Manuel Cueto, said, "There is the greatest natural hitter in the world."[23]

In the Negro League he was equally impressive, with a career average (1919–1928) of .327.[24] He even had a winning record as a pitcher (15–5) during his professional career in the United States.[25]

The oft-told story of Torriente outslugging the Bambino in an exhibition game in Cuba in 1920 is legendary. As usual, John McGraw had scheduled his team for a series of games in Havana. As an additional draw, Babe Ruth was offered a sizeable amount of money to join McGraw for several games.

The showdown between the two sluggers took place on November 4. Ruth went 0 for 3, reaching base only on two walks and an error. Torriente drove in six runs, hitting three home runs and one double.

Although this output was impressive it is only fair to note several points. First, Torriente was not facing the Giants' starting rotation. McGraw was using his regular first baseman, George "Highpockets" Kelly, as the starting pitcher. Kelly, who had pitched in his younger days, yielded ten hits in eight innings. In the fifth inning he handed the ball to Ruth, adding a new dimension to the showdown.

Although the Bambino was out of shape, tipping the scales at 240 pounds, he was still the same man who had dominated the American League pitching statistics four years earlier.[26] With Babe Ruth on the mound Torriente slashed a double to left field to drive in two runners. The Cuban fans went wild and Ruth, disgusted with the outcome, made some unfortunate and disparaging remarks.

Torriente's achievements that day cannot be invalidated by the shortcomings of Ruth's girth nor Kelly's inexperience. McGraw wanted to sign him on the spot, but he openly expressed his frustration: Torriente's kinky hair would not pass the censors.

It was a dramatic display of power, but Torriente's reputation was not founded on the fields of Almandares Park that day in 1920. A full three years before his face-off with Ruth, *Baseball Magazine* had made a stunning proclamation:

> One of the greatest batsmen in the world is free and foot-loose, unsigned, open to bids from any manager or magnate. He is Senor Jose [sic] Torrente [sic], of Cuba, an outfielder and mighty slugger such as Cuba has not seen in many and many a year. A lefthanded hitter, he pulverizes southpaws as well as righthanders; he drives the bullet to the end of any field and his baserunning is a picture of perfection.
>
> Why then doesn't some club seize him without delay? Why is he not seen before this week is out clad in a big league uniform?
>
> Alas, Senor Jose Torrente, the wonderful batsman, is as black as the ace of spades.[27]

According to that same article, Christy Mathewson exclaimed, "I don't remember many big league batsman who can even compare with this fellow…. He has the speed of Cobb on the bases."[28]

There were two men who remember seeing Torriente in his last nomadic years. Orestes "Minnie" Miñoso was in his first week of professional ball in Cuba when he was stopped by Torriente on the field. Miñoso recalled, "He was sitting (near the dugout) and he came up to me and said 'Hey kid, *chicito*, don't do that.'" Jolted by the unexpected confrontation, Miñoso listened.

"He told me that he didn't like the way I tied my shoe. I had a ring on my shoe, tied on to the shoe lace. He said, 'If you tripped you would break your leg; you might never play again.' So (out of respect) I put the ring a different way."[29] According to

Miñoso, Torriente had been given some type of coaching position with the Cienfuegos team.

In the summer of 1935 Torriente was back in Chicago. Rodolfo Fernández was a pitcher for the New York Cubans that season and his team was finishing a long road trip with a stop in Chicago to play the American Giants. Just as he was preparing to leave for the stadium he saw Torriente in the hotel lobby, looking for the Cubans' field manager, Martín Dihigo.

When he found him, Torriente begged, "Well I don't have a job or anything. Can you give me a job?" Dihigo took him up to his room and called the team owner, Alex Pompez.

"Mr. Pompez, you know Torriente. He's in poor condition. Can you help him?" asked Dihigo. Pompez, sensing the desperation, said, "Allright. Have him come with us. Come back with us to New York and be a coach."

Fernández knew that this was a mere band-aid to a larger wound. He recalled, "Torriente wasn't in good condition. He was once a powerful hitter and a good pitcher but finally he had nothing left. In 1935 Torriente couldn't play ball, so it was a pretty good thing that Dihigo wanted to give a chance to him."[30]

As word of Torriente's plight spread among those who had known him, the St. Louis Cardinals' manager Frankie Frisch commented to a writer, "In those days Torriente was a hell of a ballplayer. Christ, I'd like to whitewash him and bring him up."[31]

In 1938 Torriente endured a miserable and lonely death in New York City from the complications of tuberculosis. When some of his former Cuban teammates heard about his death they purchased a wooden coffin and draped a Cuban flag across it. Then they contacted a politician in Havana and shipped his body back to Cuba. Felo Ramírez noted, "I think he was buried in a special cemetery with many monuments in Havana. Many important people are buried there and it was popular with the tourists."

In judging Torriente's career and personal life, the "what-ifs" must be weighed against those of other great players. One has to wonder what great heights Mickey Mantle, Jimmie Foxx and Grover Alexander could have scaled if they had been freed from their addictions. What unreachable records could Martín Dihigo, Rube Foster and José Méndez have set if there had been no color line?

The great Cristóbal Torriente struck out on both counts.

Emilio Palmero

"Palmero the ageless marvel."

At the turn of the twentieth century John McGraw tried to sign dark-skinned Cuban infielders Antonio María García, Luís Bustamante and Pelayo Chacón. Later he coveted Cristóbal Torriente and publicly offered tens of thousands of dollars for José Méndez.

In the end, John McGraw got southpaw pitcher Emilio Palmero. This time McGraw found someone who seemed to be a perfect fit, because Palmero not only exhibited marvelous control on the mound but was also physically acceptable to major league baseball. This Cuban had reddish-blond hair, blue eyes and freckles.

At first, the press actually fawned over Palmero, remarking on his size and raw strength. The scribes had reasoned that if McGraw saw greatness in him then it must be a story. One writer introduced him to the nation by announcing, "In answer to many inquiries: No, Palmero is neither a new pitcher's delivery nor a soap. Palmero is a ballplayer who may yet stick around in the majors."[32]

Emilio Palmero was born on June 13, 1895, in Guanabosa, Cuba. After completing his schooling he went to work for the Remington Typewriter Company in Havana as an office clerk. Most likely he was not hired because of his extraordinary ability to deliver interoffice mail. Emilio Palmero was a former high school pitching star who could deliver victories for the company's amateur baseball team — the Remingtons.[33]

His life changed in 1913 when he was spotted by an eccentric newspaperman and part-time bird dog named Pepe Conte. After arranging a tryout for Palmero with one of the professional clubs in Havana, Conte launched a one-man publicity campaign targeting McGraw and other big-league club owners. Conte's original press releases in October of 1913 stated that his protégé was an amateur phenom, having been awarded a medal in high school in 1911 for being the best pitcher on the island. Conte added that Palmero was 20 years old and "by far the best pitcher that Cuba has produced."[34] In an effort to cleanse Palmero's background, Conte told writer Bozeman Bulger that Emilio had "Irish blood in his veins and that his ancestors were originally called Palmer."[35]

Another New York paper characterized Palmero as being 17 years old. Inspired by the Cuban promoter's cheerleading efforts, the press referred to him as a "real phenomenon: in fact the boy wonder in and around Havana."[36]

To the frustration of the local sportswriters, Conte changed Palmero's age several times. New York writer Harvey Conover reacted with anger: "The Cuban has been seventeen, eighteen, nineteen and twenty respectively, according to how well Pepe remembers the last lie he told about the boy's age." Conover sarcastically bannered his article with the headline "Palmero, the ageless marvel."[37]

Despite the confusing assertions by Conte, Palmero lived up to the hype. During the winter league season of 1913–1914 he pitched a one-hitter against the Brooklyn Dodgers in Havana, and one week later he held them to one run.

Jake Daubert, the Dodgers' first baseman and National League batting champion, urged manager Wilbert Robinson to sign the southpaw immediately. However, Conte had other plans. The Dodgers were perennial losers and had a meager budget. The Giants were consistent pennant winners and they had money to spend. With the help of his brother Rafael, who was also the sports editor of the newspaper *La Lucha*, Conte convinced Palmero to wait for McGraw's offer.

On January 13, 1914, Palmero signed a contract and was invited to attend the Giants' spring training camp in Marlin Springs, Texas. With Conte in tow, the 6' tall Palmero reported to camp in March 1914, barely weighing more than his uniform and cleats—130 lbs. In addition, he could not speak a word of English.

At 6'5" and 230 pounds, the Giants backup catcher Larry McLean loomed over

Palmero in the clubhouse while teaching him how to respond to umpires who made bad calls. "You're a hell," Palmero would repeat over and over in his broken English, trusting that McLean was giving him accurate tutelage.[38]

His nonsensical reply would no doubt evoke laughter throughout the entire spring schedule. Having trouble ordering food, Palmero relied on the Giants' second baseman Larry Doyle, who taught him to say "Give me what you got."[39] Finally, in desperation, Palmero requested that he be allowed to room with catcher "Chief" Meyers, an American Indian who spoke fluent Spanish.[40]

With only a few days of spring training remaining, anticipation turned to disappointment when McGraw announced that Palmero's contract had been sold to Toronto in the International League. New York baseball writers had originally predicted that Palmero would be sent to the minors, but one suggested that "he may be taken to New York and kept a while for advertising purposes."[41]

It didn't take very long for the disillusioned Palmero to send a telegram to his old Cuban teammate Armando Marsans, who had just jumped to the outlaw Federal League. An invitation to try out with the St. Louis Federals soon followed.

Before Palmero could leave for St. Louis, McGraw dispatched his friend, umpire Charles Rigler, to mediate a reconciliation with his Cuban hurler. Rigler spoke Spanish, but more importantly had an imposing physical presence at 240 pounds. He caught the Cuban in his hotel room as he was packing his grip. Employing basic psychology, Rigler pelted him with questions.

"How old are you? How much experience do you have in professional ball?"

Palmero followed his interrogator right down the path he had paved.

"Ah, yes, yes Señor, you are hardly 18," said Rigler. "And yet you are angry because the leader of champions [McGraw], whose club now stands at the top, without having called you to help, wishes to send you where you shall pitch often, get the experience you need, learn English, and be always ready to return to him."

The umpire continued his verbal assault: "He keeps a claim on you, thus showing that he esteems you and that he considers you a sure comer in the future. He sent [Jeff] Tesreau to the minors as he has done with you, and look at Tesreau now! Should you not be well satisfied? Should you not appreciate his fine intentions? Go now, boy, to this high-grade club to which he has assigned you and do the best you can!"[42]

Chastised and penitent Palmero agreed to take the Canadian assignment. Actually, Jeff Tesreau was an excellent example for Rigler to use. After reassignment to the bush leagues Tesreau returned to the Giants in 1912 and became one of the best pitchers in the league.

But Rigler could not tell Palmero the truth. No matter how brilliantly he had performed in spring training it would have been impossible to qualify for a spot in a rotation that included Tesreau, Rube Marquard and Christy Mathewson.

As he watched the Federal League gain public acceptance Palmero recorded a 0–3 record for the Toronto Maple Leafs in the International League and then was mysteriously sold to a Toronto team in the Canadian League, where he had a 5–4 record in 16 games.

During the winter season of 1914–1915 Palmero pitched for the Havana Reds, managed by Mike González. Although it was only his second year in professional

baseball in Cuba, he threw a no-
hitter against the Fe team. Buoyed
by his phenomenal success in the
winter league, Palmero prepared
himself for another try at major
league baseball.

Still reserved by the Giants,
Palmero attended spring camp in
1915 and surprised writers by
answering questions in English.
This time he was able to articulate
his feeling about wearing the uniform of the Giants. "I see Mr.
McGraw, Larry Doyle, Mike Don-
lin and all the boys in Cuba when
I am a young boy. I never think
then I play with the Giants," he
said.[43]

Encircled by an army of writers McGraw issued an evaluation
on his hurler's progress.

"The remarkable thing about
Palmero is his control," McGraw
declared. "I never saw a left-hander who could put the ball where
he wanted it so readily as this
Cuban boy. That's why I liked him
from the start."

After spring training he was
assigned to Rochester in the Inter-

Emiliano Palmero, McGraw's young Cuban star.

Emilio Palmero pitching for the New York Giants
in their spring training camp of 1915. He would see
action in three games, finishing with a record of
0–2 and a respectable ERA of 3.09. (Source: Nick
Wilson collection.)

national League and caught fire, winning 19 games for a team that had only 69 victories all season.

In mid–September Palmero received the call he had been waiting for. He was
ordered to join the Giants during their series against the Cubs in Chicago. On September 21 Palmero, the first Latino to wear a New York Giants' uniform, took the
hill in the second game of a doubleheader at Wrigley Field.

The next afternoon the New York newspapers told the ugly story: "GIANTS'
CUBAN PITCHER ROUTED," screamed a headline in the *Times*. The chilly wind
and low temperatures could not be blamed entirely for the poor debut. Palmero lasted
a mere two-thirds of an inning, yielding two hits, two walks and a hit batter.

He returned to the mound on September 25 against the Browns in St. Louis. In
the sixth inning the Browns were leading 3–1 and Palmero was summoned from the
bullpen to relieve William Perritt, a twelve-game winner for the Giants. Redeeming
his reputation, Palmero seemed to glide through his three-inning assignment, allowing only two hits, striking out two and allowing no runs.

Palmero is pictured in the back row, fourth from the left, in this 1915 picture of the New York Giants' spring training pitching staff. Future Hall of Famers Rube Marquard and Christy Mathewson are second and third from the left, respectively, in the middle row. (Source: Nick Wilson collection.)

There was a certain irony in Palmero playing in St. Louis on this day. One year earlier he had been offered the possibility of a lucrative contract as a starting pitcher with the St. Louis Federals of the renegade Federal League. His decision to stay with McGraw netted him a few innings and a splintery seat in the bullpen. Only 1,200 fans made the effort to see the Browns–Giants contest, while across town the St. Louis Federals were turning people away after filling the stadium with 15,000.[44]

With the Giants languishing in last place, McGraw had nothing to lose by starting Palmero in a game during the last weeks of the season. Palmero's second start was more impressive, but resulted in another loss because of poor run support. He ended his freshman season with a 0–2 record, but an admirable ERA of 3.09. In 11⅔ innings Palmero struck out eight major league batters, allowing ten hits and walking nine.

As McGraw's enthusiasm for the Cuban hurler began to cool so did the press coverage. A national publication stated, "Palmero the Cuban, came back from the international league heavier and stronger than ever. Though Emilio is a good average player he is hardly in the 'probable star' class."[45]

Traditionally, baseball players in New York had a chance to earn a little extra money after the season ended in the regularly scheduled "City Series" among the Dodgers, Yankees and Giants. In 1915 the games were cancelled because as the *Times* reported, "the chief owners are of the opinion that the baseball fans of New York are not enthusiastic about such a series."[46] With one more disappointment to digest, Palmero returned to Cuba with very little to show for his first season in the big leagues.

The next season, 1916, McGraw was equally stingy, starting him in only one game. After a total of fifteen innings and a ballooning ERA of 8.04 he was sold to Louisville in the American Association on May 31. Once again the Giants commented on Palmero, but gave him a more impartial assessment. The press echoed the report: "Palmiero, [sic] a Cuban left-hander, whom McGraw farmed out for two or three seasons, has shown a lot of cleverness, but has been jinxed and unable to win."[47]

That was his last season in a Giants uniform. McGraw had given up on him and had turned his attention to a Cuban infielder named "Joseíto" Rodríguez. After Rodríguez failed to make an impression, McGraw did not introduce another Cuban rookie to the Giants' roster for the remainder of his career.

From 1917 through 1920 Palmero pitched for Louisville, Little Rock, Minneapolis and Omaha. He re-entered the big leagues in 1921 after a career-high 28 wins with Omaha in the Western League the previous season. Again he suffered through a disappointing stint, this time in the St. Louis Browns' bullpen. After the 1921 season he spent the next five years back in the minors.

In 1925 he seemed to come alive again, notching a 18–10 record for Columbus in the American Association. His contract was purchased by the Washington Senators in May of 1926, but again he failed to make the big-league grade. He could not crack the rotation, which included two future hall of famers, Walter Johnson and Stanley Coveleski. The bullpen was the sole domain of baseball's first great reliever, Fred "Firpo" Marberry, who pitched in 64 games and was credited with 22 saves.

After minor league work in Birmingham and Toledo Palmero played his last major league season at the age of 33 with the Boston Braves in 1928.

Although Palmero's major league career was not successful and his minor league record was sporadic, he managed to find work in various professional leagues for over 15 years. While keeping busy in the Cuban League in the winter, he is also said to have pitched in the Negro Leagues, although documentation is not available. His major league career record was 6–15 with an ERA of 5.17 in 41 games. His minor league records are incomplete, but between 1914 and 1927 his record was 165–144.[48]

His one season in Toledo in 1927 seemed to result in more than just a nifty 14–5 record. Realizing that his career was nearing its end, he returned to Ohio, where job opportunities in its numerous factories were plentiful. After he hung up his spikes, Palmero, who had never married, found employment in Toledo. After several decades of factory work he retired as an order assembler in the DeVilbiss Company.

His final battles in life were staged against diabetes and high blood pressure. On July 15, 1970, he died of uremia, a disease of the kidneys. Alone and forgotten by the baseball world, Palmero was laid to rest in Toledo's Ottawa Hills Memorial Cemetery.

Palmero's one claim to fame is that he was the first Latin member of the Giants franchise, opening the historical path for players like Juan Marichal, Felipe Alou and Orlando Cepeda.

Jacinto Calvo

He burned up the Texas League circuit with his hitting.

Jack Calvo paved the way for Latins in two leagues, but failed to make his mark in the league that counted the most. A Cuban by birth, Calvo was one of the first

Latin position players to play in the Texas League when he signed with the Ft. Worth Panthers in 1922.[49] Before that, Calvo (along with "Merito" Acosta) was the first Latin-born player to be signed by the Washington Senators, debuting in the 1913 season.

His offensive numbers belied what he was eventually capable of achieving. In 16 games for the Senators he scratched out eight singles and one home run for a batting average of .242. His boss, Clark Griffith, saw little potential and cut him from the roster. After playing for the Long Branch Cubans for the next four years he again proved that he had potential. Sensing that Calvo was reborn, Griffith brought him up for one more try during the 1920 season, during which he hit .043 in 17 games.

Calvo spent the majority of the 1920s playing center field in the minor leagues, where he burned up the Texas League circuit with his hitting. Although he had a solid .305 batting average during his years in Texas, Griffith never attempted to give him a third try.[50] Calvo died in Miami, Florida, on June 15, 1965, four days after his 71st birthday.

More Cubans Are Signed for Major League Duty

"But they couldn't kiss the onion."

During the nineteen-teens, thirteen Latinos (twelve Cubans and one Spaniard) made their debut in the major league ranks. Although this number seems anemic compared with the 200-plus Latinos in baseball today, it was a benchmark decade. Only eleven Latin-born players joined the majors in the following twenty years!

Major league owners began to window-shop more frequently in Cuba as news of the Cubans' victories in exhibition games became more common. Not all of the reports were positive, however. In 1918 *Baseball Magazine* reported, "A well known big league scout, after returning from Cuba some years ago, imparted this informa-tion to a New York daily scribe: "Them Cubebs are fast, snappy fielders, but they cant hit. And that was the impression fandom had of cubban [sic] ball tossers for a long time. They could field like blazes but they couldn't kiss the onion."[51]

Nevertheless, nearly fifty Latins made the rosters of black teams in the United States during this decade. Several of them earned induction into the Cuban Hall of Fame after their careers had ended.

Gervacio "Strike" González is still considered one of the greatest defensive catch-ers ever to come out of Havana. John McGraw wanted to offer him $50,000 to play for the Giants to complement their highly touted rookie catcher, "Chief" Meyers. Obviously both Gonzalez and his battery-mate José Méndez were too dark-skinned to play. González caught for five years in America with the Cuban Stars (West) and the Long Branch Cubans beginning in 1910.

Alejandro Oms was another marquée player who came to the United States in 1917 and played for a total of 14 years. A classy outfielder and a heavy hitter, Oms never hit below .308 during his six years in the Eastern Colored League.

Many of the Cubans who made it into the major leagues during this decade came from the expanding white minor league circuits that were developing along the

Eastern seaboard. One Cuban who drew a lot of attention from major league scouts in 1915 was second baseman Ramiro Seigle.

Inspired by his friends "Merito" Acosta and Jacinto Calvo, he sent a letter directly to Washington Senators' manager Clark Griffith requesting a tryout. But before the invitation from Griffith could reach him in Havana Seigle received transportation fees from the Philadelphia Phillies.

Caught in a moral dilemma, Seigle first appeared at the Phillies' tryout camp, and then defected to the Senators' training facilities in Charlottesville on April 26. The writer who covered the story said, "Circumstances have combined to give this youngster an unusual amount of advertising."[52]

Although Seigle never made it to the majors he enjoyed a long career in Cuba which stretched into the mid 1920s. At one point his teammates called the aging veteran "Tutankamico" after the mummy recently uncovered in Egypt.[53]

Balmadero "Merito" Acosta

"[Wee Willie] Keeler in embryo."

When Clark Griffith came to the Senators in 1912 he sought to build on the success he had had with Armando Marsans and Rafael Almeida. Relying on reports from his Cuban bird dogs, he brought over a 5'7", 140-pound outfielder from Havana named Balmadero Pedro "Merito" Acosta. The first Washington Senators' player to hail from a Latin country played in only nine games in 1913, but showed some promise by hitting .300.

Before the start of the 1914 season one scribe, who was evidently searching for a thread of gold in the Senators' burlap quilt, wrote, "Washington is holding a still undeveloped jewel, the Cuban Acosta, a mere child not yet 17, who is believed to be a [Wee Willie] Keeler in embryo."[54] (Keeler was regarded as one of the greatest hitters at the turn of the twentieth century)

Acosta patrolled the outfield as a utility player for the Washington Senators for 4⅓ years and in his final season, 1918, he played for the Philadelphia Athletics for a mere 49 games.

"Merito" Acosta was born June 2, 1896, in privileged surroundings. His father, Balmadero Acosta Sr., was the mayor of Marianao, the town that hosted one of the most important baseball franchises in the country.

His brief major league career was uneventful except for one week during the 1918 season. On July 28 his name appeared in the *New York Times* in the list of the top batters in the American League. With 16 games under his belt, left-handed hitter Merito Acosta was the best hitter in the league with an average of .396. Following him were such household names as Ty Cobb at .376, George Sisler at .328 and Babe Ruth at .319.

Glory was sweet, but fleeting. He finished the season with a .298 batting average and was not asked to return to the big leagues. That winter, while playing for Havana, Acosta was the first and only player to complete an unassisted triple play in Cuban League history.[55]

On August 22, 1915, Acosta was involved in one of the most peculiar plays that

A rare photograph of Balmadero "Merito" Acosta (center right) reveals that he managed the Marianao team in Cuba during the 1923–1924 season. Playing on his club was a minor league infielder named Charlie Dressen (top, second from right), who would eventually manage the Brooklyn Dodgers to NL pennants in 1952 and 1953. (Source: Jay Sanford collection.)

has ever been transcribed on a scorecard. In the second inning of a game against the hometown Detroit Tigers, the Senators' first baseman, Chick Gandil, drew a walk. Then Acosta came to the plate and was passed on four balls. Both runners moved up a base on a bunt by catcher Rip Williams, followed by a George McBride sacrifice fly which scored Gandil. Moments later Acosta was picked off second base to end the inning. Studying his notes, the scorekeeper found that a run had scored without an official at-bat.

Late in the 1918 season Acosta was sold to the Louisville Colonels, where he finally found his personal secret to success. Overcoming his weak hitting with some fancy footwork on the base paths of love, Merito Acosta married the daughter of the team's owner.[56]

Manuel "Melo" Cueto

"A terrific wallop that looked like a fat home run."

He was only 5'5" but he was one of the most feared batters in Cuban professional league history. Manuel Cueto began his professional career in 1912 and eventually set a record in the Cuban League by hitting .300 or better for 11 seasons.[57]

His incredible offensive numbers made him a prime target for scouts from professional teams in the United States. In 1913 Cueto signed with the Long Branch Cubans, joining fellow countryman Dolf Luque.

His major league career began in 1914 when he was lured by Armando Marsans to the ill-fated St. Louis club in the Federal League. That season he played in 19 games and batted .093.

Batting from the right side of the plate, Cueto kept up his impressive offensive pace in the Cuban Leagues, earning himself another shot at the majors. This time he joined the Reds for the 1917 season and hit .200 in 56 games. His best big-league season was in 1918, when he hit .296 as a utility player. Cueto was joined that year on the Reds' roster by his former teammate Dolf Luque. He played briefly in 1919 but, unlike Luque, was not on the club when they went into the controversial World Series against the Black Sox.

Although small in stature and tipping the scales at barely 160 pounds, the athletic Cueto played every infield position (save first base), every outfield position and catcher during his four-year major league career. His 21-year tenure in the Cuban League and a lifetime batting average of .298 earned him induction into the Cuban Hall of Fame.

In the major leagues he compiled a batting average of .227 and made 13 errors in 42 games playing shortstop, second base and third base. His one memorable moment of big-league glory came during a game between Cincinnati and Chicago that was once called the "greatest game ever pitched."

The date was May 2, 1917, and a seamless blanket of clouds hung over Wrigley Field as huddled Cubs fans prepared to see the ace hurlers of both teams face each other for a historic battle. Fred Toney of the Cincinnati Reds and southpaw Jim "Hippo" Vaughn of Chicago were the starters.

Cueto had been given the nod to play left field for the Reds. This was his rookie year and he was destined to appear in only 56 games, rotating between the outfield, second base and catcher. As Cueto braced his small frame against the frosty Lake Michigan wind, he witnessed one shutout inning after another.

As the game moved into the seventh inning neither team had made a hit. By the end of the eighth inning both pitchers had allowed two walks each and still no hits. The only defensive blemish came early in the game when Chicago's powerful center fielder, Cy Williams, misplayed one fly ball for an error.

Jim Vaughn didn't realize that both he and his opponent had no-hitters going until late in the game. He explained, "At the end of the eighth I was sitting on the bench and happened to make a remark that we weren't hitting Toney very much. One of the fellows assented to this and then added that they weren't hitting me very much either. Then I recalled that they hadn't made a safe hit off my delivery."[58]

The Cincinnati Reds gather for a team photograph in 1917. Manuel Cueto (center) is seated next to manager Christy Mathewson (far right). (Source: Nick Wilson collection.)

The fans, who had been clamoring for offensive action, now watched in silence as the last inning approached. The Cubs faithful stood for the entire frame as Vaughn retired the Reds one-two-three, registering a three-pitch strikeout of the last batter.

Now it was Toney's turn. As a minor leaguer in Kentucky, Toney had pitched a remarkable 17-inning no-hitter, finishing the game with a 1–0 victory. He once told a reporter that it was his dream to pitch a no-hitter in the majors and now he was a mere three outs from seeing that happen. It didn't take long for the 6'4" 215-pound bruiser to retire the Cubs in order in the ninth, and secure a piece of immortality with a matching no-hitter.

In the tenth inning Vaughn gave up a single to the first batter, Larry Kopf, the Reds shortstop. Vaughn retired Greasy Neale and Hal Chase, but the fourth batter, Jim Thorpe, laid down a perfect bunt and beat it out for a single. With runners at first and third and two outs, the Cubs shortstop mishandled a grounder and an unearned run crossed the plate. Vaughn had struck out ten Reds batters and finished ten frames of work with a two-hit, no-earned-run game.

With the side finally retired, the Cubs had one last chance to not only tie the game, but also ruin Toney's chance for an extra-inning no-hitter. Cueto moved into position as the first batter for the Cubs approached the plate. It was right-handed-hitting Fred Merkle, the eternally abused author of the "Merkle boner"—a mental error which changed the course of the pennant chase in 1908. Merkle carefully timed Toney's hanging fastball and smashed it deep into left field.

Racing back as fast as he could, Cueto desperately tried to beat the ball to the fence. Just as it seemed that Merkle had hit a home run, Cueto leaped into the air and caught it one-handed as he hit the fence. Cueto brushed himself off and remained in the game.

Redetermined, Toney struck out Larry Doyle and Cy Williams with fastballs and secured a remarkable ten-inning no-hit game. Toney later confessed, "That Merkle nearly spilled the beans for me. He hit a terrific wallop that looked like a fat home run into the stands. But I will have to thank Cueto for keeping the score safe."[59]

Cueto's one big-league claim to glory is now preserved forever on library microfilm.

Manuel Cueto died in Havana at the age of fifty-two.

The Cubans Taste Defeat

"Even the black ones being the most polite."

It was now time to heave a big sigh of relief. The Athletics had returned to Cuba during the 1911–1912 exhibition season and had won ten out of twelve games. These victories proved that the major leaguers were finally capable of defeating their Cuban rivals. An editorial in *Baseball Magazine* pronounced, "I fancy we will not hear so much from our Cuban Brothers in the future. They will not crow over us as they did after they flailed the lining out of the Athletics in 1910.... This shows that, great as the dark athletes may be, a big league team that goes down there with anything like its full strength, and pays attention to business, can defeat them." In a sadly appeasing gesture the editor concluded, "The Cuban players are a great lot of fellows, even the black ones being the most polite," and "The charm of the Cubans, to my mind, is not so much in the ball playing as in their glorious hospitality ... they have the art of hospitality down to a fine point."[60]

José Acosta

A diplomat from Abyssinia.

José Acosta was a diminutive pitcher who came to the United States with a group of fellow Cubans to play for the Long Branch, New Jersey, club in 1914. Although the Long Branch team was destined to dissolve after the 1915 season, Acosta and fellow right-hander Dolf Luque honed their skills playing along the Eastern seaboard for the next several seasons. In 1916 Acosta played briefly for Vancouver in the Northwest League. Although he proved himself to be a proficient pitcher, he did not cut a very athletic figure at 5'7" and barely 140 pounds. (Hence his nickname, "Joseíto").

Acosta had one distinguishing pitch which made him unique among Latin hurlers. Some writers referred to his knuckleball as a "floating pitch," and the Washington Senators were anxious to see how it worked on major league turf.[61] The dismal Senators had finished the 1919 season in sixth place and their pitching staff and bull pen were staffed with unreliable cast offs. Only Walter Johnson and "Grunting Jim" Shaw provided the Washington fans with any semblance of proficiency.

Throwing open the clubhouse gates to many aspiring hurlers, the Senators debuted José Acosta on July 28, 1920. After 17 games, 12 in relief, the rookie compiled a record of 5–4 and a not-so-impressive ERA of 4.03.

On the other hand, in the fall of 1920 John McGraw led his team, plus guest-player Babe Ruth, to Havana to play an exhibition series. Playing for the Havana Reds, Acosta took the hill in the second game and struck out Ruth three times.[62]

In 1921 the Senators' manager, George McBride, used Acosta twenty-six times out of the bull pen while only allowing him to start seven games. As a starter he was 2–3, but he saved three games and posted a 3–1 record as a reliever. For the second consecutive season he finished with a 5–4 record, and an ERA above 4.0.

In 1922, his final major league season, Acosta was traded to the Chicago White Sox, where he gave up 25 hits in 15 innings and registered an ERA of 8.40. Despite his poor performance with the White Sox he is now recognized as the first Latino signed by that organization.

A humorous anecdote involved Acosta while he was struggling to make the Senators' roster during the 1922 spring training period in Florida. He had befriended the comical third-base coach Al Schacht—a man who imparted more belly-laughs than strategic instruction.

Because of his reputation for his parodies and on-field antics, Schacht was known throughout the country as the "Clown Prince of Baseball." Through sheer guile he had wangled an invitation to accompany Acosta and teammate Ricardo Torres to a banquet sponsored by the Tampa Cuban community honoring the players.

When Acosta warned him that the entire evening would be spent listening to laudatory speeches in Spanish, Schacht assured him that he would not only enjoy the evening, but would be honored to give a speech of his own.

Unable to utter even one phrase in Spanish, Schacht requested that Acosta introduce him as a diplomat from Abyssinia. Schacht strode to the lectern with an elegant bearing and delivered a monologue of utter gibberish, gesturing towards his teammates and pronouncing their names with enthusiasm. The zany coach did such a convincing job that the crowd rose to its feet and gave the departing Schacht a standing ovation.[63]

Jose Acosta died in Havana at the age of 86 in 1977.

World War I and Its Effects on Baseball

The major league season was terminated on September 2nd.

In 1917 baseball had been adversely affected by America's entry into World War I because it had lost so many of its prime players to the draft. However, the following year saw unprecedented action on the part of the government to stop the national game altogether. When the provost general declared a "work or fight" order, players either joined the military or sought employment that was considered essential to the war effort.

Despite its importance to morale on the home front, baseball was deemed nonessential. The season was terminated on September 2, 1918, with approximately 125 games having been played by each team. In response to the national uproar, the secretary of war acquiesced and allowed a World Series to be played, featuring the top teams in each league (Red Sox vs. Cubs).

During the three years of the First World War, only three Latinos were signed to major league contracts, while the World War II years of 1942–1945 saw sixteen make their debuts. Many more jobs opened up in the Negro Leagues, however, after twenty-two African American players went off to military service from 1917 through 1919.[64]

Baseball hit its lowest point during the 1918 season, and newspapers even began to lament the lack of play among black ball clubs. One magazine editor noted, "Where, oh, where have the colored ball clubs gone? What has become of the dusky entertainers?"[65]

José Rodríguez

His huge, protruding ears and dark features stood out in a sea of white.

If baseball was America's number one sport, the Great War in Europe was its number one preoccupation. And the mood at the New York Giants' spring training camp of 1917 reflected the tenor of the times. As cameramen lined up along the foul lines a sharp-looking army officer stood patiently in full military dress. On cue he led the entire Giants' squad, bats steadied on broad shoulders as if they were rifles, in a march up and down the field. The ownership of the Giants along with the other fifteen clubs in major league baseball wanted to send a clear message to the government. They were firmly behind the war effort. It was also a plea not to shut down the game entirely.

This was José Rodríguez's first major league spring training camp and the disturbing rumors of a shutdown threatened to disrupt his young career before it had a chance to bloom. During the previous year, 1916, the Giants had used him as a pinch runner in the last game of the season.

But this year, he hoped, would be different. With many well-known players joining the military Rodríguez had suddenly emerged as a valuable asset because of his foreign status. In addition, John McGraw was not going to give up on his quest for the perfect Cuban, despite the disappointing performance by Emilio Palmero.

After the military exhibition had concluded the players were herded into groups for a series of photo sessions. Rodríguez looked out of place as he posed with ten other infield candidates. His huge protruding ears and dark features stood out in a sea of white.[66]

José "Joseíto" Rodríguez was born on July 25, 1894, in Havana—three years after John McGraw had first set foot on the island. Although Rodríguez had been playing professionally in the United States since 1913 with a series of black barnstorming teams, he was first noticed by McGraw during winter league play in Havana. When McGraw spotted him around 1912, Rodríguez was considered to be the best defensive first baseman and catcher in the Cuban League.

Prospective infielders for the New York Giants gather for a spring training photograph in 1917. José Rodríguez is in the middle of the back row. (Source: Nick Wilson collection.)

It wasn't until late in the 1916 season that the Giants finally brought him up to the majors, however. His big-league debut on October 5 was disheartening for a couple of reasons. First, the man he wanted to impress the most, John McGraw, had vanished.

After timidly migrating to a fourth-place finish the Giants' skipper was forced to watch the Brooklyn Dodgers capture the National League pennant. As the final week of the grueling campaign approached, McGraw finally exploded, and on October 3 he bluntly announced, "I am through with the Giants for the season."[67] He walked out of the visitors' clubhouse at Ebbets Field and left his coaches to finish the season.

Then, in the seventh inning of the final game of the season Rodríguez was inserted into the game as a pinch runner and was left stranded on first base. Rodríguez would not have an opportunity to impress McGraw for another six months.

When the spring training camp of 1917 finally broke and the Giants headed north to begin the regular season, Rodríguez was on the roster. However, the manpower vacuum left by the war did not automatically earn the Cuban a permanent place in the lineup. McGraw used him as a first baseman in only seven games, where the speedster stole two bases, collected only four hits and registered a batting average of .200.

In 1918 Rodríguez was moved to second base, where he played in fifty games, stole only six bases and ended his major league career that autumn with a season batting average of .160.

He continued to play in the United States with the Detroit Stars and later joined José Méndez and the Kansas City Monarchs in the Negro National League during its inaugural season of 1920. In the black leagues Rodríguez was an accomplished catcher, while in the major leagues he played second, third and first base.

Beginning in the 1920s Rodriguez tried his hand at managing in the Cuban

Leagues. He also allied himself with the Washington Senators' super-scout Joe Cambria in the 1940s, foraging through the Cuban countryside in search of the next José Méndez.

His successful career at the helm of several Cuban teams stretched across nearly three decades, ending with his death in Havana in 1953. Two years prior to his passing Rodríguez was inducted into Cuba's baseball hall of fame.

Angel Aragón

The first Latin signed by the Yanks

Angel Valdes Aragón made history with his timing, not his bat or glove.

With a large Cuban community settled in New York, the 5'5" third baseman was a perfect fit for the struggling Yankee organization. In 1914 his presence was supposed to bring a new community of paying customers to a ballpark that drew anemic attendance, especially when compared to the crosstown Giants, who were a perennial powerhouse. At that time, the Yankees were the piñata of the American League, having finished no higher than sixth place during the previous three years and drawing an average of 3,966 fans per game.

Aragón, the future box-office draw of the Bronx, was literally snatched out of obscurity, having played for the Long Branch Cubans since 1913. His big-league career was launched on August 20, 1914, at the Polo Grounds against the Cleveland Naps (a.k.a. Indians), and his debut performance earned him flattering reviews from the New York press. The *Times* printed the headline, "ANGEL PINCH HITS, BUT YANKEES LOSE." The subhead read, "Cuban Player's Timely Single Not Enough to Turn Tide Against Naps"

In the second inning the Naps were leading 4–1 and Aragon was called from the bench to pinch hit for the pitcher, Ray Fisher. With runners at second and third and two out Aragon was facing Cleveland's ace hurler, Willie Mitchell. The diminutive Cuban slashed a single through the infield, driving in both runners. The *Times* referred to his clutch hit as "the aid of a Cuban angel."

That event marked the first time that a Latino had ever appeared in a Yankees uniform.

Unfortunately, August 20 was Aragón's finest moment. Before the season was over he played in five additional games with a mere six plate appearances, and no hits.

Aragón, known by his teammates as "Pete," made a comeback with the Yanks in 1916 for thirteen games, and again during the manpower-short season of 1917 for fourteen games in which he hit an embarrassing .067. That season the Yankees averaged only 2,158 fans per game and finished in sixth place.

The great Angel Aragón experiment was scrapped. Remarkably, it wasn't until 1987, seventy years later, that the Yankees signed another Cuban-born rookie to make his debut with the club.

Aragón may not have made an impact on the diamond, but his stories of the beauty of the Caribbean must have impressed one impressionable Yankee. Ray Caldwell was not only one of the best pitchers that the moribund Yankees had on their

1916 staff, he was also their most erratic. With three-quarters of the season behind him and 35 starts under his belt the hard-drinking Caldwell disappeared after a game in St. Louis.

New York papers treated the mystery with as much devotion as they would a lost child. Efforts to find him continued through the winter holidays until a dispatch arrived at the Yankees' offices suggesting that a man named Ray Collins, pitching for the baseball team in Colon, Panama, might be the "deserter," Caldwell.

It seems that the *Panama Herald* and its crack team of investigators finally solved the mystery in mid–February. After having his picture published in the Panamanian paper with the caption, "Ray Caldwell is Ray Collins," the Yankees hurler decided to return to his team for spring training. It wasn't until the first week of spring camp that the *New York Sun* broke the story to American readers, noting with unbridled hope "that he has cured himself of bad habits."[68] Had Angel Aragón stoked the imagination of Ray Caldwell with his exotic visions of the Caribbean?

Aragón stayed in the city which gave him his first major league opportunity and raised a son, Angel "Jack" Aragón Jr., who made a brief appearance with the Giants in 1941. Angel Aragón died in New York City in 1952, at the age of fifty-eight.

Cubans Were Fair Game for the Press

"The admiral of the Cuban navy goes barefoot?"

It seems that no one was immune to being branded with a nickname based on their ethnicity or religion. A hurler for the Phillies named Erskine Mayer was referred to as "Mayer, the Hebrew pitcher."[69] Even Lou Gehrig, the most respected of all major leaguers, and a first-generation German-American, was hailed in a banner headline in the 1920s as "Little Heinie."

Former New York sportswriter Harold Rosenthal explained that it was not uncommon for writers to assign caustic or even racially-charged nicknames to ballplayers on a whim. Rosenthal had a seventy-year career documenting the legends of sports and could easily recall the open hostilities of the times.

"People were more open in their prejudice back then than they are today," he said. "Back then if there was [a player of an ethnic background] they would call him a name and think nothing of it. If there had been any blacks in the major leagues God only knows what they would have said and done back then."[70]

Billy Rogell, who began his professional career in 1923, remembers the anger directed at Detroit first baseman Hank Greenberg: "I never heard the people call someone the names that he was called: just because he was Jewish. Some guys ... even hated us because we played with a Jew. They were no angels in my day," Rogell declared.[71]

One writer in 1914 encouraged cultural stereotypes by describing, in exaggerated detail, a prank that was pulled on several unsuspecting Cubans:

> Reverting to our Cuban friends: we had five minutes of rich, unalloyed fun out of them one night in New York. Having learned that a number of Cubans, ballplayers, scribes, and collegians were assembled at the home of one of them on Central Park

West, some cruel sinners called up by phone and got a prominent Havana writer. "Ah, Senor ___," suavely spoke the sinful man, "this is the *New York Sunday Whirl*. We would be deeply grateful to you if you could supply us with some valuable Cuban information."

"Anysing zat ees een my power," replied the courteous hidalgo. "What ees eet you weesh dat you sall know?"

"Why, Senor, we would like to know if it is really true that the admiral of the Cuban navy goes barefoot?"

There is really no word-painting which could do justice to the adjectives, expletives, and exclamations which hissed and flamed around the home end of that telephone.[72]

Oscar Monzón Tuero

One of the first Latin-born pitchers in the Texas League.

A native of Havana, Oscar Tuero was born eight days prior to Christmas, 1892. He made his first pitching appearance in the major leagues for the St. Louis Cardinals in 1918, and was primarily consigned to relief duties.

Tuero is a particularly interesting figure because, after being cut by the Cardinals in the early part of the 1920 season, he returned to Cuba and enjoyed his best seasons. Extracting sweet revenge, the 5'8" right-handed fastballer proved his unfulfilled promise by shutting out John McGraw's Giants in an exhibition game in Havana on October 19, 1920. During the 1920 and 1921 seasons Tuero proved that he was worth more than a slot in the bullpen when he led the Cuban league in complete games and games pitched.[73]

After being rejected by the Cardinals Tuero became one of the first Latin-born pitchers in the Texas League. Despite a ban imposed by the league on the use of the spitball, Tuero and several other pitchers were "grandfathered" and allowed to use the pitch until they retired from the game.[74]

The Cuban also did a stint with Atlanta in the Southern Association in 1923. His stateside career lasted until the 1932 season.

Tuero then returned to Havana, where he passed away at the age of 67 in 1960.

Eusebio Miguel González

González slashed a line drive that landed between two outfield defenders.

Until very recently, the year 1918 has always been remembered by baseball fans in Boston as the last time that their beloved Red Sox ever won a World Series. Babe Ruth patrolled left field, filled in at first base and won thirteen games as a pitcher. Future hall of famer Harry Hooper played right field while their catcher, Wally Schang, was heralded as one of the best defensive backstops of his time. Besides Ruth, the pitching staff also included Dutch Leonard, Carl Mays and "Bullet Joe" Bush. Team owner Harry Frazee had so many stars on his roster that the loss of a utility player was a mere clerical inconvenience.

On July 26 the Red Sox were about to introduce another fill-in shortstop to give

Everett Scott a rest as they sped towards their fourth pennant in seven years. Although Scott was a light hitter he had led the league in fielding percentage for the past two years and was an integral part of Boston's defensive prominence. (In fact, the Indiana native would eventually lead the league in fielding for eight years in a row.)

Scott's temporary substitute on that warm July day at Comiskey Park was Eusebio González, the first Latino to ever appear in a Red Sox uniform. That week González had joined the team in Chicago during one of their lengthy road trips and now his big debut came in the eighth inning when he was used as a pinch hitter for Scott. The Boston team had nothing to lose since the White Sox ace hurler, Ed Cicotte, had limited them to three hits, and they were being battered by a score of 7–1.

Batting right-handed against the right hander Cicotte, the 26-year-old Gonzalez slashed a line drive that landed between two outfield defenders. When the ball was caught by the infield cutoff man, González was standing on third base.

The next hitter, third baseman John Stanbury, hit a single and the Havana native scored easily. In the ninth inning he took his position at shortstop, but didn't handle a play.

Two days later the scene was replayed, with the White Sox comfortably ahead 8–0 and González once again relieving Scott late in the game. This time the Cuban failed to reach base in his only at-bat, but he did field two grounders successfully. (Babe Ruth, who was playing left field that day, didn't get a hit either.)

The next day González was cut from the team. During the course of that season the Red Sox field-tested five utility players at shortstop; González was the only man who lasted more than one game. It may seem strange that a rookie who hit a triple off one of the best hurlers in the American League in his first major league at-bat was treated so indifferently.

Was he too dark-complected to bring back to Boston? Did his previous minor league club demand too high a payment for his services? Whatever the reason for his abrupt departure, Eusebio González had nothing to be ashamed of: There aren't many men who could boast of having a lifetime major league batting average of .500 and a 1.000 fielding percentage.

4

Adolfo Luque

"His blue eyes blazed malevolently at each hitter."

The first week of October 1923 belonged to Adolfo Luque.

It seemed that the entire city of Havana was standing at the edge of the harbor, waiting to celebrate the return of the greatest pitcher in the major leagues. Their native son had not only captured honors for the most wins, the best ERA, the most shutouts and the best winning percentage in all of baseball, he had also defended the integrity of Cuban manhood against the entire New York Giants ball club with his fists.

Luque (pronounced Loo-Kay) had been the seventh Cuban ballplayer to make it to the big leagues, but no Latin had ever reached this level of success before. He was hailed as *The Pride of Havana.*

The thirty thousand people who greeted him at the docks now followed him along the parade route that wound through the capital city, accompanied by military marching units, the fire department, politicians and musicians. The honorable leaders of Cuban politics lined up at the podium to give elaborate and eloquent speeches, suggesting a welcome that Caesar would have received in Rome.

The next day Luque was transported to a theatre where he reenacted the famous fight he had had with the American ballplayers who taunted him with racial slurs on the ball field in Cincinnati. His celebrated beating of the Giants' outfielder, Casey Stengel, had been covered by the Cuban sportswriters who followed him throughout the season. They had cabled back to Havana the news of the historic fight so that their newspapers could describe the details in print. But now it was demonstrated live on the stage of the Martí Theatre with Luque playing himself.[1]

When the celebration migrated to Havana's Gran Stadium, Luque was presented with an automobile while the laudatory speeches continued. But the Cuban Caesar had noticed José Méndez sitting nearby. In a profound gesture of compassion and respect he addressed the *Black Diamond*. "You should have gotten this car," he said to Méndez. "You're a better pitcher than I am. This parade should have been for you."[2] Luque's light skin and blue eyes allowed him entry into the big leagues while Méndez's superior talent was trumped by his black skin.

If the audiences at the Martí Theatre and Gran Stadium felt a thrill at seeing Luque accepting the part of a mythological hero, they would have been mesmerized by the half-dozen other real-life roles he was scripted to play during his 65 years on earth. There was the sinister Luque, waving a loaded pistol and threatening the lives of fellow players. There was the sensitive Luque who created a roster position for a troubled friend. On the field he was known as a hard-luck pitcher, although he never complained to the press about the lack of run production from his club. But when a teammate criticized his pitching, Luque chased him through the clubhouse with a pair of scissors.

Historian Roberto González Echevarría called him a "snarling, vulgar, cursing aggressive pug," while others referred to his "displays of fiery temper and volcanic outbursts." One of his obituaries read, "Luque never learned to master the English language or his own temper."[3]

But historians and authors also address the immensely positive aspects of his personality, such as his durability, courage and dominance. *New York Times* writer Arthur Daley said, "When Luque got out on the mound his blue eyes blazed malevolently at each hitter and he defied them. He was a mean cuss at times and they said he never threw a beanball by accident."[4]

His final epitaph is a confusing merger of contradictions—gentleman, thug, hero, gambler, teacher.

Like the other Cuban players who came to the United States during the early years of the century, little is known about Luque's family or childhood. He was raised in humble surroundings and at a young age played amateur ball for the exclusive Vedado Tennis Club in Havana. He served in the artillery division of the Cuban army and earned a spot on their baseball team playing third base.[5]

There are conflicting stories about his first step into professional baseball, but it appears that the Cuban promoter Abel Linares discovered Luque and recommended him to Dr. Hernández Henríquez, who was forming a barnstorming ball club for the 1912 summer season.[6]

Henríquez had quartered his team in Long Branch, New Jersey, and was scheduled to play the best semipro clubs in the eastern United States.

Henríquez correctly reasoned that if his team, called the Cuban Stars (like so many other clubs of that era), could prove its mettle with semipro teams they could also draw major leaguers to Long Branch for profitable exhibition games. The prohibition against playing baseball on Sundays in New York forced idle big-league ball clubs to find quick methods of generating income. (As Clyde Sukeforth, who played his first professional game in 1921, noted, "In those days if you had a day off you didn't grab your golf clubs and head for the golf course."[7]) Geographically, the oceanside town of Long Branch was an ideal location, positioned just south of Manhattan.

The 1912 barnstorming season brought Luque his first taste of big-league competition. When the Pittsburgh Pirates arrived one Sunday afternoon in Long Branch Luque took the hill and defeated them, despite the fact he had pitched on three consecutive days before this game. One newspaper noted that "his Pirate victory had been his fourth win in four days."[8]

Although there are no surviving records to prove how well Luque performed in 1912, he must have impressed Dr. Henríquez, because he was offered a chance to return to Long Branch for the next season. We can only judge the environment that Luque experienced on the semipro circuit by comparing the notes of surviving players.

Bobby Robinson, who started his twenty-eight-year career with a semipro team in 1916, could never forget the conditions that he endured. "It was pretty rough with all that traveling," he said. "We would travel long distances by car…. In the semipro towns the fields were pretty rough. The ball would sometimes hit a rut or land in cow manure in the infield." Regarding the meager finances that each team was forced to budget, he said, "We had about fifteen or sixteen men when I played … but sometimes the other team wouldn't have but twelve."[9]

During this period Luque also started his professional career in the Cuban Leagues, but found less success. In 1912 he made seven appearances for Club Fe, pitching two complete games and posting an inauspicious 0–3 record. In the 1913 Cuban League season he pitched in only three games and completed the season with a 0–2 record.[10]

Before the start of the 1913 campaign Henríquez folded his Long Branch Cubans (He had dropped the "Stars") into the newly formed Class D, New York–New Jersey League. Luque's teammates included four other Cubans—catcher Miguel González (who would prove to be the only source of stability in his private life); pitcher Luís Padrón; outfielder Jacinto Calvo and infielder Angel Aragon.

Dolf Luque warming up before a game in 1923. Luque led all major league pitchers that season with a record of 27–8 and an ERA of 1.93. (Source: Jay Sanford collection.)

The inaugural season of the New York–New Jersey league was, in the words of Fred Lieb, "one of the freakiest ever played in Organized Baseball." The Long Branch Cubans were the only team, in a six-club league, to finish with a winning record. They compiled a winning percentage of .691, and a team batting average 40–50 points above those of the other teams.[11] Luque was their ace, winning 22 games while also playing third base and outfield, and hitting over .300.[12]

The 1913 season showed the first glimpse of the true determination and grit of Luque. Between June 4 and July 12 he pitched in thirteen games, winning all but one. After being soundly defeated by the Middletown team on July 11 by a score of 12–3, he told Henríquez that he wanted to avenge his humiliating exhibition by starting the next day. And so on Sunday, July 12, Luque returned and pitched a six-hit shutout of Middletown, allowing his team to win 12–0.[13]

Seven days earlier Henríquez had sent his ace to the mound on successive days against the Newburgh team with Luque winning both games, 3–2 and 7–3. By mid-season Luque had played at least one position in every game and was leading the league in victories (12) and shutouts (3). He also had a batting average of .290.

The Boston Braves and Washington Senators were actively scouting the ace, while one New York paper reported that the Yankees had their "eyes peeled" for Luque. With a biographical note that was carefully prepared to assuage the fears of segregationists, the newspaper stated, "Luque is a very light skinned Cuban, in fact lighter than Marsans or Almeida, and looks more like an Italian than a full blooded Cuban."[14]

At about this time Luque was introduced to an aggressive and unsettling cultural phenomenon — racism. Although Cuba was not totally free of segregation, the light-skinned Luque had little experience with being stigmatized.

Other players complained of harsh treatment at the hands of angry fans, during that time including hall of famer Al Lopez, who was a light-skinned blend of Spanish-Cuban and Italian ancestry. Lopez admitted to his biographer that he faced taunts of "Cuban nigger" during his minor league years in the mid 1920s in Florida.[15] Luque's experience was not dissimilar.

As the big-league scouts prepared to make their bids for the Cuban ace, Dr. Henríquez began to question whether he was ready for the big time. He told Lieb that Luque's curve ball was so effective that "those poor bush leaguers never see it." Then he cautiously added, "But maybe in the big leagues they straighten out that curve."

Henríquez also averred, however, that he expected Luque to be a successful third baseman. "They try to hit one past him and he just gobbles it up, they try to bunt and he is on the ball like a cat." Regarding the offensive side of Luque, Henríquez predicted, "And hit. My how he can hit.... If he advances from my team he would hit too hard to be a pitcher."[16]

In the end, Luque was sold to the gutter-dwelling Boston Braves, who had finished in last place in the National League four times in the previous five years. His contract was for the un-princely sum of $250 per month.[17] Back home in Havana, Luque increased the value of his stock by defeating the New York Giants in an exhibition game early in 1913.[18] Then he set his sights on the major leagues and the city of Boston.

What Luque could not have foreseen was that he would be under the thumb of a man who was best described as unrelenting and demanding — Boston's manager George Stallings. Stallings had taken over the reins of the Braves in the 1913 season and had forcibly dragged the franchise out of the cellar and into a semirespectable fifth-place finish. One biographical outline on Stallings read, "As flexible as an iron truncheon and as forgiving as a French guillotine."[19] The superstitious skipper drove his players with intimidation and humiliation, dispensing individual tongue-lashings in front of the entire team.

According to Fred Lieb, Henríquez had sold the rights of both Miguel González and Luque to the Braves at the same time, but Lieb questioned whether Stallings had consented to the purchase. When Stallings heard that he had inherited two Cubans he told Lieb, "What are you going to do with a bunch of birds that you have to talk to in sign language?"[20]

Although González never made it to the Braves' big-league roster, Luque enjoyed a brief cup of coffee.

How deeply Luque was influenced by Stallings is open to speculation. Certainly the future "Pride of Havana" did not walk into the Braves' clubhouse as an innocent lamb, looking for a personality to embrace. However, he must have been impressed by the success that this unrelenting slavemaster had with his ball club. Could it be that Luque concluded that the formula to success lay in an amalgam of anger and physical intimidation?

And, despite all the pressures of his rookie season, the Cuban hurler refused to be unnerved by the rantings of his new skipper. "No man has ever scared the señor," Lieb wrote.[21]

The beginning of the 1914 season started out as a dismal reminder of the previous five years. During one point in the early 1914 campaign the Braves lost a game to an amateur soap company team. Frantically searching for a formula to lift themselves out of last place, they shoved a league-leading twelve starting pitchers through the revolving doors of the club

George Stallings, of the Boston Braves, was Luque's first major league manager, in 1914. Stallings, and later John McGraw, had enormous influence on Luque's managerial techniques. (Source: Nick Wilson collection.)

house. (The second-place New York Giants had seven starters)

On May 20, 1914, Dolf Luque made his first big-league start, against the Pirates in Pittsburgh. His appearance on the mound that day represented the first time in history that a Latino pitched a major league ball game. Although Luque showed flashes of brilliance in limiting the Pirates to only five hits, he ended up taking the loss by a score of 4–1.

After watching the contest one writer commented, "Luque, a Cuban, pitched a good game, but was accorded poor support."[22] The Braves' future Hall of Fame shortstop, Rabbit Maranville, committed four errors and Boston hitters left seven runners stranded. This was the first time that a scribe had publicly attached the "hard-luck" moniker to Luque, and it would follow him throughout his career.

After one more appearance, this time in relief, he was demoted to the Jersey City team in the International League, where he floundered for the next three months.

The 1914 season was the worst experience of Luque's entire career. Between the Braves and the New Jersey team Luque had amassed a record of 2–11, walking 69 batters in 115 innings while striking out only 41. His combined ERA exceeded 5.50.[23] But the Braves saw something in the Cuban hurler, because they invited him back for the next spring training camp.

Meanwhile, the Boston club finally had an epiphany. With Stallings kicking and screaming, the Braves pushed their way from last place on July 4–10 games out of first place—to win the National League pennant, 10½ games ahead of McGraw's Giants. Luque may have missed the 1914 "miracle" finish and the four-game World Series sweep of the Philadelphia A's, but he wasn't oblivious to one glaring fact: The madman Stallings had forged a mountain of granite out of a hill of mud.

During the winter of 1914–1915 Luque signed with the Almandares team in the Cuban League and started to develop a new pitch—the change of pace, which, according to Felipe Alou, he referred to as the "change of space."[24] Up to that time Luque had relied on spotting a good fastball.[25] He completed the winter season with a respectable record of 7–4, and returned to the Braves' spring training camp displaying a new confidence.

During the training camp of 1915 manager Stallings boasted about Luque's new-found pitch and proclaimed that he expected "great things from the youth" for the upcoming season. One reporter noted that Luque was "a puzzle to all the men in batting practice."[26]

The season began with promise and ended quickly with disappointment. Whatever Stallings had expected, it wasn't good enough—and it wasn't quick enough. Luque started one game and worked out of the bullpen for another before he was shipped out to the Toronto Club in the International League. If the 1914 season was the ultimate nightmare, the 1915 season wasn't starting out any better.

Again, Luque picked himself up and charged back into the game. In Toronto he excelled by registering a 15–9 record, with an ERA of 1.18.[27] Towards the close of the 1915 season he was offered a contract with the Brooklyn club in the outlaw Federal League, but fortunately the league disbanded before he could make a commitment. From 1916 through a short portion of the 1918 season Luque labored in obscurity as a starter and spot reliever for the Louisville Colonels, while perfecting an unworldly curve ball. In those three years he amassed a record of 26–14, with an ERA that stayed between 2.00 and 2.64.[28]

But the Colonels and the American Association suddenly suspended play in mid–1918 because of the war. Luque was nearly 28 years old, out of work and his future was darkened by insecurity. Seemingly out of the heavens, an angel of mercy in the form of a Cincinnati Reds scout appeared with a contract. Luque was once again a major league pitcher, and this time he would never look back.

At the close of the dismal and disappointing 1917 season the Reds had decided to rebuild their pitching staff. In February of 1918 they began the transformation by selling one of their starters, Clarence Mitchell, to the Dodgers. Before the year ended they had sold two other starters, Fred Toney and Pete Schneider, plus a reliever, George Smith.

Luque's manager in Cincinnati for the 1918 season was the complete opposite of Stallings in every manner. Christy Mathewson was an icon—an all–American boy whose striking good looks only enhanced his image as one of the greatest pitchers who ever lived. Mathewson took over the helm of the Reds on the 86th game of the 1916 season. Despite his prestigious presence, the final 69 games of the season were a disaster. During the 1917 campaign he could only lift his team two games over .500. When Luque arrived at spring training the Reds seemed to have improved their roster, but they struggled throughout the season, barely staying in the top half of the National League.

As a teenager, Luque had seen Mathewson pitch during his many exhibition trips to the island republic. Later in his life he admitted that he learned his craft by studying the Giants' ace hurler.[29] Many years later a seasoned baseball scribe observed that Luque's curve ball was not unlike Mathewson's, "a dazzling pitch, a low-breaking and controlled delivery."[30] Mathewson actually threw a reverse curve, called a screwball or "fadeaway," which, because of the unnatural twist of the arm, could only be employed a dozen times during a game.[31]

The reunion between Luque and Mathewson was short-lived because of the war. Late in the 1918 season Mathewson enlisted in the Army and was given the rank of captain. While the student's star was quickly rising, the teacher's world was collapsing. In 1918 Luque was amassing a 6–3 record and Mathewson was battling the effects of being gassed during a military training exercise. Because of the accident he developed tuberculosis and died seven years later in a sanitarium in upstate New York. It was "Matty" who had gotten the Reds back on a winning track in 1918, but he could not fully enjoy the enormous success his team would achieve in the following year.

Dolf Luque was now 29 years old and had finally proven that he could handle the rigors of major league pitching. He glided through the 1919 season with an impressive record of 10–3 and an ERA of 2.63. (He also appeared briefly in one game at third base.) The team's new manager, Pat Moran, started the Cuban in nine games, including a 6–2 victory in the home opener, but used him out of the bullpen 21 additional times.

Remarkably, Luque was one of six Reds' hurlers who won ten games or more in the pennant-clinching 1919 season. Hod Eller won 20 games and Slim Sallee won 21 while Edd Roush led the league with a batting average of .321. The Reds won the pennant with timely hitting, exceptional defense and a pitching staff that was extremely deep in talent. For the second time in his major league career Luque had pitched for a pennant-winning team, but this time he would be on the World Series roster.

On October 3, 1919, at Chicago's Comiskey Park, Luque became the first Latin to play in a World Series game when he pitched one inning of relief. His christening was in game three, which, according to historians who have researched the scandal-ridden series, was the first game in which the White Sox made a legitimate attempt at winning. In game seven he pitched in relief for four innings and again the White Sox won.

When the dust settled on October 9, the Reds had won the series in game nine with a 10–5 slugfest victory. Luque was impressive with a total of five innings pitched, allowing no runs on one hit and striking out six batters.

The Reds' hard-fought pennant drive and World Series championship was to be effectively invalidated by the revelation that several of the games had been fixed by eight White Sox players. As Luque pitched in his first World Series, his boyhood idol, Christy Mathewson, sat in the press box circling the plays in his score book that he thought were suspicious.

Unaware of the tainted Series crown, Luque returned to Cuba and displayed his championship talents to his Cuban League fans by notching a 10–4 record in 15 appearances.[32]

An interesting story to come out of the 1919 major league season involved Luque and one of the most unusual acts of cooperation between two clubs in the history of baseball. In May of 1919 an automobile filled with St. Louis Cardinals players was struck by a streetcar, with injuries sustained by five of their pitchers. At first, the Cards' general manager, Branch Rickey, thought that it would take months for two of his prominent hurlers, Red Ames and "Spittin' Bill" Doak, to return to play. With the baseball season in full swing and his team depleted of pitchers, Rickey reportedly placed a call to the president of the Cincinnati Reds, Garry Herrmann. Shortly thereafter, the press was alerted to the unprecedented news: According to *Baseball Magazine*, Herrmann had offered, as a temporary loan, to transfer Luque to the Cardinals to help bolster their staff.[33]

Days after the news report, however, nothing had transpired. Either Hermann backed out of his offer or the injuries suffered by Ames and Doak were exaggerated. Official baseball records reveal that Luque never pitched one day in a Cardinals uniform and Doak recovered quickly enough to log 31 games as a starter.

Prior to the 1921 season the balance of power on the diamond was tilted decidedly in favor of the pitcher. Baseballs were "adjusted" with razor cuts or sandpaper, and intentionally discolored with tobacco juice and dirt. Pitchers' spit and emery abrasions caused the ball to move wildly and hitters were forced to swing at balls that were weathered and soiled. During the 1920 season, Cleveland Indians shortstop Ray Chapman became the first major leaguer to die from head injuries sustained when he was hit by a pitch.

In December of 1920 the baseball rules committee outlawed the spitball, shine ball and emery ball pitches. They decreed that the prohibition would go into limited effect for the upcoming 1921 season. In consideration to those pitchers who relied on spitballs for their livelihood, 17 men were allowed to continue using that pitch. The effect of this ban was immediate and astounding.

Between the years of 1910 through 1919 there were 76 pitchers who registered a season ERA under 2.0 (minimum 20 games per season). During the decade of 1920 through 1929 the number of pitchers with ERAs under 2.0 plummeted to just two. Home runs and high-scoring games soon became commonplace while an army of pitchers found themselves emasculated. Only a few hurlers were able to make a successful transition from the epoch of the dead ball to the era of offense and double-digit ball games, among them Dolf Luque.

In 1920 Luque was used as both a rotation starter and a spot reliever, completing ten of the twenty-three games he began and coming out of the bullpen fourteen times. His record of 13–9 was the third-best won-lost record on the team and his 2.51 ERA was second best. By today's standards Luque's pitching performances in the offense-driven seasons of 1921 and 1922 were extremely effective. Although his two-year record was 30–42, he maintained an ERA in the 3.30 range.

It was at this point that he started to wear the label of "hard-luck" pitcher on a regular basis. Fred Lieb wrote, "whenever he used to take the mound for the Reds that was the office for the Cincinnati team to go into a hitting trance."

Does this mark the beginning of Luque's famous temper flaring against his teammates? According to Lieb the answer is no. He wrote, "[Luque] never showed the white feather, nor did he complain. Even though he lost one close game after another, he always was living in the hopes that someday the Reds would have a real hitting team."[34]

Despite Lieb's characterization of Luque as humble in defeat there is proof that his volcanic emotions did erupt against at least one teammate during this period. (This story has been retold so many times that the exact details have been blurred by overuse.) Sometime in the mid-twenties Luque's teammate Ralph "Babe" Pinelli hit a raw nerve when he suggested that Luque try a different pitching strategy (or, depending on the source, he criticized his performance). Luque exploded in anger and chased the third baseman around the clubhouse with a pair of scissors (or an ice pick). After being restrained, Luque demanded that Pinelli meet him at another location for a gun duel. When passions had subsided the two players made up and became close friends.

In the face of repeated losses by major league clubs during barnstorming tours in Cuba in the early 1920s, baseball commissioner Kenesaw Mountain Landis decided to take action. In order to avoid further embarrassing defeats at the hands of the dark island race, Landis banned tenured big-league ballplayers from participating in tours after November 1— or more than thirty days after the end of the regular season.

The rumor that Luque was actively participating in the Cuban League after the cutoff date had reached the offices of Landis in January of 1923. The commissioner cabled Reds' president Garry Herrmann, demanding an investigation. Herrmann cabled his subordinate in Cuba, Pepe Conte, to address the accusations. After nearly two weeks without a reply Herrmann sent another urgent cable. On January 21, 1923, Conte finally responded. He reassured the Reds' boss that Luque was not pitching, but he also added an unsolicited and rambling editorial on his Cuban hurler. This letter, preserved in the archives of the Hall of Fame, has served as a source of great amusement and deep insight into the volatile side of Luque's personality.

In his reply Conte seemed both anxious and angry, stumbling through a forest of typing errors and misspellings. Conte began, "Adolfo has grown a head large-enough to wear a number 47 hat."

His frustration with Luque came through in subsequent paragraphs: "I read your letter to him and as he is the most illiterated [sic] man on captivity, he raised cane and started to say at top of his voice that you and Landis could go pllump [sic] to…. And that when he got to training camp he would repeat this." The paragraph ends with a personal editorial, stating that Luque is "a most perfect jack-ass."

In the fifth paragraph he stated that Luque packs a "gat" (pistol) and he has been "in the habit of threatening [Cuban sportswriters] and is getting to be a public nuisance." In the seventh paragraph Conte acknowledges that Luque "is a good man at heart," but is also "a most perfect savage." The correspondence includes two emphatic pleas that Herrmann not disclose the contents of the letter.[35]

Conte may have been sloppy with his grammar and spelling, but he was crystal clear with his concerns. He knew better than to publicly insult a man who carried a pistol in the clubhouse.

Despite Conte's assertion that the ban was being observed, Luque received credit for pitching in 23 games during the 1922–1923 winter season.[36] It might be assumed that Luque, like so many other players, pitched under a false name. One alias he seemed to prefer was J. Cabada, the name of his chauffeur.[37]

The following winter baseball season Conte was ordered to investigate Luque's activities for the second consecutive year. In response, he sent a reassuring telegram to Herrmann, dated December 29, 1923, stating that his star pitcher was not playing past the November 10 deadline.[38] Again, despite the emphatic denial, Luque's Cuban records indicate he went 7–2 in 11 games.[39]

Pepe Conte's remarks in his January 1923 letter were not the first indication that Luque had personal problems. He had gotten himself involved in the world of cockfighting and was losing much of his earnings in gambling. Some have asserted that Luque also was involved in drinking and womanizing.

A cable sent to Herrmann on February 17, 1922, may have been a first signal to the Reds' front office that something was wrong. Luque, writing from the offices of a Havana-based promoter named Abel Linares, requested that the Reds' paymaster advance him the sum of $500 so that he could arrive at their Mineral Wells spring training camp in time. With apologies for his dire financial condition, he stated that he had not pitched during the 1921–1922 Cuban winter league season and he was short of cash.[40] Records indicate that indeed, Luque did not officially play that season.

The 1923 season was destined to be the greatest year that Luque would enjoy in a major league uniform. In fact, it would eventually prove to be the second-greatest single-season pitching performance of the entire decade.

At the Reds' spring training camp in Orlando, Florida, Luque was not reticent about making bold predictions for the upcoming season. When asked how he felt, Luque informed New York writer John B. Foster that he "was going to lead his league" in pitching.[41] The Pride of Havana proved to be incorrect in his estimate.

He actually led both leagues in a variety of pitching categories, including most wins, reflected in a 27–8 record, best winning percentage at .771, an ERA of 1.93, most shutouts (6) and fewest hits per nine innings (7.80). He also placed near the top in both leagues when he finished second in strikeouts, third in complete games and fourth in most strikeouts per nine innings. Columnist Bob Considine would later claim, "With a little better support his record would have been thirty-one and four."[42]

Luque's statistics seem even more extraordinary because the National League had exploded offensively in 1923, just as the American league had done in previous years. In 1919 the senior circuit's top home-run hitter clubbed 12 long balls while the top player in the category of slugging percentage topped out at .436. In 1923 the top home-run hitter had 41 and Rogers Hornsby of the St. Louis Cardinals led the league with a slugging percentage of .627.

Despite this offensive onslaught, Luque owned the league. Buried deep inside the calculations that made up his miniscule ERA are several interesting facts. He allowed only two home runs all season and held opposing batters to the lowest average of any National League pitcher, at .235. In addition he completed 28 games. Only one other man, Hall of Famer Dazzy Vance of Brooklyn, was able to record a season-low ERA under 2.0 during the entire decade of the twenties.

Despite his stunning successes on the mound in 1923, the Reds finished in second place for the second consecutive season. Again, Luque was saddled with a team that finished in a league tie for fifth-worst batting average and seventh worst in team home runs.

As Cuban journalists followed Luque through this incredible season they witnessed one event that came to epitomize the struggles that many Latin players had to endure. Luque's light complexion had not exempted him from racial taunts during his eleven previous years in the United States. The midsummer contest against the Giants may have been the last time he held back his fury in public.

The stands at Redland Field in Cincinnati were overflowing with fans eager to watch the defending world-champion New York Giants take on their pennant-contending Reds. From the first pitch of the game the Giants' bench corps were hurling insults at Luque, who was the starting pitcher that afternoon. Offensive suggestions about his family heritage and epithets such as "Cuban nigger" filled the air. The chief antagonist was New York's utility outfielder, Bill Cunningham. With the Giants' hard-hitting right fielder, Ross Youngs, waiting at the plate Luque decided that he could not tolerate the taunts any longer.

As columnist Frank Graham later explained to his readers, "Luque took off his glove, placed the ball in it, put it on the ground and, walking straight to the Giants' bench, punched Casey Stengel in the eye, Casey having the misfortune to be sitting next to Cunningham."[43] Stengel's biographer Robert Creamer said that Casey was expecting to watch a good fight, but Luque had completely ignored Cunningham. After Casey had been struck and knocked backwards, Luque then jumped on him. By this time, Ross Youngs had raced over to pull the angry Cuban off his teammate.[44]

The writers from Havana struck gold with this story. They concluded that Luque's heroics did not lie in the fact that he hit Stengel, but rather that he advanced against a bench full of players who were obviously hostile to him. He may have selected the wrong player for his wrath, but he challenged the entire New York Giants team, face to face.

As the fight continued, four Cincinnati policemen grabbed Luque away from Youngs' grasp and escorted him to the Reds' dugout. The officers then raced back to the mob scene across the field because the Reds' outfielder Edd Roush had re-ignited the brawl — much to the delight of the Cincinnati faithful.[45]

It wasn't over yet. Luque apparently generated a great deal of steam while pacing in the dugout because he grabbed an ash bat and returned to the Giants' bench for one more round. Again he received an escort, but this time the police secured him safely in the Reds' clubhouse.

Luque's reaction to his adversaries that day gained him the respect of the most grizzled combatants in baseball. Stengel, who was the Giants' veteran center fielder at the time of the incident, confessed a deep respect for Luque twenty years later when he told Al Lopez, "Never saw a pitcher who could do it better than Luque."[46] Likewise the Giants' manager, John McGraw, an infamous brawler in his own right, respected the Cuban's courage. McGraw called him "The greatest Cuban player ever produced."[47] And Frank Graham of the *New York Journal-American* later wrote, "He was a tough man, this one, stocky, gnarled, hard-visaged, hard thinking, unyielding in combat."[48]

In an era of hard-fisted baseball, Luque was now respected and feared. And it really didn't matter how large his opponent was. A case in point was a game against the Brooklyn Dodgers on May 10, 1925.

When the Dodgers' pitcher, Ernest "Tiny" Osborne, threw a high, hard fastball at Luque's head he had invited disaster. Luque stood 5'7" and weighed 160 pounds while Osborne was 6'5" and weighed 215 pounds. Luque responded by dusting himself off, picking up his bat and hurling it at the mammoth pitcher. After the ensuing brawl was broken up, the president of the National League, John Heydler, decided that the most aggressive offender should be punished. Luque was fined $50.[49]

If size didn't matter, neither did stature, because in April of 1925 he aimed a head-high fastball at the Cardinals' second baseman, Rogers Hornsby, that sent him sprawling in the dust, unconscious. It was four days before the "Rajah" could return to action. Luque had apparently taken offense at Hornsby's successful hitting streak against him.[50]

Luque did not confine his temper to the sovereign borders of the United States, either. While pitching for the Cienfuegos team in winter ball in November of 1928, he managed to incite a brawl and ended up with a $200 fine for disorderly conduct and "Public scandal." He told a reporter that he was banned for life from the Cienfuegos team because of the disturbance.[51]

In most instances, however, Luque held his temper and did not retaliate. If he had struck back every time his nationality or manhood was insulted he would never have survived, emotionally or physically.

For example, there was an incident in 1924 when the Reds played a spring training game against the Cardinals and Luque restrained his famous temper. An overconfident bush leaguer named Stan Smith had been boasting about his big-league abilities during training camp. Despite Smith's open disdain for the veterans on the club, Cardinals manager Branch Rickey decided to give him a tryout. The youthful braggart was placed in the lineup to face the Cincinnati ace Eppa Rixey and responded by hammering three consecutive hits.

When Luque replaced Rixey later in the game the next hitter was Smith. Luque's heavy accent captured the attention of Smith, who stepped out of the batter's box and irreverently walked toward the mound. Smith began assaulting Luque with sarcastic questions:

"Hey, you, what kind of language do you speak?"

"What's your name?"

"Adoolfo what?"

"Where are you from?"

"Where the hell is that?"

Luque's teammates braced themselves for the inevitable retribution. Nervous about a possible fight, the umpire intervened and ordered Smith back into the batters box.

Then Luque responded to the disrespectful youth, saying proudly, "Now you will know where Cuba is." He toed the rubber and struck back with two fast balls that caught either corner of the plate. Then he launched a curve ball that froze Smith stiff. Three pitches, three strikes. The cocky youth slunk back into the bush, where he vanished, along with his career.[52]

Luque was a fiery character for sure; however, objective research reveals that his antics were a mere sideshow in comparison to those of some of his teammates. From a sane distance it appeared as if the Reds' clubhouse was a version of the Mad Hatter's tea party.

First there was Carl Mays, the only 20-game winner on the Reds staff in 1924. Mays had a reputation for being a headhunter and was credited with beaning 54 batters in six seasons.[53] He had earned the infamous distinction of killing Cleveland's Ray Chapman with a pitch in 1920. Mays was heavily criticized by the press for not meeting with Chapman's widow and not publicly expressing his sorrow. In November of 1920 he admitted that whereever he had played during his career he was always unpopular in the locker room and that he didn't care.[54] In addition there were persistent but unfounded rumors that Mays had thrown the fourth game of the 1921 World Series.

The other staff ace was Eppa Rixey, a 6'5" future Hall of Fame left-hander who wasn't afraid to show his displeasure. Clyde Sukeforth, the team's catcher, told a writer, "When he pitched you didn't have to ask who won the game.... If he'd lost, the place would look like a tornado had gone through it. Chairs would be broken up, tables knocked over, equipment thrown around."[55]

The Reds briefly had another hurler named Clyde Day, a native of Pea Ridge, Arkansas, who demonstrated his hog-calling talents from the mound. Insanity prevailed in the Reds clubhouse in the 1920s.

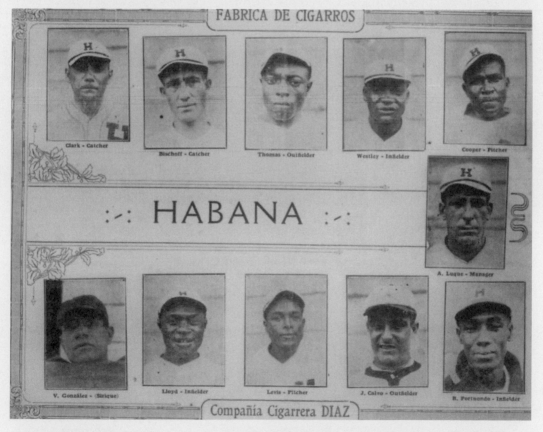

During the 1923–1924 winter league season Luque managed a truly integrated Havana Reds' ball club. Included in this composite are Negro League great and hall of famer "Pop" Lloyd (bottom, second from left), and major leaguers Jacinto Calvo (bottom, second from right) and John Bischoff (top, second from left). (Source: Jay Sanford collection)

Spring training camp of 1924 began on a positive note, but ended in tragedy. Pat Moran had taken over the manager's job in 1919 and engineered the Reds to their first World Series championship in club history. He also saw potential in the fiery Cuban who was struggling to make the starting rotation. In 1920 he gave Luque the break he had been waiting for and it paid off with four consecutive seasons of double-digit wins.

But Moran's lifestyle and a kidney ailment were affecting the 48-year-old skipper. When camp began in Orlando in February, Moran was a shadow of his former self. He would skip meals and spend much of the time alone in his hotel room. In early March he was rushed to an Orlando hospital while his "boys" waited and prayed. On March 7, 1924, Pat Moran died of Bright's disease, a kidney ailment.

Jack Hendricks, a one-time manager with the Cardinals, took over the helm. His first job was more psychological than tactical, because he had to rally the team back from the sudden and stunning loss.

Misfortune struck again early in the season when the team captain, Jake Daubert, was nearly blinded from a beaning at the hands of a St. Louis Cardinals pitcher. Daubert never regained his old form and eventually died during a blood transfusion in Cincinnati on October 9, 1924.

During the 1924 season Luque returned to the starting rotation, but achieved only lackluster results. His record of 10–15 and ERA of 3.16 were hallmarks compared to the Reds' continued anemic offensive numbers. Although they finished in fourth place, the pitching staff led the National League in fewest runs surrendered, fewest walks allowed, fewest home runs allowed and lowest ERA. On the other hand, aside from the consistent offensive brilliance of outfielder Edd Roush, they were the second worst team in the National League in runs scored.

Just as preparations were being made for the 1925 season Luque began a bit of hard-nosed negotiating by returning his contract unsigned. In a letter to Herrmann dated January 27, he stated that the salary offered "is not satisfactory to me." He countered with an demand for $9,500. In February Luque signed the contract for an amount he deemed satisfactory. He also attached a short note to Herrmann asking for an advance of $500. No explanation of financial need was given.[56]

In spring training camp of 1925 Luque was suddenly stricken with a case of "grippe" (contagious viral disease resembling influenza). A sportswriter from New York commented, "He was coughing for the first time in his life and he was worried to death about it. The doctor had prescribed castor oil and the famous player was making more fuss over the dose than any child ever made."[57] Perhaps it was the Cuban's fear of becoming the third Reds player to die within a one-year period that led to his distress. The visions of Moran and Daubert were still hauntingly clear to each of the Cincinnati players.

In 1926, *Baseball Magazine* published a detailed profile on Luque, acknowledging that he was one of the premier pitchers in the game. Commenting on his physical stature the article revealed, "beneath his well-tailored suit are muscles like whipcord, as strong and as tough. Even more than deceptive strength, Luque has endurance.... He has never been crippled by a sore arm."

The article also revealed a personal milestone: Luque had married a Cincinnati girl sometime during the year.[58]

In 1925 Luque was once again the best pitcher in the National League, posting a leading ERA of 2.63. But because of his teammates' languorous hitting he ended the season with a record of 16–18. Reflecting on the 1925 campaign, he told writer Cullen Cain, "I had one lucky year, 1923. Last year I have the lowest earned average and yet I lose more games than I win. Can you imagine that?" Cain responded in his column by saying, "This was the lone word of protest of a pitcher who has lost more hard luck games than anybody. They say he never complains when his team fails to make runs behind him."[59]

Late in the winter of 1925 Luque underwent surgery and missed the entire 1925–1926 winter league season in Cuba. He wrote to Garry Herrmann on February 4, 1926, assuring the Reds' president that he would be fully prepared for spring training, but needed an advance of $500 to "meet certain payments regarding the operation in question."

By the time spring training exercises began in 1926, Luque was a 35-year-old veteran and was expected to be the #4 rotation starter for the sixth year in a row. The Reds had come off a disappointing third-place finish in the previous year, but their powerful submarine pitcher, Carl Mays, was expected to return to the squad after an injury-riddled season.

Joining the Reds' camp was a rookie catcher named Clyde Sukeforth, who, 19 years later, would help change the course of baseball by delivering Jackie Robinson to the Brooklyn Dodgers. Sukeforth remembered seeing Luque that spring, describing him as, "a short, little right-hander: kind of stocky with one of the greatest curveballs you ever looked at."[60]

The Reds' front office had planned to audition a large group of pitchers that spring, just in case Carl Mays could not return. Sukeforth recalled, "I reported to the Reds in 1926 in Orlando, Florida, and the club came in a little heavier [on catchers]. They added two catchers and I guess the only reason they took me was because the [additional] pitchers wanted to throw a lot in spring training. So there was always room for an extra catcher and I was one of them. They had two veteran catchers already."[61]

When you hear Sukeforth describing the pregame preparations between catcher and pitcher it seems elementary compared to the extravagant analysis conducted today: "We had clubhouse meetings before the game and [I'd] just listen to him [the pitcher]," said Sukeforth. "The manager would want to know how you're going to get so-and-so out, but everything depended on the pitcher."[62]

Willis Hudlin pitched for the Cleveland Indians in the 1920s and he echoed Sukeforth's claim that the responsibility of planning for the game fell upon the pitcher. "Back then," Hudlin said, " when you knew which day you were going to pitch you would start studying three days ahead of time. You would take the lineup for the opposing team and go over it by yourself and figure how you would pitch to those guys. I would review their weaknesses."[63]

By all accounts Luque was a very smart in matters concerning baseball, and he would mentally catalogue the many hitters he had faced during his career. "He was a very intelligent guy. He could tell after studying what the [opposing] pitcher was going to throw," claimed former teammate Bill Werber. "Sometimes he would come up to me and say, 'Beel, you want to know what he will throw?' And sometimes I would say no. I'd say, 'If you're wrong you might get me hit in the head.' But he could tell what a pitcher was going to throw next."[64]

The cold weather that blanketed the East during the early spring of 1926 affected Luque adversely. He complained about the frosty conditions and admitted he hated the cold. "Arm hardly ever gets sore. But him sore now," he said.[65]

Luque's dream of having offensive firepower behind him came true during that season when catcher Eugene "Bubbles" Hargrave led the National League in hitting with a .353 average. Center fielder Edd Roush, right fielder Curt Walker and rookie left fielder "Cuckoo" Christensen all hit over .300.

Although the Reds led the league in hitting with a .290 average and finished only two games out of first place, however, Luque had an undistinguished season. His 13–16 record and ERA of 3.43 were the worst performance among the four starting pitchers in the rotation.

More unsavory information on Luque's personal life became public after the close of the 1926 season. On the afternoon of October 28, 1926, a woman walked into the law offices of Arthur C. Fricke in the Second National Bank Building in Cincinnati. She demanded that action be taken against her husband, a Cuban pitcher for the Reds named Adolfo Luque. Giving an address of 951 Pavilion Street, the scorned female argued that she had been cast aside by her spouse, leaving her to face the world sick and penniless.

Attorney Fricke penned the following letter to Herrmann:

> I represent Mrs. Luque.
>   She tells me she is in a delicate condition and will shortly give birth to a child. Luque has abandoned her and has sent her a cablegram stating that he has left the country and is not expecting to return. Do you know anything about his contemplated plans, and is there any money in the hands of the ball club coming to him?
>   The woman is destitute and someone will have to take care of her.
>   Very truly yours,[66]

Shortly after this letter arrived at Herrmann's office the rumor started to circulate that Luque would not return for the 1927 season. Responding to the stories that were now appearing in the press, Luque cabled Herrmann, confirming that he had "no intentions of quitting professional baseball and expected to be back in the States next year."

Despite his response, the Reds' front office had already begun to act.

Another phantom story was leaked indicating that Luque might be "one of the first men traded … provided any trades are made."[67]

When first light broke on the Reds' 1927 spring training camp, Luque was in attendance; the subtle threats seemed to be put away for another season.

Gambling was a problem that ran throughout baseball from its earliest days. After Commissioner Landis took office in 1920 he expelled many well-known ballplayers who were implicated in fixing ball games. Indeed, even the slightest hint of impropriety set his moral scythe in motion. John McGraw was forced to give up his investment in a racetrack in Havana, while American League first baseman Art Shires was advised to abandon his part-time boxing career because of possible gambling influences. Fifteen ballplayers were banished from the game during Landis's first few years as commissioner and many more, including Dolf Luque, were being watched carefully.

Suspicions that Luque pitched illegally in Cuba during the early 1920s, and his well-documented battles with teammates and opposing players, put him in a high-profile position. It was rumored that he enjoyed public gambling, but this behavior never received the public scrutiny that dogged Rogers Hornsby during his career.

It is doubtful that Luque ever fixed a game to win a bet, given his enormous competitive drive; however, one man held a secret about Luque that would have destroyed his career if the details had been divulged. A few short months before his death in 1951, Hall of Fame umpire Bill Klem revealed that he had been approached with an offer, way back in the 1920s.

He mused, "I wonder what Judge Landis would have done had I reported the colorful Cuban pitcher, Adolfo Luque, for twice attempting to 'tip' me." Recalling the incident, Klem revealed to writer William Slocum that Luque had entered the umpires' dressing room prior to a game he was scheduled to pitch.

"Who is going to work behind the plate today?" Luque boldly inquired.

Klem told him that Barry McCormack would be the umpire calling balls and strikes and asked him to explain his inquiry. Luque answered, "Beel, I give you ten dollars you work behind plate today." Klem ordered him out of the dressing room after telling him that he would get into trouble for "that kind of nonsense."

Two months later Luque returned, now increasing the offer to twenty-five dollars. Klem exploded: "I gave the Cuban quite a tongue-lashing and he left."

At the age of 77, and sensing that he had very little time left, Klem reflected on his five-decade career and defended his decision not to report Luque to the commissioner. He argued, "Technically, I suppose, I was being bribed. But Luque didn't mean it that way." Interpreting his motives Klem added, "It means a lot to a pitcher to know a curve that nicks a corner of the plate will be called a strike and Luque simply thought I would not only call 'em as I saw 'em, but also see 'em correctly."[68]

In 1927 Luque was asked to collaborate with a group of high-profile players on an instructional manual called *Secrets of Baseball*. He joined future hall of famers Rogers Hornsby, Eddie Collins, Pie Traynor, Tris Speaker, Lou Gehrig and George Sisler in contributing chapters on how to play the game. Certainly the publisher employed a ghost writer for Luque, but the fact that a Cuban was chosen over many well-deserving American pitchers is remarkable.

In chapter three, titled "*The Work of a Pitcher*," Luque states, "I've always played ball — as a boy in Cuba I learned the game, and I kept at it until I landed in the big leagues. But when I was young, fortunately, I didn't overwork myself."[69] His repeated admonitions of "pacing the stress on your arm" seemed to be advice that he followed religiously in his personal life.

(His ghost writer was either sloppy or knew nothing about baseball. Halfway through the chapter he fabricated this Luque quote, "Babe Ruth, extremely successful with the Boston Braves as a twirler, became an outfielder so that his batting ability could be brought into every game...." Every red-blooded baseball fan knows that Ruth had pitched for the Boston Red Sox, not the Braves.)

Between 1927 and 1928 Luque won 24 and lost 22 and the Reds finished in fifth place both seasons. By 1929 the trade rumors were thick again.

Luque's worst performance since the debacle in 1914 occurred in the last year of the roaring twenties, when he notched a 5–16 record with an ERA of 4.50. Although they had the third-best ERA in the league, the Reds finished in seventh place with the second-worst batting average. To use a tired analogy, the 1929 Reds were like cheap luggage: Although they looked good at home they fell apart on the road (28–49).

That winter Luque received a cable at his home in Havana informing him that he had been traded to the lowly Brooklyn Dodgers. The trade could best be described as a lateral move for the Cuban hurler. Under the direction of the seemingly befuddled Wilbert Robinson, the Dodgers had strung together a sadly consistent record. They had managed to finish in sixth place seven times in eight years.

When the trade of Luque was announced the local scribes, and many Cincinnati fans, expressed their disapproval.[70] But, although the Reds front office felt he was washed up, Robinson saw years of potential left in the 39-year-old warhorse.

In exchange for Luque the Reds received a burned-out right-hander named Doug McWeeny, who was destined to last only eight games in the 1930 season. The Dodgers certainly got the better end of the deal; Luque would make fifty appearances in two winning seasons for the Bums of Brooklyn.

It is important to note that Luque became the first Latin ever signed by the Dodgers organization; and when Robinson signed a 21-year-old catcher named Alfonso Lopez in 1930, the big leagues had their first Hispanic Spanish-speaking battery. (Lopez, born and raised in Florida, was of Cuban, Spanish and Italian heritage.)

Reminiscing over a hall of fame career that spanned 19 years, Lopez credited Luque with teaching him how to become a major league catcher. "He'd shake me off until I knew exactly what to signal for," Lopez would explain to reporters. "After a while I was thinking just like he was."

The old Cuban taught Lopez the most important responsibility of a catcher — "getting the pitcher's confidence ... (so) he doesn't have to worry about thinking.... He just takes the sign."[71]

When Brooklyn rebounded in 1930 with an 86–68 record, one New York newspaper exclaimed, "these two bronze-skinned individuals are accounting for many of the team's victories." The article also noted, "Luque has achieved one of the most remarkable comebacks in baseball this year, pitching winning ball from the start and turning in many low-hit pitching accomplishments."[72] His first season with Brooklyn ended with a record of 14–8, second only to Dazzy Vance in team victories.

In the spring of 1931 a Cuban brewery invited the Brooklyn Dodgers to Havana to play a series of exhibition games, betting that the Lopez-Luque battery would create a profitable draw. However, Luque envisioned an embarrassing series of defeats for his Dodgers against the highly talented black players of Cuba. He persuaded manager Robinson to stage intra-squad games instead.

The Dodgers may have avoided defeat against the Cuban players, but they could not avoid the lure of Havana's free-for-all nightlife. One player was forced to pay a Cuban lawyer for time lost when he kept the barrister's secretary out late during a week of partying.[73]

During one of the first evenings in town Luque gathered a group of young, naïve players together at a beachside bar and recommended that they drink a concoction called piña fria. For several hours the group consumed drink after drink without effect. Eventually they realized that they had been drinking only crushed pineapple.[74]

In later years more and more anecdotes about the fun-loving, prank-playing Luque seem to emerge. But so also do more stories about his violent nature. There are few photographs of Luque smiling. His dour image appears over and over in the earliest pictures from the late 1910s through the 1950s. One strained smile appears in a 1930 photo when Luque posed near Al Lopez.

His two-year tenure in Brooklyn was modestly successful, and although he proved he could still pitch in the major leagues at the age of 41, his ERA was over 4.0. In 1932 Wilbert Robinson was replaced as the Dodgers' manager and Luque became expendable. Brooklyn's loss was New York's gain as the Giants' John McGraw finally got his wish, and Luque inked a contract with New York nationals for the 1932 season.

McGraw knew that his Cuban gem had seen his best days in the starting rotation, but he felt that he had a new bullpen ace. Luque was seen as the vintage filigree that the Giants needed to complement the organization.

John McGraw was entering his forty-third year of professional baseball and his thirtieth season at the helm of the Giants when spring training drills commenced in Los Angeles in February of 1932. As usual, McGraw and his family had spent much of the winter in Cuba enjoying the mild temperatures. In February, McGraw (and later Luque) made the arduous, time-consuming trip from Havana to the training facilities in California. The players lodged at the Hotel Biltmore and were soon stunned by the high cost of getting from place to place in a city that seemingly sprawled forever.

McGraw was the first member of the team to check into the Biltmore and when he held court with the press he pronounced, "I feel confident we will be in the thick of the fight from start to finish."[75] But the 59-year-old warrior was ill. Besides his weight problems he was suffering from high blood pressure, an enlarged prostate and continuing bouts of sinusitis.

As the regular season began in the chilly climes of the Northeast McGraw's health problems multiplied. The last straw was a case of ptomaine poisoning he picked up in Pittsburgh. After forty games and a dismal record of 17–23 John McGraw handed over the managerial reins to his star first baseman, Bill Terry. Months later McGraw and his wife Blanche boarded a ship and sailed back to their beloved city of residence, Havana. With Terry at the helm, the Giants played close to .500 ball for the remainder of the 1932 season, and Dolf Luque found a comfortable new niche.

Joe Culinane is a writer and broadcaster who began his career in 1937 as a junior sportswriter for the *Chicago Times*. He had the chance to observe the Cuban hurler for several years and concludes, "Luque was the first successful relief pitcher in the history of the National League."[76]

Luque appeared in 38 games in 1932, finishing the season with a team-high five saves and a four-year-low ERA of 4.01. Under Terry's leadership Luque's natural abilities came to the fore as the manager attempted to change some of the defensive strategies for the Giants. *New York Times* baseball writer Arthur Daley wrote that Luque was one of the best fielding pitchers in the game. He observed, "Few pitchers could field their position with the cat-like agility that made Luque sure death on ground balls."

Manager Terry had devised a strategy built around Luque's quick defensive skills. With opposing runners on first and second base and a probable bunt situation, Terry would order his shortstop to straddle second base and his third baseman to do the same at his position. Naturally the shortstop would be so close to second base that the runner could not take a long lead when the bunt was laid down. Luque would then hang a sucker pitch — a "tantalizingly slow" curve ball, and the ball would be bunted easily into the infield grass. According to Daley, "Luque could cover all that territory, compelling the batter to bunt where he wanted him to bunt." Luque would handle the bunt and easily throw out the runner going from second to third. "It was the prettiest defensive strategem this reporter ever saw."[77]

When Harry Danning arrived as a rookie at the Giants' camp in 1933, he was not expecting to learn his greatest lessons of the game from an old Cuban pitcher. A native of Los Angeles, Danning was not isolated from the growing influence that Hispanics were having on this country, however, so was open to listening to Luque's unique philosophy of the game.

"He was one of the best baseball men I ever met," Danning later declared. "I spent a couple of years with him in the bullpen when I was a second- and third-string catcher and he taught me more about baseball and catching and pitching than anyone in my whole career. He was my mentor."

When the bullpen phone rang, Luque was like a prizefighter, ready for war. He had his attack strategy all mapped out. Danning watched the process and remembered, "In fact when he was called in to relieve I said, 'What are we going to do Pops?' and he said This is what I'm going to do and that's what I'm going to do. He was a very smart man."[78]

Although Luque had lost the steam on his fastball, Danning recalled how he utilized his other strengths. "He had great control and he had an overhand curve ball. Anywhere you wanted it, he put it…. Left-handed hitters had a tough time hitting him."

Danning further observed, "I don't care who you were, you'd have a hard time stealing when he was pitching…. He was very fast and he would fake towards home plate and you couldn't steal on him because he got that ball away fast."[79]

Danning, who had a successful ten-year major league career, particularly remembered one incident in spring training camp of 1935 when Luque was attempting to display his accuracy. Teammates Mark Koenig and Joe Moore had set their bats on either side of the plate and dared Luque to keep his pitches within those boundaries. Danning then set himself behind the plate wearing all of his catcher's equipment. Luque was intent on demonstrating his skills, but his bullpen catcher was holding up the process. Suddenly, Danning saw a flash of the old Cuban's temper: "So I put on my catcher's mask and Luque came running down there, took the mask off me and threw it away. And then he threw curve balls and fast balls right between those bats."[80]

Nothing would obscure the full spectacle of Luque's exhibition — not even a catcher's mask.

In 1933 Luque made 35 relief appearances and compiled an impressive ERA of 2.69 and a record of 8–2. His risk-taking mentality sometimes emerged when he was pitching, according to baseball veteran Dave Garcia:

> When Luque was pitching for the New York Giants it was a very hot day, maybe 100 degrees.
> It was a tight game and the first hitter of the inning was the pitcher. He walked the pitcher and when his manager came out to ask him what was going on Luque said, "If I get him out he will go back into the dugout and cool off with a cold towel. I want him to stand out in the hot sun for one inning and get tired."
> Luque then went on to retire the next three batters. He had made his point.[81]

Luque regaled his bullpen catcher Harry Danning with a similar parable involving an incident in the 1920s: "Luque told me a story once about when he was pitching for Cincinnati against [Dodgers' pitcher] Dazzy Vance," said Danning. "It was very hot in Cincinnati and he walked Vance on purpose. And then he tried to pick him off, over and over, so he would get him tired. This thinking was over and beyond a lot of players."[82]

With a team that included Luque and three future hall of famers— Carl Hubbell (23 wins, ERA 1.66), Bill Terry (.322 batting average) and Mel Ott (23 home runs)— the Giants easily beat the second-place Pittsburgh Pirates by five games for the 1933 National League crown. They would now march into the World Series to meet the surprise winners of the American League title — the Washington Senators.

The *Pride of Havana* had pitched for world-champion teams before and he had pitched in World Series games before, but neither Luque nor any other Latino pitcher had ever won a game on America's largest sporting stage.

The Senators were managed by Joe Cronin, who had succeeded Washington's heroic icon, Walter Johnson, after the 1932 campaign. It was a nice coincidence that both Cronin and Terry were manager/players who led their teams to the World Series in their first full seasons as skippers. Six of Washington's eight starting-position players hit .295 or better in 1933, while the Giants had three starting pitchers with ERAs under 3.0. It was a classic matchup of offense vs. defense.

The Giants had won the first two games of the series in New York, but the Senators' Earl Whitehill shut out the Giants in game three, in Washington. In game four the Giants squeaked past the Senators in the eleventh inning with a 2–1 victory.

New York's Carl Hubbell was physically spent after hurling all 11 innings, limiting the hard-hitting Senators to only eight safeties.

Meanwhile, the Giants' bullpen was like a morgue. Luque had spent the entire series riding the bench, while the only New York relief pitcher to see action was Herman Bell, who pitched one uneventful inning in game three. The Senators, on the other hand, went to the bullpen five times in the first four games.

In game five the Giants started 19-game winner Hal Schumacher, while the Senators gave the starting job to General Crowder, an eight-year veteran who had won 24 games. The contest was played in Washington on October 8 before a crowd of 28,454. With the Giants ahead in the series three games to one, the Senators were desperate for a victory.

By the top of the sixth inning the Giants had reached a 3–0 lead by piecing together scratch hits and sacrifice bunts. But the Senators fought back by tying the game in the bottom of the frame. Schumacher managed to retire the first two Senator batters but gave up singles to Heinie Manush and Joe Cronin. Luque had begun to warm up in the bullpen when centerfielder Fred Schulte came to the plate and hit a long drive into the deep left field seats to tie the score. Schumacher earned a trip to the showers after he gave up consecutive hits to Joe Kuhel and Ossie Bluege.

With runners at first and third, the forty-three-year-old Luque walked across the diamond to take his position on the mound. Employing his deadly curveball, he got Luke Sewell to hit a harmless grounder to second baseman Hughie Critz for the last out of the inning.

In the seventh inning Luque had to face relief pitcher Jack Russell and then two of the Senators' best hitters, Buddy Myer and Goose Goslin. Russell struck out swinging and Myer froze on a curve ball for a called strike three. Goslin couldn't connect and struck out swinging.

It couldn't have been scripted better by a Hollywood writer: The grizzled veteran making one last stab at the greatest prize, with what one *New York Times* writer described as "slow and deliberate" concentration.[83]

In the Giants' half of the eighth a minor rally had begun with one out. Suddenly a strange-looking blue pigeon landed on the infield. Washington fans regarded the familiar bird as a sign of good luck and the omen proved true again. New York's infielder Travis Jackson promptly hit into an inning-ending double play. The score remained deadlocked at 3–3. In the bottom of the eighth Luque got Heinie Manush to hit a grounder for the first out. Manager Cronin hit a solid single to left, but was stranded after Luque retired home-run hero Fred Schulte on a fly ball and Joe Kuhel on a grounder to third.

In the Giants' half of the ninth inning Luque came to the plate with two outs and rapped a single up the middle. In the Senators' half of the ninth Luque struck out Bluege and got Luke Sewell to ground out. Then he walked the pitcher Russell. Was it a lapse of control or did he do it purposely to keep him from resting on the bench? It didn't matter, because Buddy Myer grounded out to end the inning.

But trouble was brewing because Luque had been coming off the mound so hard on his fastball delivery that he broke the nail on his big toe. In the Giants' tenth inning Mel Ott drove a fastball over the wall with two out to break the tie and put New York ahead. Now it was up to Luque to finish off the middle of the Senators' order in the bottom of the tenth.

Giants' manager Bill Terry considered removing the aging veteran for a fresh arm when he scanned the lineup card and saw that the first three Washington batters were Goose Goslin (.297), Heinie Manush (.336) and Joe Cronin (.309)—all future hall of famers. Terry dismissed the idea of relief despite the fact that Luque's toe was bleeding and he was limping on the mound.[84]

Goslin swung at a breaking curveball and hit a grounder to Terry at first base. Luque, moving as quickly as he could through the pain, rushed to cover the bag in time for the first out. Manush, who came in second to Jimmy Foxx for the American League batting title that season, hit a bullet which found its way directly into the glove of the Giants' second baseman, Hughie Critz. Two out.

Luque found himself in serious trouble for the first time in the game when Cronin slapped a single to left and Fred Schulte took ball four on a 3–2 count. After signaling for Carl Hubbell to start warming up in the bullpen, manager Terry walked to the mound, intending to remove Luque to the showers.

"I peetch," The Cuban forcefully told the skipper.

Terry hid his face in his glove to conceal a wide grin and replied, "Go ahead and peetch."[85]

With that annoyance out of the way, Luque set himself to face Joe Kuhel, who had hit a career-best .322 that season. He was also the Senators' second-best run producer. Kuhel stood deep in the batter's box and Luque placed a curve on the outside corner for strike one. Then Kuhel moved up, and, according to Luque, his feet were practically on the plate. The Cuban sent another curveball, this time on the inside half. Strike two. Kuhel then moved back, and Luque responded with a curveball on the outside of the plate and Kuhel swung.

"Strike three!" the umpire bellowed.[86]

The Giants' catcher, Gus Mancuso: "Leaped far off the ground waving both arms in the air and letting out a victory whoop that could be heard above the noise of the crowd." Manager Terry raced to the mound and draped his arm over the Luque's shoulder and shoved the gameball into his pocket.[87] Bob Considine later declared that Luque started sprinting for the clubhouse yelling, "I feexed heem, I feexed heem. I geeve heem Numbaire Two!"[88]

Luque had won the game and clinched the World Series for New York. He would later admit that this victory was his number-one thrill in baseball.[89]

In the clubhouse the players were drinking champagne when a figure — larger than life — entered the room.[90] John McGraw, now sixty years old and only five months away from his final breath, wanted to pay his boys one last tribute. McGraw had not engineered a world series title since 1922, and had not managed the team for the last two seasons, but his name was still synonymous with the New York Giants. He had earned the right to join in the celebration.

More than two thousand Giants fans met the team at Pennsylvania Station at 9:25 that evening. With a marching band playing on the station platform each team member walked off the train and was hustled through a cordon of police. They walked to the Hotel New Yorker where they were honored in an all-night banquet in the grand ballroom. Every player received a share of approximately $4,600, the lowest world series payout since 1922.

It would be another 21 years before the Giants would win another World Series, and another 24 years before a Latin-born pitcher would appear in the post season. Placing this game in historical perspective, it was more than just an old man facing three future hall of famers in the last inning of the last game of the World Series. It was the first time that a man over the age of 40 had won a World Series game and it was the first time that this feat was accomplished by a Latin pitcher. The world was changing.

Within a short period of time the Senators ownership would hire a full-time scout named Joe Cambria and send him to mine the untapped wealth of talent in Cuba. But still, changes came slowly for Latinos in the post season. The reappearance of a Caribbean or Latin American pitcher in the World Series did not happen until 1957 when Puerto Rican Juan Pizarro pitched in relief for the Milwaukee Braves. A Latin-born pitcher would not win another championship series game until Puerto Rican reliever Luis Arroyo of the New York Yankees beat the Cincinnati Reds in 1961.

The next season, 1934, would be Luque's last full campaign. The Cuban made 26 effective relief appearances and then retired from active play in 1935 after two games.

Manager Bill Terry asked Luque to stay on as a Giants coach beginning in 1935, but eventually Luque chafed under Terry's strict methods. When he failed to show up for the first days of spring training in 1938, Terry cabled his famous assistant in Cuba, telling him that he had 24 hours to report to Hot Springs, Arkansas. Luque's reply was terse and definite: "Get somebody else to coach. I'm through."

One writer reported that Luque was planning to "retire to his ranch and raise fighting cocks" full time.[91] Three years later, after Terry was fired, Luque returned to the Giants and remained a coach with them for five more seasons.

During the 1930s Luque started to phase himself out of pitching duties in the Cuban League and concentrate more on management. He began to make a greater impact for his team by directing young players from the dugout. As a manager in Cuba he demanded that his players follow every directive to the letter and they would later admit that they feared his wrath.

Adrian Zabala played for Luque beginning in 1935 and he remembered, "He wanted you to do it just like he'd say or he'd get mad at you. I had a fuss with him a couple of times but, the next day we'd just forget about it."[92]

Former Washington Senators great Camilo Pascual recalled how Luque acted towards his players. "Luque was very aggressive," he said. "If things didn't go his way he became a maniac. But he was a nice guy as long as everything went his way."[93]

There are two stories which illustrate how Luque could restrain his volatile temper when dealing with players who had earned his respect. A youthful Minnie Miñoso played under Luque in Cuba and admits that he was temperamental, but had the capacity to exhibit fairness. "He was managing me at Marianao and I had a charley horse and it bothered me for a couple days," said Miñoso.

"I had put lamb grease on it so I thought I would try it out. I was on first base playing against Cienfuegos and I wanted to find out if my leg was good. So I took out running without a signal to steal, and the catcher, Ray Noble, threw me out."

When Miñoso returned to the dugout Luque was fuming. "Hey Negrito!" Luque shouted. [*Negrito* is a unflattering term meaning "little black man."]

Miñoso shot back, "What is it?"

"Who told you to go? Who gave you the signal to go? That just cost you $50."
"OK, you're the boss," Miñoso replied, stonefaced.

Later that afternoon Luque found out that Miñoso had been keeping his injured leg a secret, and had just wanted to test it. When he saw the outfielder the next day he said, "No, I cannot fine you. You give 100% all the time."[94]

Felo Ramírez also knew a story about Luque's evenhanded treatment of his players. "Luque managed Marianao," Ramírez remembered. "He had the great Pedro Formental playing for him in the center field. They called him '300' Formental because he always hit .300. So one day [Luque] went out and told Formental to play deeper in the outfield ... [but] he didn't obey the order." Luque stood fuming on the dugout steps as the hitter drove the next pitch over Formental's head.

A quick smile crossed Ramírez's face as he continued with the story: "When he came from the outfield Luque was waiting for him, furious and angry. Pedro told Dolf, 'Don't say anything to me — it was a *Tremendo Palo*.' It was a very Cuban expression meaning great, great hit. Luque backed down and smiled. Luque was enamoured and disarmed and intimidated by the response."[95]

In most cases, however, Luque would stand his ground. Zabala recalled an episode in 1935 in Cuba:

> One time we were playing against Almandares in Tropical Stadium and Luque was our manager. I was pitching and the game was 3–2 in our favor. In the ninth inning Almandares got two men on base with two outs.
>
> So the batter was Hector Rodríguez, who eventually played with the White Sox. He hit a fly ball to right field which was an easy play. So we all started running to the clubhouse because we thought the game was over. It was around five o'clock and it was hot. We wanted to take a shower and go home.
>
> Our right fielder, Pedro Formental, came in on the ball and it hit him right on top of the head. The ball was hopping all over the outfield.
>
> I was walking across the infield to the clubhouse and people started yelling [to go back].
>
> Well, Pedro was looking for the ball and the two runners scored and we lost the game.
>
> Oh boy, Luque was mad and he started getting on everybody because we left the field before the fly ball catch. He fined everybody five or ten dollars. I can't repeat what he said.[96]

On the other hand, Bill Werber pointed out that the Cuban would go out of his way to compliment a player who distinguished himself. Werber was playing third base for the Giants in 1942 while Luque was a coach. "I remember right now a game when Whitey Kurowski hit a curving line drive that landed in fair territory and I slid and caught it in foul territory and I threw him out at the plate," said Werber. "And when I came into the dugout Dolf hurried down from one end of the dugout to where I was and said, 'Beel, you're the only man in baseball who could make that play.' And I felt that was a high compliment coming from him. He ought to be in the Hall of Fame for what he did in his career."[97]

Projecting a Jekyll-and-Hyde personality, Luque exhausted or inspired a small army of players who line up on both sides of the issue. Did Luque derive the core of his tough management techniques from watching George Stallings in 1914 and John McGraw in 1932?

Preston Gómez, the first Latin to sign a contract as a big-league manager, was a student of Luque in the early 1940s and he believes that McGraw had the biggest impact. Gomez said:

> Since Luque played under McGraw he was very strict and very demanding. And when I became a professional I was very glad to play for a man like that. In those days you respect the manager. Whatever he says goes. And he taught me to be disciplined and to be organized and to respect people. He was strict. When he said something you had better be there. When a game was over you could not shower and change clothes until he came into the clubhouse and told you to. If we lost we would have to go back out on the field and practice.

In retrospect, Gómez concluded, "I was very fortunate when I broke in my first year in Cuba to play for Dolf Luque."[98]

In the last week of September 1945, Luque coached his final major league game. After cleaning out his cubicle he walked over to the locker of a struggling freshman pitcher named Salvatore Anthony Maglie and offered him a job in Cuba.

Sal Maglie was a 28-year-old rookie for the New York Giants in 1945 when he first met his Cuban-born coach. When the season ended Maglie walked away with more than a modest 5–4 record. He had a friend for life.

Years later he reminisced to a reporter, "[Luque] liked the way I pitched, and I liked Luque. He was going to manage Cienfuegos in the winter league in Cuba and he suggested that I play for him."[99]

Following the advice of his new mentor Maglie won nine games in the Cuban League and learned the art of the brushback. "Luque believed in protecting the plate, and I became a believer, too," said Maglie. He memorized the #1 rule of his new "bread and butter" pitch — "You have to knock them down twice before they know you really mean it."[100]

When he returned to the Giants' spring training camp in 1946, Maglie pitched very well, but failed to make the roster. Meanwhile, Luque had been lured into Jorge Pasquel's Mexican League, joining the Puebla club as a manager and emergency pitcher in the spring of 1946. During his one-year tenure in Mexico he played a big part in grooming a hard-hitting second baseman named Roberto "Bobby" Avila. He would also be reunited with Maglie.

Frustrated and angry over the way Giants manager Mel Ott had treated him, Maglie joined the exodus of American ballplayers to the Mexican League. Luque welcomed his protégé to the Puebla team and set out to remold the former pipefitter by teaching him a new arsenal of pitches. In a short autobiographical article for *Sports Illustrated* Maglie said, "Once Luque got me throwing the fastball, I could get three different curveballs, breaking across, breaking down and breaking out, depending on when I released the pitch."[101]

He now parted his two fingers, shortened up on his delivery and snapped his wrist harder when he threw the curve. He also learned how to sequence pitches and adapt to his physical surroundings. Pitching at high altitudes, Maglie repeated Luque's mantra, "Show them your curve ball but make them hit the fast ball." At sea level he would reverse the theory.[102]

For four decades Luque had relied on three things—his sweeping curveball, a fearful inside pitch and a reputation as a madman. Now he had a student with the physical and mental makeup to replicate all three. Fans in Puebla dubbed Maglie "Luque's Little Warhorse."[103] (Years later Maglie would pass down those skills to another famous intimidator, Don Drysdale.)

When Maglie returned to the major leagues in 1950 he became an overnight success, notching a record of 18–4 with the Giants. The next year he led the National League with 23 wins, followed by another 18-win season. Long after his ten-year major league career had ended, Maglie never failed to mention the impact that Luque had on his life.

While the *Pride of Havana* was changing the course of many youthful careers in Puebla he was privately steaming over the way that Pasquel was operating the league. In the last game of the 1946 season, Luque, now 56 years old, placed himself on the mound to pitch in relief. Squelching a rally by the opposing team he induced a double play in the ninth inning to secure his team's victory. As the fans swarmed onto the field Luque walked to the clubhouse, ignoring the celebration.

The next day he vented his frustration to a local journalist. In his usual unapologetic style he criticized Pasquel and his brothers for their business decisions, saying, "When they pay a little bit more attention to the game and a little less to the show, then they'll be on the right track." He added that the Pasquels lacked the experience and organizing skills to run the league. Understandably, Jorge Pasquel never offered him a contract for the 1947 season.[104]

Because of his participation in the Mexican League, Luque was banned from participating in baseball in the United States, at any level. Three years after his final game for Jorge Pasquel and his brothers, Luque submitted an appeal. On June 7, 1949, Luque recruited a friend at the central radio facilities in Havana to help him draft a formal request for reinstatement. With uncharacteristic humility he petitioned the National League president, Ford Frick, using such "Un-Luque-ish" words of diplomacy as "please ... kind regards ... thanks ... sincerely." The letter of contrition worked, and he was soon advised that his request was approved.[105]

Did Dolf Luque pack a gun?

Minnie Miñoso claims that he never saw a gun, but Negro League great Buck O'Neil did. "He hung it up in his locker when he came to the ballpark," O'Neil said.[106] In the early 1940s the Negro league legend Ted "Double Duty" Radcliffe not only saw Luque's pistol, he once found himself on the business end of it:

> We were leading the [Cuban] league by ten games and I had won eleven straight games that year until this one game.
> We had this boy named Rodolfo, a Cuban-born player, at short. He threw the ball away on a play to first. Martin Dihigo pitched against me in that game and he beat me 2–1 in twelve innings.
> That was the first game I lost.
> So in the clubhouse Luque and I got into an argument over the loss, and he called me a son-of-a-bitch and I called him a son-of-a-bitch.

Then he pulled out a gun and shot at me.

The owner of the Cuban Stars, Mr. [Alex] Pompez, was in the room and he hit his arm. If he hadn't hit him he would have shot me in the head.

Well, [later] Luque came after me and wanted me to come back to his team, but I wouldn't talk to him.

He shot at me, I'll tell you.[107]

(Although Radcliffe steadfastly maintains that it was Pompez who pushed the gun away, others believe that Cuban hurler Rodolfo Fernández was the real hero. When questioned, Fernández told a reporter that he ran into Radcliffe the following day in front of the Colón Cemetery. The Negro League star told him, "Look Rodolfo, I owe you my life. If it weren't for you I would be buried in this cemetery."[108])

Unlike Radcliffe, Negro Leaguer Terris McDuffie was at least given an option. While he was pitching for the Almandares team in the 1940s, manager Luque announced that McDuffie would pitch in an important game that day. McDuffie refused the assignment, citing overwork. Angered by his pitcher's insubordination, Luque ordered him into his office, where he confronted him with a ball in one hand and a pistol in the other. McDuffie was able to translate the mute option, choosing the round object rather than the pointed one.[110] Chastened, and filled with limitless adrenaline, he left Luque's office and pitched a brilliant two-hitter.

And for every reckless incident there are half-a-dozen stories of humor or compassion. Fausto Miranda has spent nearly seventy years as a journalist and is proud to say that Luque gave him his start:

When I was trying to become a sportswriter Dolf Luque helped me.

He was a close friend of my father and my father spoke to him and said, "My boy wants to write about the sports," and Luque told him, "Send the boy to me."

At that time [Luque] was still in the major leagues with the Giants and Bill Terry, 1932 and '33. I had to stop my studies in the university so I could work, so I decided to go for the journalist job. Luque told me how I could get started and introduced me into the league and introduced me to all the ballplayers. Luque did me many favors and gave me inside information. So I started to write from 1934 until now. Luque, two or three times, visited my home. He taught me many things about baseball because he was a very smart man.[110]

Camilo Pascual recalled his early days playing in the Cuban League. "When I was a very, very young age I always fooled around, trying to throw a curve," said Pascual. "And [when I made the] reserve squad my first manager was Adolfo Luque. And you know, he worked with me a lot in the bullpen and he really helped me develop that curveball."[111] Luque's curveball became Pascual's signature pitch and helped him become a major league star in the 1950s and 1960s.

Another Cuban "iron man" saw Luque's sense of determination as a model for his career. Tony Taylor, a veteran of six decades of playing, managing and coaching professional ball, states, "Luque was tough. A tough pitcher and a tough manager. He never did take anything from anybody."[112]

While managing Almandares in 1945 Luque allowed the once-great Cuban outfielder Alejandro Oms to play on the team out of sympathy. Oms was in his fifties and ill when he returned to Cuba from Venezuela, but Luque found a position for him on the roster.[113]

The humorous side of Luque seemed to show itself more in his later years. Bill Werber still remembers one hot night in St. Louis in 1942 when, as he was struggling to get to sleep in his hotel room, the phone suddenly rang. On the other end of the line were Luque and another Giants coach, Bubber Jonnard. They insisted that Werber allow them to bring a bucket of hot crawfish and bottles of beer to his room.

Werber was reluctant to allow them in to his room because the Giants were scheduled to play a doubleheader the next day, and he was going to play third base in both games. But, after protesting, he finally relented. After the food and beverages were consumed Werber retired to the bathroom to wash off the foul smell of crawfish. During his brief absence Luque and Jonnard hurriedly unwrapped the remaining food and stuffed the crawfish shells into Werber's pillowcase. During the night the shellfish leavings soaked through the pillow, staining Werber's hair and leaving red scratch marks all over his face.[114]

Later in the season Werber got back at his Cuban coach. "Once we gave him a birthday present," said the veteran infielder. "We cut a tie and sewed buttons and screws and bolts and nuts into the tie and when he opened it up he said, 'How the hell I wear that thing?!'"[115]

There are several anecdotes that illustrate how the older, more rational Dolf Luque was capable of laughing at disappointment rather than exploding in anger. Buck O'Neil remembers how committed Luque was to one other sport in Havana. "He liked cockfighting and he would enter his rooster in the fights on Saturday night," recalled O'Neil. "One time he came to the park on a Sunday and I asked him, 'Luque did your cock win last night?' He said, 'No; I had him for breakfast this morning.'"[116]

Adrian Zabala tells of an incident in a winter league game in which Luque surprised everyone with his response. "One time one of our players was on second base, and Luque was coaching at third," said Zabala. "This guy tried to steal third base and they threw him out. We didn't know how Luque would react, but we figured he was mad. Luque didn't want him to try to steal.

"Suddenly (Luque) started to play like he had a machine gun in his hand and he pretended to point it at the player on the ground and went, 'Tat-tat-tat-tat!'

Everybody started laughing. Including Luque."[117]

It was inevitable that time would catch up to the aging veteran. After 28 years of pitching professionally, the Cuban iron man announced his retirement on March 24, 1940. He had pitched three innings in an exhibition game in Havana against the visiting Cincinnati Reds, giving up three runs.[118]

Despite the awful results of that final game, Felo Ramírez recalled that Luque was still a hero to the Cuban people. "He did a good job for his age and the fans all applauded him," said Felo.[119]

Later that day Luque announced the end of his playing career to a New York reporter by saying, "I'm going to be 50 in August, I cannot pitch any more, so I'll never pitch again." He then said something that no one had ever expected him to admit: "Tomorrow I will stay in bed all day. I must have rest. I'm not as young as I used to be."[120] And in a private moment that evening he told Cincinnati writer Tom Swope, "I am just washed up, Tom. I tell you my arm is so sore now I can hardly raise it."[121]

In fact this was not Luque's last outing. During the winter league season of 1945–1946 he pitched one scoreless game in relief for his Cienfuegos team, at the age of fifty-five.[122] But his magical playing career had been unofficially terminated at the beginning of the decade.

Nothing in Luque's private life held his passion and devotion like the game of baseball. It was all he had to bolster his ego and finances. Outside the chalk lines Luque experienced divorce, banishment from baseball, racism and the negative results of his temper tantrums.

The only other positive constant in his life seemed to be his friend and catcher, Miguel González. From their early playing days with the Long Branch Cubans, González seemed to be the ballast that kept Luque from capsizing. Felo Ramírez said that they enjoyed a good relationship despite the fact that they were personality opposites: "Miguel was a relaxed guy and Luque was explosive," he said. Ramírez noted that González was thrifty and accumulated great wealth, but "Luque died with very little money because he liked gambling too much."[123]

González purchased his own ball club in Cuba and prospered while Luque depended on a paycheck just to get by. González was a guardian angel who saved his friend from sinking too deeply into self-made quicksand. When the Cuban League banned Luque from managing and playing in the 1948–49 season, because he had participated in Jorge Pasquel's outlaw Mexican League, González hired him as a coach. In 1955, when Luque was fired as the manager of the Marianao team over a dispute, González hired him again.[124]

Rumors had circulated that the two Cubans were at odds with one another. After Luque announced his retirement from coaching the Giants in early 1938 one writer noted, "For almost 25 years, Luque and his fellow Cuban, Miguel González of the St Louis Cardinals, have made plain that they entertained a cordial dislike for each other."[125]

Both Camilo Pascual and Felo Ramírez challenge that assertion. Luque's dependence on González was apparent to everyone who was on the inside. Pascual noted, " Luque and González had a good relationship and when González owned a baseball club in Havana, Luque [was invited to] manage his ball team."[126]

Ramírez saw the same mutually dependent relationship: "Miguel González and Dolf Luque were very good friends despite they were rivals," argued Ramírez. "When González bought the Havana franchise from Mr. Linares he offered a contract to Luque during the last years of professional baseball in Cuba to manage."[127]

In the 1920s the duo had even formed their own league in Havana, which operated for a short period of time.

As Luque entered the final years of his life he must have been overwhelmed by the bittersweet memories. At one time he was on top of the world. He had employed a chauffeur and purchased a handsome ranch on the outskirts of Havana. He had been hailed, both in Cuba and in the United States, as the greatest ballplayer of his homeland. One of his daughters, Olga, carried the famous Luque pedigree forward when she became a swimming champion and represented Cuba in international competition.[128] (According to Felo Ramírez, Luque had fathered only daughters.)

Since he was still accorded the title of a national hero Luque often associated with other Cuban sports stars. When Kid Gavilán, a boxer from Camaguey, won the World Welterweight title on May 18, 1951, Luque joined in the celebration in Havana when the champion returned home. According to Gavilán there was a large parade and a public ceremony with the president of Cuba presenting an award — not unlike Luque's celebration 28 years earlier.

Gavilán said that all of the athletes in Cuba knew each other at that time. "We were all friends and we sympathized and admired each other. We all socialized together." Regarding Luque, the former boxing champ declared, "He was eccentric, but he was good. We had respect for each other."[129] No doubt Luque probably placed a bet or two on his friend, since Gavilán started boxing professionally in Havana in 1943.

Prior to the opening game of the 1954 winter season in Havana, the president of the Cuban Baseball League, Dr. Arturo Bengochea, walked out on the field to make an announcement. With Luque at his side he presented the 64-year-old veteran with a gold medal for his many years of service to Cuban baseball.[130] The angry fights and suspensions were all forgotten. The year of banishment because of his association with the Mexican League was in the past.

He had been only the seventh Latino admitted to the modern major leagues and had achieved stardom far beyond any of his predecessors. No foreign-born player would attain his level of greatness in the big leagues until the Latin Revolution of the 1950s.

Hall of famer Tony Pérez was fifteen years old when he met Luque in 1957. Naturally he had heard of Cuba's legendary pitcher all of his young life, and he would never forget their first meeting. Pérez remembered that Luque and Mike González were joking with each other during a ball game in Havana when he was introduced to them.[131]

On that day both old warhorses were nearing their sixty-seventh year on earth, but González had twenty years of life left in him; Luque was in his final months.

On Tuesday June 25, 1957, *The Pride of Havana* suffered a heart attack. Felo Ramírez believes that Luque's final hours were spent at his ranch in the company of his Mexican-born wife. He was rushed to Havana's Anglo American Hospital but succumbed to another heart attack on the evening of Tuesday July 2.[132]

It must have been appropriate that, while he was struggling in his final battle, his protégé Sal Maglie was shutting out the New York Giants at the Polo Grounds.

For the Record

Adolfo Luque was...

- The first Latin to appear in the World Series.
- The first Latin to win a World Series game.
- The first Latin to pitch a major league shutout.

• The first Latin pitcher to hit a home run in the major leagues.

• Only the second man in the 1920s to hold a single-season ERA under 2.0.

• A major league veteran of twenty years, retiring with a record of 194–179.

• One of the great pitchers of all time. His career ERA of 3.24 was better than those of hall of famers Bob Feller, Robin Roberts, Nolan Ryan, Herb Pennock, Burleigh Grimes, Waite Hoyt, Jesse Haines, Ted Lyons and Red Ruffing. He won more games than hall of famers "Dizzy" Dean, Lefty Gómez, Sandy Koufax, Dazzy Vance and Rube Waddell.

• Ranked fourth among all Latin American pitchers in total major league victories behind Juan Marichal, Dennis Martínez and Luis Tiant Jr. Out of these four pitchers only Marichal has a better lifetime ERA than Luque. (Pedro Martinez is expected to surpass Luque in 2005.)

• The best-hitting Latin pitcher in major league history, holding a batting average of .227.

• One of the greatest pitchers in Cuba for 22 seasons, retiring with a record of 103–68. His career batting average in the Cuban League was .252.[133]

• A successful manager, leading championship teams in Cuba eight times.[134]

And yet, he is not in the National Baseball Hall of Fame.

5

The 1920s

In 1928 a respected baseball writer named John J. Ward must have had a glimpse into the future when he predicted, "Perhaps some day Havana, which is becoming one of the great cities of the world, may have a team of native players able to compete on an equality with the best America can produce."[1] Years earlier another scribe had quipped, "The day is not far distant when the Champions of the American and National Leagues will have to contend with some of their hustling South American rivals for the title of the world."[2]

Martín Dihigo

"His was the greatest name that existed at the time."

In the summer of 1977 the veterans committee at the Baseball Hall of Fame made a special announcement. They had elected a black Caribbean-born athlete to the hallowed and elite fraternity at Cooperstown. He was a man who was barely known outside of the Negro and Cuban Leagues, but was, by most accounts, the greatest baseball player who ever lived.

The Cuban people called Martín Dihigo *el Inmortal* because they truly believed he possessed talents which eclipsed the most gifted players of his time. While Babe Ruth's reputation transcended the confines of sport in the United States, Dihigo (pronounced Dee-Go) had also become a living national treasure in his native land. The reverence they paid him was staggering.

Rodolfo Fernández met him as a youth, and remembered the impact he had on the entire country. " One day in 1929 my brother took me to a ball game in Havana and I met Martín Dihigo," said Fernández. "He was, what one could say, the biggest baseball figure in Cuba. He was an extraordinary figure. His was the greatest name that existed at that time."[3]

He was a rare physical specimen for his era. The average size of an American male in the 1920s was 5'6" and 160 pounds, while Dihigo was 6'3" and 200 pounds. Born in Matanzas Province in 1905, he was endowed with all the qualities that make a superstar athlete — blinding speed, deceptive power, exceptional coordination and a sharp intellect.

In the United States he was judged to have only one flaw. He was black. In Cuba, not a day passed in which a Cuban ballplayer was not forced to measure himself against the Dihigo yardstick.

Bobby Robinson made his first dollar in professional baseball in 1916 and played for semipro, barnstorming and Negro League clubs for the next 28 years. In the mid-twenties he played against Dihigo. More than seventy years later Robinson remembered him clearly.

"He was playing in the East," said Robinson. " Yes, Martín Dihigo. I think he was one of the greatest that has ever lived."[4] That is no small admission for a man who played with the likes of Oscar Charleston, Satchel Paige and Josh Gibson.

A review of Dihigo's career is possible today only because of the tireless research of baseball historians such as Peter Bjarkman and John Holway. Bjarkman penned an article for *Elysian Fields Quarterly* (Spring 2001) in which he concluded that Dihigo is ranked in second place — just behind Lefty Grove — among the all-time leaders in won-lost percentage for professional pitchers. His career 288–142 record amounted to a .670 won-lost percentage and places him ahead of Christy Mathewson (third) and Sandy Koufax (fourth) .

If pitching had been his sole vocation he would have richly deserved his enshrinement in Cooperstown, but the mound was not his only domain.

If he had been judged by his hitting alone it, too, would have been enough to earn him a place among the gods. Former American League slugger Minnie Miñoso said, "The best hitter I had ever seen in my life was Ted Williams. Martín Dihigo is right up there with him."[5] When Dihigo retired from his near–quarter century of play he had compiled a lifetime batting average of .305.[6]

Even his defensive skills earned him a second glance from influential baseball figures. When Preston Gómez made it to the major leagues he had a conversation with an astute judge of talent who had seen *el Inmortal* play. Gómez recalled, "Leo Durocher said to me, 'If Martín Dihigo had had the opportunity to play at the big league level in those days they would have made him a center fielder.'"[7]

The right-hander played in the American Negro leagues, the Mexican League, the Venezuelan League and the Cuban Leagues, earning a place in each country's hall of fame. Additionally, he played for a short period in the Dominican Republic and Puerto Rico. Miñoso added, "Sometimes you see a guy who might be great, great, great in one league, but when he comes up to another league he cannot do it. But (Dihigo) could do it."[8]

And it wasn't just his bat or just his pitching that netted such great honors. Rodolfo Fernández said, "He had extraordinary qualities, because he could play any position, which is something that not anybody can do. A pitcher usually knows only how to pitch and a third baseman can only play his position. Martín was the greatest player of all times."[9]

Just as Babe Ruth's shadow has extended over subsequent generations so did Dihigo's. Lester Rodney, a baseball writer whose career extended from 1935 to 1957, recalled one revealing conversation he had in the late 1960s with another Latin superstar: "I remember (Roberto) Clemente talking about him and he said, 'When we grew up we had idols in Latin American ball and Dihigo was one of the best.' Rodney reflected for a moment on what he had just said and concluded, "He was a legendary figure to a guy like Clemente."[10]

Dihigo honed his numerous skills under the watchful eyes of African American ballplayers who came to the island to play winter ball prior to 1920. He began his professional career in Cuba in 1922 and was introduced to Negro League fans the following summer season when promoter Alejandro "Alex" Pompez signed him to play for the Cuban Stars in New York.

Negro League great Ted "Double Duty" Radcliffe was a close personal friend and eventual battery-mate of Martín and he remembers seeing him for the first time in 1928. "Martin Dihigo was one of the best all-around players that ever lived," said Radcliffe. "Later I caught him in two no-hitters in Mexico."[11]

Emilio Navarro, an infielder from Puerto Rico, said, "I played with him on the Cuban Stars in 1928 and later in Venezuela." It wasn't difficult for Navarro to remember one incident in particular:

Martín Dihigo played professional baseball from 1922 to 1947, excelling at all nine positions. He is now considered by many historians to be the greatest player who ever lived. (Source: National Baseball Hall of Fame Library, Cooperstown, N.Y.)

> I was playing in Venezuela in the championship game and a little [guy] named Radamef Lopez came up and he hit a triple off of Dihigo. Then Martín Dihigo was so surprised he walked over to third base and told him, "Oh, little man. You hit a triple off of me, like a man. But I'm sorry you will stay at third base." And he did not score. But after he made that one hit off of Dihigo they called Lopez the "Little Giant."[12]

Santos Amaro, the patriarch of a three-generation baseball family, also played against Dihigo in the twenties. At the age of 98 he told the author, without the slightest hesitation, "The man I admired most was Martín Dihigo."[13] Amaro felt that he became a hero to all young Latin players, even though most would never be able to see him play.

Rodolfo Fernández said that in Cuba during the twenties and thirties, blacks were not allowed to play on the exclusive amateur teams in Cuba, but Dihigo gave them hope. "He was a hero and inspiration to the black ballplayers in Cuba, because he was so good."[14]

Fernández and Navarro both remembered that Dihigo gave young Latino boys a sense of pride not only through his athleticism on the field, but also in the way he carried himself in public. Navarro said he was impressed with Dihigo's style and flair for clothes. "He liked to dress very well and he got custom-made pants and shirts and suits."[15]

Back in the early thirties, when Minnie Miñoso was just a young kid, he approached Dihigo and boldly asked him if he could carry his shoes and glove as he walked to the stadium. Cuba's greatest sports hero graciously obliged the youngster and offered him a free pass to get into the park. Later, he took the time to give Miñoso private instructions. The youngster was inspired to push forward, telling everyone, "Dihigo was my idol."[16]

All three men agreed that Dihigo proved to them that talented black men could beat the odds and pull themselves out of poverty.

With a lifestyle resembling that of a desert nomad, Dihigo set records in at least four different countries. In the Mexican League he threw their first no-hitter, completing a 119–57 record during 10 summer seasons there (1937–1947). During that time in Mexico he also had a career batting average of .317. In 1938 he led the league in both hitting (.387 BA) and pitching (18–2, 0.90 ERA).[17]

In the Cuban League he was the league leader in an assortment of batting categories for three seasons and in numerous pitching categories for four seasons. In the 12 years he spent in the Negro Leagues he won three home-run crowns and hit .370 or better six times, including breaking the .400 level twice. He left the Negro Leagues in 1945 with a pitching record of 30–21.[18]

Negro League great Buck O'Neil remembers playing against Dihigo later in the Cuban's career. "The best Latin ballplayer I've ever seen was Martín Dihigo," said O'Neil. "I played against him when I went to Cuba [because] he was managing the Marianao ballclub. And I played against him here in the U.S. in the thirties. He pitched and played any position so well."[19]

Hall of famer Buck Leonard saw Dihigo in the mid-1930s in the Negro Leagues and declared in his autobiography, "Dihigo was the best all-around ball player I ever saw."[20]

In total, Martín Dihigo played from 1922 through 1947, pitching no-hitters in three countries—Mexico, Venezuela and Puerto Rico.

Immortality seemed to fit Martin like one of his hand-tailored suits, but his exclusion from the big leagues chafed him like a coarse collar. Navarro remembers Dihigo's reaction: "[He] hated the way white people treated the blacks [in the United States]. He felt a strong hatred for those who discriminated against him."[21]

Something happened to the Cuban star while he was in the United States and he spat anger when the smoldering embers were disturbed. During an interview in Puerto Rico a commentator once asked Dihigo, "Are you sorry you are not white?" He scolded the interrogator, his voice rising with passion. "But what is worse?" he responded, "To be black and good, or maybe be white and be a thief? I could be a thief but I'm not. Is it better to be white and be a thief? That would be a shame."[22]

Later in his life Dihigo used his ugly encounters with bigotry to guide other black Latin players. The flashy rookie shortstop for the Chicago White Sox, Chico Carrasquel, was mentored through his first tough years in America by Dihigo. "He could tell you about his experiences in the Negro Leagues because those were the days you could not play in the big leagues because of racism," said Carrasquel.[23]

It was obvious to everyone who saw him, whether they were white or black, that he deserved a better lot in life. Myron Hayworth had sterling credentials in white leagues, having once been the star catcher on the 1945 American League champion St. Louis Browns. After World War II Hayworth met Dihigo south of the border and was awed by the talent that he saw in the 43-year-old Cuban.

"Martín Dihigo was playing with me in Mexico (1946–1947) and I caught him when he pitched," said Hayworth. "People don't realize he was good as any athlete in this country. He could swing the bat and run. He's the one who caused me to go to Cuba and play." Hayworth continued, "I went to play two years in Cuba (1948–1949) because Martín Dihigo wanted me to come. He asked and I went!"[24]

When Dihigo took up the responsibilities of managing he was equally successful, because he had the ability to push players to their highest levels without losing their trust and respect.

Adrian Zabala, a former pitcher with the N.Y. Giants, began his professional pitching career under the tutelage of Dihigo. He recalled:

> If you did something wrong he'd just say, "You know you did this wrong. Next time do this and this." He tried to teach you. He was much different from [Dolf] Luque. One day he said to me, "I know you had only one day rest, but today is the last day of the season and we have to win. You've got to pitch today. I don't want to finish in last place."
> Even though I had no rest I agreed with him. We respected him because he knew a lot about baseball. I always listened to him because he was a very good teacher.

One incident in particular stuck in Zabala's memory:

> We had a poor guy on our team playing shortstop who was also from my town [San Antonio de los Baños]. He was married and had two or three kids and he wanted to play baseball real bad so he could make a living. One day he made an error on a play and we ended up losing the game.
> Of course Dihigo wanted to let him go, but I told him he was poor and he had three kids. If he didn't have a job playing ball he would have a very hard time. So Dihigo went over to the guy in the locker room and told him he could keep his job. He didn't let him go because Dihigo wanted him to support his family. The guy wanted to cry. Dihigo knew how to treat people.[25]

Chico Carrasquel, who enjoyed a ten-year career in the major leagues, added,

> I was already playing in the major leagues when I went back to Venezuela for the winter leagues.
> I played there with the Lions team [1953] and Martín Dihigo was my manager. We won [the league championship] and went to the Caribbean series in Cuba. [He] could talk about baseball all the time and teach you and give you good advice. He didn't care where you were from, Cuba, Venezuela, anywhere. I was lucky to meet him and play with him.[26]

As a field manager Dihigo guided teams to league championships four times, including twice in Cuba. He briefly seized upon an offer to umpire in Cuba and Mexico and later became a radio personality, broadcasting games in Havana.

As he approached his fifth decade of life he seemed to enjoy the simple plea-sures that eluded him during his wandering years. A then seventeen-year-old Cuban boy named Tony Taylor remembers how they spent their time together. "I played dominos and played cards with him in those days because a friend of mine intro-duced him to me," said Taylor. "He was very elegant. A gentleman and very intelli-gent and a very great man." Taylor, who was just starting a baseball career that would last over fifty years, learned a lifetime of baseball strategy over the card table. "Any time I had a chance to talk to him about baseball he always gave me good advice."[27]

In March of 1952 Fulgencio Batista overthrew the government of Carlos Prío, and Dihigo packed his well-traveled suitcase one more time. In protest he left Cuba, eventually moving to Mexico. He did not return until Fidel Castro took power in the 1959 revolution.

(Ironically, his second son, Gilberto, who pursued a career as a sportswriter, abandoned Cuba in the early 1990s in protest over Castro. Like his father, he then settled in Mexico.)

In the early 1950s Dihigo was introduced to a young Argentine medical doctor named Ernesto, who inspired many Cuban exiles with his fiery views on the island's political future. Dihigo was captivated by the doctor's passionate vision of over-throwing Batista. (One decade later Ernesto's stern visage would grace the walls of American college dorms in the turbulent 1960s, because his nom de guerre became synonymous with revolutionary thought. Ernesto was "Che" Guevara.

As time went on Martín Dihigo became an avid supporter of Fidel Castro's cause and helped fund the growing insurrection from his home in Mexico. The most famous operation that Dihigo helped finance was the clandestine invasion of Cuba in 1957 when Guevara, Castro and a small group of revolutionaries set sail from Mexico on the rickety boat named *Granma*.

After the overthrow of Batista, *el Inmortal* announced that he himself would return. Just before Dihigo repatriated himself to Cuba he was introduced to an Amer-ican-born ballplayer of Spanish ancestry named Dave García. "I replaced Dihigo as manager at Jalapa, Mexico, in the winter league," recalled García.

"When he left I took his place."[28]

This time Dihigo had unpacked his bags for the last time. He would never live anywhere else again. Months after the revolution Dave García reappeared. As a newly hired scout for the Giants, he began recruiting in Cuba and was reintroduced to Dihigo.

García said, "Alex Pompez (then a Giants scout) took me over to Martín Dihigo's house and we had dinner there. His home was in Santa Clara and it was a real nice house. He didn't have a lot of money but it was a very nice [place]. He was still very handsome and well dressed. A really great guy."

García now saw a man who was settled and happy. All night they laughed and exchanged baseball stories. Dihigo admitted that he was the same age as his old neme-sis, the great Satchel Paige. García asked him, "When you pitched against Satchel Paige, who won?" Dihigo took in a breath, proudly smiled, and said, "Sometimes he won 1–0 and sometimes I won 1–0."[29]

The Cuban recalled a day in September of 1938 when Paige and he were duel-ing for the Mexican League crown. The teams were locked in a 1–1 tie going into the ninth inning when Paige was lifted for a relief pitcher. It was Dihigo who broke the deadlock in the ninth with a thunderous home run.

Garcia thought that Dihigo's joyous attitude that evening reflected the public mood at the time. "It was in 1959, because that's the year Castro came in there," García explained. "There were a lot of people who were happy, but not too many of them knew what Castro would do."[30] Despite the radical changes that would eventually affect baseball on the island, Dihigo had earned the right to maintain and enjoy his status as a hero.

His eldest son, Martín Jr., earned some recognition in baseball as well, eventually signing a minor league contract with the Cincinnati Reds in 1959. Future hall of famer Tony Pérez got a chance to meet *el Inmortal* through his relationship with the eldest son.

"I met Dihigo in Havana in 1960 because I played with his son in Geneva, New York," said Perez. "When I came back to Cuba he introduced me to his daddy."

Like most young Cuban men, Pérez knew Dihigo as an icon, even though he had never seen him play. Pérez explained, "I heard about him because my father loved baseball and he used to tell me about all those great players from the past. Dihigo was one of his favorites."

Pérez recalled their first meeting: "He looked big and he looked like a guy who had a lot of confidence. He was elegant and well dressed. At that time he was working for a newspaper in Havana."[31]

Later, Dihigo was granted a position in the ministry of sports and helped dismantle the professional league and create the famous amateur leagues that now exist on the island. He spent his final years living with his son Martín Jr., and died in 1971, possibly of cerebral thrombosis.

The man who first sponsored Dihigo's debut in the United States in 1923, Alex Pompez, had become an influential member of the baseball Hall of Fame in Cooperstown. Pompez made sure that no one could bury the achievements of the man who was considered the greatest player of all time.

Author's note: I feel especially privileged to have interviewed the five surviving men who knew Dihigo during the 1920s. Messrs. Fernández, Robinson, Radcliffe, Navarro and Amaro all joyfully volunteered their recollections. The passion they showed for advancing Dihigo's story was inspiring. I also want to thank baseball historians Bjarkman and Holway for their tireless work in compiling Dihigo's statistics and uncovering details of his illustrious life.

Miguel "Mike" González

Stallings replied, "That Gonzales [sic]
is frightened whenever I look at him."

He was perfectly proportioned to be a banker. Tall, gaunt and bookish. At 6'1" and 160 pounds he resembled a coat rack more than an athlete. But underneath his tropical suits lay a band of sinewy muscle that fought for space alongside his exposed rib cage.

His contemporaries laughingly called him "*Pan de Flauta*" after the long slim loaves of bread sold in neighborhood stores. But one enthusiastic writer described him as being "endowed with a whip-like throwing arm and good fielding ability."[32] Miguel Angel González was a catcher for the Havana Reds when he wasn't counting money in a Havana bank.

González was born in Regla, Cuba, to a working-class family in 1890; for a while, he delivered bread to make a living.[33] At the age of 17 he was employed as a bank teller and played baseball professionally on weekends. Young Miguel would often day-dream about leaving the island and traveling to the United States as he worked in the confined environment of the bank.

His life took a dramatic and permanent turn in 1911 when he was signed by the Cuban Stars, a team of Cubans and American blacks who barnstormed through the eastern United States.

He later mused, "If I had remained in Cuba no doubt I would have stayed at the bank. But there came a chance to come to America. I wanted to see the country, to travel. I had no idea at the time that I would make good in the big leagues."[34]

After spending a few months of 1912 playing "battery-mate" to his friend Dolf Luque on the Cuban Stars (West), González was picked up by the Boston Braves in the late summer. In subsequent interviews he did not talk publicly about coming from a black team to the majors because of the possible inference that he might have black African blood.

His first, and only, major league appearance that year was September 28, when he faced the fearsome New York Giants. Squeezing out a walk was the only memorable event of that game. The rest he wanted to forget. The gangly rookie not only went hitless in two official at-bats (including a strikeout) he also failed to throw out Giants base stealers in four attempts. A post-game quote attributed to him was, "She run. I throw. She safe."[35]

During his short stay in Boston, González had to endure the explosive antics of the Braves' manager George Stallings. When writer Fred Lieb asked the punishing skipper about his new players Stallings replied, "That Gonzales [sic] is frightened whenever I look at him."[36]

Shortly after that first game González was released. It was a humiliating introduction to a career that would eventually span six decades.

Joining Luque once again, he was signed by the Long Branch Cubans in 1913 and hit .333 in 95 games.[37] That effort earned him another chance at the big leagues with the Cincinnati Reds in 1914, where he caught in 83 games and hit .233.

During the 1914–1915 winter league season in Cuba González took his first managerial job when he assumed the reins of the Havana Reds.

Then, just before the Cincinnati Reds arrived at spring training camp in 1915, Gonzalez learned that he had been traded, along with another catcher, Bob Bescher, to the St. Louis Cardinals. In return, the Reds received one of the best catchers in the National League, Ivy Wingo. Replacing Wingo, González became the primary catcher for the Cardinals from 1915 through 1918. The once-timid Cuban was evolving from a cautious and scrawny young rookie into a confident and robust team leader.

Facing the great Grover Cleveland Alexander in a 1917 game, González made it all the way to third base on a series of errors and hits. Ignoring his manager, González started running as Alexander was going through his windup and slid across home plate for a rare stolen run.

The Cardinals' skipper, Miller Huggins, immediately confronted him in the dugout.

"You stole without my signal! You've got plenty of guts." Not intimidated, González aggressively replied, "I got plenty big lead."[38]

Records show that he reached 200 pounds during his career and one scribe noted his fiery competitiveness: "Gonzales [sic], the Cuban player, talks Spanish, strikes out in English and gets fined by the umps in United States."[39]

His maturation was manifested in greater form off the field, however. González had a dream of becoming wealthy. Working in the bank he had learned the value of saving and investing his earnings, and by the mid-1920s he owned a real estate business in Havana. In the 1940s he purchased his former employer, the Havana Reds baseball club. Felo Ramírez, a hall of fame broadcaster, explained, "González had a lot of money. He could save what he earned."[40]

Outside of his successful investments there are few details about his personal life. In the endless debate about which major league ballplayers from Cuba had black African blood, he was not spared. When Willie Wells, a speedy Negro League shortstop, returned from playing winter ball in Cuba he commented that he had seen González's mother and she was a black woman.[41]

Another legend that kept reappearing was about a fight that he had with Giants manager John McGraw in 1911. During his annual exhibition tour of Cuba that year McGraw had reportedly scouted González, but didn't think he could pass the color-test. McGraw's biographer, Charles C. Alexander, confirmed that the two men "had a run-in" during a game that was marred by several other incidents as well. Later that evening a group of Havana street thugs threatened the Giants' skipper and his entourage with knives because of the on-field incidents.

The confrontation turned into a brawl and McGraw was arrested. The next day the court ordered him to write an apology, which was subsequently printed in the *Havana Post*.[42]

The hot-tempered McGraw had seen his fair share of fights and public humiliations during his tumultuous 38 years on earth, so when he had a chance to grab González in a trade after the 1918 season, it appeared that all was forgotten. But the Cuban spent most of the 1919 season catching batting practice or warming up pitchers in the bullpen. His activity dropped from 117 games with the Cardinals in 1918 to a mere 58 with the Giants. In 1920 and 1921 he appeared in only 24 total games, because of a series of injuries.

On December 6, 1921, McGraw packaged González in a blockbuster trade with the Cincinnati Reds. In a desperate search to find a capable third baseman the Giants gave up their star outfielder, George Burns, plus González and an extraordinary amount of money — $150,000 cash — to acquire the Reds' slugger Heinie Groh.

The trade had mixed results. Burns hit an impressive .285, Groh slumped 66 batting points to a .265 average, and González was cut before the 1922 season started.

Returning to the bush leagues, he spent 1922 and 1923 with St Paul in the American Association, rebuilding his reputation as a solid hitter. González not only hit .298 and .303 respectively for St Paul, but he stole a total of 31 bases.[43]

That success earned him the right to return to the Cardinals in 1924, where he enjoyed the best season of his big-league career. In 120 games he hit .296 and clobbered 27 doubles. Only two other catchers in the National League did as well offensively. His defensive numbers were equally impressive, because he led the National League in games played, putouts and double plays.

(Despite the fact that the Cardinals had four future hall of famers on their roster they finished in sixth place in 1924 and fourth place in 1925. But success was just around the corner. Grover Cleveland Alexander would join Rogers Hornsby, Chick Hafey, Jesse Haines and Jim Bottomley for the world championship season of 1926.)

González's offensive numbers improved even more during the early part of 1925, but the Cardinals unexpectedly traded him in mid-season to the Cubs for their hard-hitting catcher, Bob O'Farrell. In 1926 he was barely hitting .250, but he shone brilliantly behind the plate, leading the National League in fielding percentage, making a mere four errors.

González, like many Latin and Afro- American players, would play throughout the calendar year, supplementing income with a string of exhibition games in Mexico before the Cuban winter league season began. After a profitable series in Mexico in 1926 he returned the following November to a less-than-enjoyable experience.

Prior to the first game of the series, a group of Mexican soldiers entered the ball field, arresting the promoter and dragging him over to a neighboring wall. After the commanding officer explained that the promoter had associated with a local rebel group, the soldiers raised their rifles and executed him.[44] Within a short period of time all of the players, including González, had boarded trains for a quick exit.

During the next three seasons he performed in only 148 games and was cut loose by the Cubs after the 1929 season. González returned to the United States for the 1930 campaign to play in the American Association.

Back home in 1932, he won the Cuban League batting crown with a .432 average.[45] He was forty-two years old.

In 1931 and 1932 he played in a handful of games for the Cardinals and then retired as an active player. But his career in St. Louis wasn't over, because he remained with the Cardinals as a coach from 1934 through 1946.

It wasn't enough of a challenge that he was the first Latin-born coach in the majors; he also had to contend with one of the most irreverent and chaotic groups of players in history — The Gashouse Gang. In 1934 some local writers came up with that moniker which aptly described a team consisting of Pepper Martin, Leo Durocher, "Ducky" Medwick, Frankie Frisch and the Dean brothers, "Dizzy" and "Daffy."

Don Gutteridge played on that team and the scenes from the locker room still play clearly in his memory. "They did everything that you could possibly imagine and then more," Gutteridge recalled. "They were a rough and tumble outfit. They would wrestle in the clubhouse and kid each other. Very rough."[46]

The only figure who could command sanity was their field-general, a future hall of famer. Gutteridge said, "We had Frankie Frisch as the manger and he just sat back and let them go. He was a type of manager who could deal with that kind of ball club because he was rough and tumble himself. He was a perfect manager for that type of ball club. I don't think any other manager would have put up with that kind of stuff. He let it go just as far as he wanted it to go and then he'd say, 'that's enough.'"[47]

Although he had the authority of a coach, González fit into the asylum more like an inmate than a warden. "[Mike] kidded everybody and he was one of us," said Gutteridge.

"In the Cardinals' clubhouse they kidded him and he kidded them right back. We considered him as one of us rather than just a coach."

When Gutteridge first appeared in the Cardinals' spring training camp of 1934 he was considered to be one of the fastest runners in the organization. Immediately they turned him over to their third-base coach González, "to learn the art of basic base running."

In 1936 Gutteridge finally made the club as a utility infielder and was scheduled to play on one of their first road trips to Brooklyn.

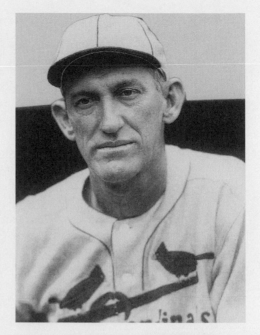

Miguel González, circa 1930. He maintained a career as a player, coach, manager and club owner that spanned five decades. (Source: Jay Sanford collection.)

Early in the game the Kansas native had made it all the way to third base and was anxious to score the first run of his major league career. He glanced over to González who was intently studying the Dodgers' pitcher, Van Lingle Mungo. González then turned to Gutteridge with a poker face and whispered, "You steal me home."

The rookie thought, "What are you talking about? I've never stolen home in my life!"

"What are you talking about?" he demanded in a hushed tone.

The Cuban persisted, "You steal me home."

González had seen something subtle in Mungo's demeanor. He was completely ignoring the runner after getting his sign from the catcher, Babe Phelps.

"You steal me home, now!" exhorted his coach.

With Mungo in his full windup Gutteridge started racing for the plate. Halfway down the chalk line he thought, "I hope the batter doesn't swing at the ball because he would take my head off."

The slide was straight-on and perfect. He didn't even have to hook to avoid Phelps's booming tag. Gutteridge recalled, "[González] was tickled to death and he was patting me on the back. He was so tickled because he told me to do that and it worked."

Max Lanier, a left-handed hurler from North Carolina, played for 14 years with the Cardinals and recalls that González was the team's base-running instructor. "He didn't teach me how to run because I wasn't too fast, but he did help the guys who stole bases," said Lanier. "He was a great helper. And, on the team, he was the man to get along with."[48]

By 1946 the rowdy Cardinals players had been replaced by a group of focused superstars led by Stan Musial, Red Schoendienst and Enos Slaughter. With Miguel anchoring the third-base coach's box they captured the pennant with a 98–58 record and earned the right to face the Red Sox for the world championship.

This was González's fifth World Series appearance as a coach with the Cardinals. He had been part of their victories in 1934, 1942 and 1944, and their loss in 1943.

The 1946 series proved to be one of the most exciting in the history of baseball. In game seven the score was tied 3–3 in the Cardinals' half of the eighth inning. Enos Slaughter led off the inning with a single, but was stranded as two of his teammates made consecutive outs. When Harry Walker popped a single into center field Slaughter started running with his head down and never stopped. Rounding third base, he glanced up and saw coach González frozen in disbelief.

Slaughter later commented, "I think he was flabbergasted."[49]

Slaughter's run from first base to home plate on a weak single was the stuff of baseball legend. It proved to be the eventual winning run that secured another world championship for St. Louis.

But González would not celebrate for long, because he was fired by an order from the commissioner before the 1947 campaign began.[50] The unfortunate and grossly unfair circumstance which led to his dismissal was nothing less than an act of vengeance by major league baseball. As owner of the Havana Reds, González had signed several renegade American players for the 1945–46 winter league season. Some of these players had broken their major league contracts to play summer ball in the upstart Mexican League. Baseball owners swore to punish anyone who harbored these outlaws.

Although many of the fugitive players were later reinstated, González would never return.

In total, he had logged seventeen seasons as a big-league player plus at least four seasons of minor league ball. His major league tenure ended with a batting average of .253 in 1,042 games.

González also played with three integrated barnstorming teams during five seasons in the United States. He played winter ball in Cuba for over three decades and managed his Havana Reds to Cuban League championships fourteen times between 1914 and 1953.[51]

Because of his prudent investing and his successful ownership of the Havana Reds for two decades his is one of the few rags-to-riches stories in professional ball during those early days of the twentieth century.

González's only World Series playing experience occurred in 1929 with the Chicago Cubs. The Cubs lost the series against the A's, four games to one; González struck out in his only at-bat.

His greatest claim to fame on the diamond, moreover, is all but forgotten. With seventeen games remaining in the 1938 season the Cardinals fired manager Frankie Frisch and asked González to act as interim field boss. When he walked out to home plate that September day to exchange lineup cards he became the first Latino to manage a big-league club.

Under González the Cardinals won nine of their final seventeen games for a .529 winning percentage. Frisch had left the team with a .463 winning percentage.

During the winter González learned that the Cardinals had hired Ray Blades to manage for the 1939 season. In 1940 he was again asked to manage the Cardinals for five games when Blades was fired and the new manager, Billy Southworth, prepared to take the helm.

It was another 29 years before another Latino, Cuban-born Preston Gómez, was hired to manage a major league club.

The fact that González was bold enough to own and operate a professional franchise in Cuba — and cunning enough to manage it to fourteen championships—carried little weight in America. He would never be able to secure a permanent management position in St. Louis. José Montiel, the former business manager of the Cuban Sugar Kings, said Mike was qualified, but his thick accent was seen as a negative. "Mike González was a very smart guy but [big-league owners thought] he didn't speak English well and that he didn't write English real well."[52]

Don Gutteridge agrees that language should not have been a barrier. "Mike spoke very good English and he really was a good coach. I admired him because he was a hard worker and he tried to help everybody."[53]

Felo Ramírez concurs that González was capable, but his alien status may have played a big part. As Ramírez explained, "When he was sent out to scout a player one time he responded one time by saying, "*Good field — no hit*." As innocuous as that statement may seem, it would become an unfortunate part of the baseball lexicon for generations.

Ramírez continued, "The phrase became very famous and, from that, many people felt he could not communicate. But he could communicate. He had all the qualities to be a good manager. A successful manager. He was very intelligent and was very scientific."[54]

It was evident that González tried to overcome the linguistic stigma that attached to him. "He was very careful about what he said," said former Cardinals pitcher, Max Lanier. Always maintaining a modest posture, González loved to tell people that he was a "smart dummy."[55]

According to Montiel, he was also successful in his private life. "He was married for many years and had one son who now lives in New York," said Montiel. From all indications González reveled in his life as a middle-aged entrepreneur in Cuba. Whenever the bygone stars of baseball visited the island they would beat a path directly to his door.

Felo Ramírez explained, "Miguel had a great friend in Rogers Hornsby. They were roommates once and Miguel invited Rogers to Havana. I interviewed Hornsby, using Miguel as an interpreter. This happened in the fifties."

When Max Lanier thought his career was finished in 1953, he was summoned by his old coach. "He helped everybody," said Lanier. "[Mike invited me] and I played for him over in Cuba after I quit playing in the major leagues."

Unlike his friend Dolf Luque, González made every effort to distance himself from controversy and scandal. Montiel said that sometime in the late 1950s there was a rumor circulating about a possible fix to the winter league championship game. González, who owned one of the participating teams, immediately intervened and told the press that he would donate the gate receipts to charity. The rumors died and the integrity of the championship was preserved.[56]

The Cuban revolution of 1959 changed the lives of everyone in Cuba and the 68-year-old Miguel González was no exception. Dave García, a professional player and scout since the late 1930s, remembered one incident in particular that sheds a sad light on González's life shortly after Fidel Castro took control.

On a February day in 1959 Dave and New York Giants' scout Alex Pompez were walking through the streets of post-revolution Havana. Both men were in town to scout for talent in the Cuban League and they decided to make an unannounced visit to the home of González.

When García and Pompez reached the González villa they knocked for several minutes before there was an answer. Peering out from the slowly moving door was a frightened old man. It was Miguel González. García was dispirited by what he saw. "He was scared to death. When he opened the door he was really frightened."[57]

It was only one year earlier that García had had a very different experience. "Before the revolution I remember visiting with him on the front porch of his house," García recalled. "We had dinner together. At that time Castro was down in the Oriente in the southern part of Cuba trying to overthrow Batista. But, back then [everything was fine with Mike]."

Almost two years later the Cuban government abolished González's beloved Havana Reds baseball franchise, along with the entire Cuban League. Nine years later González was selected to head the amateur Cuban League, a post he held until his death in Havana in 1977.

Author's note: Dave García first met Miguel in 1937 at the age of 16 while García was a high school senior in East St. Louis. During a visit to the Cardinals' ballpark the youth was unexpectedly invited by their zany outfielder, Pepper Martin, to come out on the field and join in infield practice. González was hitting infield practice and agreed to have the teenager join them. A 22-year friendship blossomed that day when García spoke to González in Spanish.

Cubans of All Shades Make the Big Leagues

A carbon-copy Cuban

During the decade of the twenties only five Latin-born players made their debuts in the big leagues. All were Cubans, three were pitchers, and none had an illustrious career.

Pitcher José Acosta, who is featured in the decade of the 1910s, and his longtime catcher, Ricardo Torres, were initiated by the Senators in 1920. The reason for the brevity of Torres' career would appear to be a mystery when evaluating his offensive output.

Ricardo Jiménez Torres became the first Latin catcher debuted by the Washington Senators when he made an appearance on May 18, 1920. He exceeded expectations as a third-string catcher and first baseman when he smacked nine singles and one double in thirty at-bats for a .333 average during his rookie year. In 1921 he appeared in only two games, but again he hit .333. His last season was 1922, when he swung the bat four times.

If Torres had proved he could hit major league pitching, why was he used in only twenty-two games? The answer might lie in the comparison of his career to that of pitcher José Acosta, his battery-mate. Acosta was expected to succeed at the big-league level as a knuckleballer and it is clear that Torres was brought up to handle the difficult pitch. When Acosta failed to impress his employers in Washington, both he and Torres were released together.

Torres did have a son named Gilberto who played a variety of positions, including pitcher, for the Senators in the 1940s.

"Mike" Herrera became the second Latin on the Boston Red Sox, but was granted only 84 games in two seasons to prove himself. The versatile infielder finished his career in 1926 with a .275 batting average.

Oscar Estrada, a left-handed pitcher from Havana, pitched for the fourth-place St. Louis Browns for one inning in 1929. After surrendering a walk and a base hit and committing a balk he was taken off the mound and never returned to a major league club.

Pedro Dibut may have been another player who slipped under the watchful eyes of the race-conscious censors. The right-handed hurler was born in Cienfuegos, Cuba, and was 31 years old when he joined Dolf Luque on the Cincinnati Reds' roster in 1924. Since Luque had just come off a 27-game winning season the previous year, there is little doubt that the Reds were searching for a carbon-copy Cuban.

Dibut's first major league game occurred in Chicago on May 1, 1924, when he was handed the responsibility of stopping a Cubs rally in the sixth inning. Chicago had amassed a seven run lead but were stopped cold by the stocky Cuban.

Cincinnati manager Jack Hendicks gave Dibut two starting assignments and four more relief appearances before the end of the season. That rookie season was abbreviated but impressive. His record of 3–0 and ERA of 2.21 earned him a contract for the following season.

The first game that he pitched in 1925 was his last in a major league uniform. Given a starting assignment, Dibut pitched to three batters in the first inning, giving up successive hits and two earned runs. Pulled from the mound, he was not offered a chance to redeem himself. Dibut was released by the Reds and eventually signed with the Cuban Stars (West) for only one season. He did achieve some measure of success back home when he tied for the lead in victories during the 1926–1927 Cuban League season.

Veteran columnist Fausto Miranda remembered Dibut and explained that there was speculation about his heritage. "He had a very dark complexion," Miranda recalled, " but there was no proof he was a mulatto."[58] Historian Peter Bjarkman also noted that Dibut was "Absolutely, very dark."[59]

The few Cubans who were admitted into professional baseball must have felt a chill when they learned that a left-handed pitcher named Jimmy Claxton had been released from the Oakland Oaks baseball club in the Pacific Coast League. Claxton, who was presented to the media as a dark-skinned American Indian, had joined the team on May 22, 1928. He was released six days later when it was discovered that he had black ancestry.

Aberlardo Rodríguez

…Might have been the first Mexican.

When Aberlardo Rodríguez first came from Mexico to attend the University of Arizona he brought with him a suitcase full of books and a love for baseball. While attending school he played on the University's baseball team and attracted the attention of West Coast scouts.

He was indeed a talented player, and in 1920 Rodríguez was offered a contract to play with the Los Angeles Angels in the Pacific Coast League. As alluring as a career in professional baseball seemed to him at the time, his wealthy and influential family had set him on a different path. After graduation Rodríguez returned to Mexico and entered politics. In 1936, the man who might have been the first Mexican in the major leagues was sworn in as president of the Republic of Mexico.

Barnstorming in Unfriendly Locales

"Only one of them is considered to be white"

In the fall of 1928 the Cuban Stars (West) of the Negro National League launched a barnstorming tour that took them to Wichita, Kansas, to play a doubleheader against the local all-star team. The Wichita city fathers found it necessary to announce that the team consisted of 14 Cubans –only one of whom "is considered to be white." The local order of the Ku Klux Klan probably appreciated the update. What they didn't appreciate were the final scores. The Cubans drubbed the white all stars by scores of 15–2 and 23–5 respectively.[60]

Alejandro "Alex" Pompez

In the twenties and thirties he was a Spanish-speaking Moses.

Alejandro Pompez was being hunted by the law.

His long run as Harlem's gambling kingpin had been lurching toward a disastrous conclusion ever since Thomas E. Dewey had become the district attorney of New York County. Considered to be a member of the notorious Dutch Schultz mob, Pompez had also made an honest buck as the owner of a successful Negro League ball club, The New York Cubans. But his connections to organized crime led Dewey, a future presidential candidate, to push for an indictment by a grand jury in 1936. Armed with an arrest warrant in January of 1937, Dewey engineered a trap which might have been successful had it not been for the elevator operator who warned Pompez of his impending capture.

Hurriedly, Pompez made his escape and crossed the border into Mexico. Discovering his location, Dewey pressed the Mexican police to make an arrest. Although the Mexican officials refused to extradite him, Pompez realized he had few alternatives remaining.[61]

In a decision his colleagues called "suicidal" Pompez agreed to turn state's evidence against his mobster friends in exchange for a safe return to the United States—and his eventual release. Within two years he returned to his responsibilities as owner of his baseball club. Threats against him never materialized, and revenge was never exacted. Once again, Alex Pompez had cheated fate.

There were other legends which, exaggerated or not, point to his survival instincts. On one occasion, it was said that he was forcibly removed from a train by a group of angry Mafiosi after he was unable to pay off on heavy losses in the numbers business.

Again he emerged intact and pressed on with his businesses. Providing a form of entertainment that was an accepted cultural pastime, this son of a prosperous Cuban businessman found himself on the dark side of the law, because betting on numbers was illegal.

That was the Alex Pompez of the demi-monde.

The Alex Pompez of the legitimate world was a genuine hero. In the twenties and thirties he was a Spanish-speaking Moses who led many Latin athletes to jobs playing baseball in the United States.

In the forties through the fifties he was involved in the transition of many Afro-American and black Latin ballplayers from the Negro Leagues into the majors. He invested heavily in Negro League baseball and was one of the first entrepreneurs to install lights in a stadium. It was a full five years before major league baseball's introduction of night baseball that he built light standards at his stadium, Dykman Oval, in 1930.[62]

Toward the end of his career Pompez was actively involved with the Baseball Hall of Fame in evaluating the forgotten heroes of the Negro Leagues. Former *Miami Herald* columnist Fausto Miranda was one of Pompez's biggest supporters. "He was the one who made it possible to put colored Cuban men in the Hall of Fame," said Miranda. "For black people who did not play in the big leagues, Pompez got them noticed. Like Dihigo and others."[63]

Because of his ability to straddle those two worlds, and to reinvent himself, he was one of the wealthiest men in Harlem at one time.

His father was José González Pompez, a successful businessman who owned cigar factories in Tampa, Florida, and was active in Cuban politics. José Pompez had immigrated to the Florida Keys from Havana with his wife, Loretta Pérez, and their young son Alex, who was born in Havana on May 3, 1890.[64]

Alex had completed only two years of high school in Florida and was exempt from military service during the First World War because of a hernia. Spending his young life surrounded by the laborers in his fathers tobacco factories, Alex learned the vagaries of gambling, especially the numbers game. Wagering was considered to be an innocent pastime by his older companions, and Alex learned a new method of generating cash.

During that period he also organized barnstorming tours throughout the United States with a group of Cuban ballplayers. He claimed that during one tour in 1916 he invited a *Brujo*, a witch doctor, to travel with the team, because six of the eleven men on the roster practiced a version of Haitian voodoo called *nanigo*. He asserted that his team had tremendous success in one crucial game because he ordered a witch doctor to bury the head of rooster beneath second base.[65]

One of the players on his 1916 team was a Cuban-born catcher named José Fernández. His younger brother, Rodolfo Fernández, said that José was forever grateful to Alex for that chance. "Too many good Cubans did not have a chance to play in the U.S. back then," said Fernández. "Pompez gave them [their only chance.]"[66] Later, José managed one of Pompez's teams in 1935 and scouted for him during the winter league season in Havana.

As a mulatto Pompez understood the limitations that existed for minorities in America, but was determined to push the limits to achieve his dreams. These dreams may have had their genesis while Cuban teams were defeating, with regularity, the major leaguers who came to Havana in the winter. Because of their rapidly growing reputation, Cubans had solid commercial value to the black teams in America.

Armed with his father's keen sense of business, and perhaps some of his money, Alex journeyed to New York in the early 1920s to seek his fortune as a sports promoter. He acquired a baseball stadium and amusement park at the northern tip of Manhattan (Tenth Avenue and West 204th) called Dyckman Oval and eventually took control of the Cuban Stars (East) baseball club.[67]

For many years Dyckman Oval had featured wrestling, boxing, motorcycle races and Sunday baseball games. It was also an integrated oasis for both white and black sports fans.

Before Pompez's arrival, Dyckman Oval had supported a local white team, named the Bears. This club, run by Jeff Tesreau, a former pitcher with the New York Giants, was drawing as many as 6,000 fans at a time. Ignoring the segregationist policies of other white clubs, Tesreau and his partners, Connie Savage and Guy Empey, urged black teams from Chicago, Philadelphia, New Jersey, Washington, and New York to play against them weekly.[68] They also attempted to lure teams from Cuba. On June 6, 1920, the Cuban Stars, led by José Fernandez, made their first appearance at the Oval, splitting a doubleheader.

When Pompez bought the complex two years later he acquired a venue that was already ahead of its time. In 1923 Pompez saw promise in a budding 18-year-old country boy named Martín Dihigo. Signing him to a contract, he brought Dihigo to New York to play with his Cuban Stars as a second baseman. Although Dihigo had displayed only mediocre success as a batsman, and had a touch of wildness when pitching, Pompez was impressed.

That was also the year that his Stars became a charter franchise in the Eastern Colored League — a direct competitor to Rube Foster's Negro National League. The arrangement was not ideal, because there were six teams in the ECL and four of them were owned by white entrepreneurs. Unable to form a majority opinion on issues that affected the Afro-American community, Pompez and the Hilldale Daisies' owner Ed Bolden held little power. Nevertheless, Pompez was instrumental in making peace with Foster and organizing the first world series between the two leagues in 1924.

There is no public record of when Pompez began his numbers business nor of when he became an associate of the notorious Dutch Schultz, but his integration into the large Cuban community in New York in the early twenties was probably a realistic date. By 1931 Pompez was a lieutenant in the Schultz mob, securing business primarily in the Harlem area.

But, as a baseball executive, Pompez was considered a god-send to many black ballplayers. Emilio "Millito" Navarro, a former Puerto Rican star, remembers that in 1928 Pompez was extremely paternal, especially if a young player felt alone or frightened.

"He was very nice, but he was very tough," said Navarro. "But at the same time he was a good guy. Alejandro Pompez was my best friend and he was the only guy who invited me to downtown New York. He didn't ask the other players. Only me. Pompez went downtown to make business and he picked me up to go with him. We went to restaurants and movies like tourists." Navarro recalled with gratitude, "He didn't leave me alone."[69]

According to biographical reports Pompez dissolved his beloved Cuban Stars after the 1929 season and formed the New York Cubans five years later. This franchise survived through 1950.

Puerto Rican-born Carlos Santiago said he made $275 per month playing for the New York Cubans in 1945. When I interviewed him 55 years later he still remembered the first time he met Pompez. "Sitting at his desk he was smoking a cigar," said Santiago. "He was well dressed and sometimes wore a [Panama] hat. If you saw Pompez from a distance you would think he might be white, but when you came closer you knew he was black."

But it was the private man that Santiago learned to respect. "He was a great man. He always wanted to help people. Alex helped us get adjusted and he told us not to be afraid and to talk to him if we needed help. He told all the Latin players that."[70]

However, it seemed that no matter how hard Pompez worked in the legitimate world, his underworld reputation followed him. Felix Delgado recalled the day he was approached in Puerto Rico by Franco Coímbre, one of Pompez's scouts. Coímbre asked, "Felix, damn, you are doing better than most of the players on the Cuban Stars in New York. Do you want me to recommend you to play for us when I go back to play in the spring?"

Delgado was interested, because he had dreamed of going to the United States to play professionally. So he asked Coímbre who he was representing. "The president of the team is Alex Pompez, a Cuban," explained Coímbre.

Delgado continued, "[At one time] Pompez was in the policy numbers—the rackets in New York—and every year he would bring the best players from Cuba and other countries for his team, to be a front so it would look like he was not in any other business but baseball."[71]

Delgado accepted the offer and when he arrived in New York he found the notorious racketeer to be a gentle and caring man. "He opened a restaurant, called the Cuban-Spanish Café," said Delgado. "All the players would go there for breakfast, lunch and dinner [inexpensively]. We would get our pay every fifteen days and then pay part of that money to him for our food."[72]

Pompez also operated a handmade-cigar factory on Lenox Avenue, employing a handful of deserving characters during a period when jobs were hard to come by. Pompez knew that opportunities to find a decent job were rare, especially during the Depression.

On May 26, 1935, a Negro League game between Pompez's New York Cubans and the Homestead Grays erupted into a free-for-all after the Cubans' shortstop was spiked by a Grays base runner. The melee spread into the stands when Cuban and American fans started fighting. When the Grays returned to New York two months later, Pompez had programs printed which hyped the previous skirmish, promising that the upcoming series would be a "Blood feud." Pompez had a flair for the dramatic, trying to excite his fans by circulating a picture of the May brawl with a promise to have his "Fiery Latins" exact revenge. The Grays' first baseman Buck Leonard revealed in his autobiography that there was never a blood rivalry and the entire promotion was a pure fabrication to attract more fans.[73]

When Horace Stoneham took over the reins of the New York Giants from his father Charles in 1935, a close relationship between Alex Pompez and the new regime took root. It was shortly thereafter that Pompez's beloved Dykman Oval was demolished by the city to construct affordable apartment buildings. Pompez went to Stoneham with a new business proposition.

Fausto Miranda said, "Pompez's relationship with the Giants owner Horace Stoneham first began when he leased the Polo Grounds to hold Negro League games. Their friendship eventually led to a job for Pompez as a scout."[74] Pompez forged relationships with all the big-league teams in New York during the 1930s, but no matter how close he got with the ownership there were always barriers.

Felix Delgado explained further: "I remember that we played one time at Ebbets Field. We would play at New York Giants' stadium and Yankee Stadium when those teams were playing away. Mr. Pompez paid to use the stadium even though we could not use the facilities in the clubhouse."[75]

After Pompez's team won the championship in 1947 Stoneham approached him with a revolutionary offer. Stoneham proposed that Pompez fold his team into the Giants organization as a minor league affiliate, renaming them the Cuban Giants.[76] He also offered Pompez a job as a scout.

Fausto Miranda explained that this was a turning point in major league scouting. "Soon after Jackie Robinson broke the color line Stoneham sent Pompez out to locate and sign talented black players in Latin America and the United States," said Miranda. For the next 25 years Pompez blended his tough street savviness with the smooth manners of an aristocrat to convince the parents of young players to sign with the Giants.

A showman all the way, he was not reticent about revealing the methods that he had used to lure prospects into signing professional contracts. He told a freelance writer that he scared Minnie Miñoso into signing a contract after threatening to unleash a witch doctor on him.[77] (*Author's note*: Miñoso told me in May of 2000 that he had never heard of such a ridiculous story.)

He also revealed that while he was the head scout for the N.Y. Giants in Latin America he would never prepare a "canned" recruitment speech. Instead, the perfect words would tumble from his mouth as if he were a "medium" for a higher power.

Pompez claimed, "I go to the mothers and fathers and I say, 'Every team has money to offer [your son] but no team has a man like me. Your boy go with the Giants and I look after him. Your boy get sick I see he get better. With the other clubs no one speak Spanish. He might die and no one give him a tumble.'"[78] Fearing his prophecies of doom and gloom the parents would readily place their child in the hands of Señor Pompez.

Indeed, he is credited with luring many future stars to the Giants, including Felipe and Matty Alou, Juan Marichal, Orlando Cepeda, Willie Mays and José Pagán.

Although Pompez wanted to sound positive he was also realistic about the challenges that were waiting for the young recruit. Referring to segregation in America he said, "When they first come here they don't like it. Some boys cry and want to go home. But, after they stay and make big money they accept things as they are. They can't change the laws."[79]

According to Fausto Miranda, Pompez also had other duties with the Giants. "He was asked to acclimate and supervise the Latin players during spring training," said Miranda.[80]

Several of the men who were signed by Pompez during the late forties and fifties spoke about him with an air of reverence. Minnie Miñoso said, "I liked Alex Pompez a lot. A very respectable guy and he had a beautiful personality. He gave me [my big] opportunity."[81]

Baseball's greatest pinch-hitter, Manny Mota, declared, "Alex was like a father to all of us. He took us under his wing and he prepared us to face baseball in the United States. He prepared us on what to expect in a different country and a different culture. And we appreciated what he did for us."[82]

Hall of famer Orlando Cepeda confessed, "Alejandro Pompez had 100 per cent to do with my career. In 1955 the Giants wanted to release me from spring training and he begged the Giants not to let me go because I had a big future in the big leagues. And he fought with them until the end."[83]

Pompez spent his final years with his wife of five decades, the former Ruth Seldon, at 69-55 44th Avenue in the Borough of Queens. On March 15, 1974, the former entrepreneur suffered a stroke and died later at St. John's Hospital in Queens. His body was interned at Woodlawn Cemetery in the Bronx.[84] Unfortunately, the flamboyant life and historical achievements of Alex Pompez are only recalled by a few. This man, although labeled a gangster, helped change the face of baseball.

Emilio "Millito" Navarro

"I imagined that I was in heaven."

Emilio Navarro remembers the day in 1928 that changed his life.

He was approached by a man representing the famous promoter Alejandro Pompez. Navarro recalled, "There was a Dominican pitcher named Pedro Alejandro San who played on the Ponce team with me. He was invited to play with the Cuban Stars in New York and he invited me to go there and [tryout] with them. I was surprised [but] I was sure I would find work with the team." Although he was brimming with confidence, the trip was a gamble: "There was no contract. I just went directly to the U.S. [for the tryout]."[85]

Although Navarro was only 23 years old, he already had six years of professional baseball under his belt. He had started playing shortstop in his native Puerto Rico in 1922, eventually moving to Santo Domingo and then Caracas, Venezuela, before returning to the fields of San Juan.

The six-day boat trip to New York was ordinary enough, but his first glimpse of the metropolis has stayed with him all his life.

He said, "I was surprised because a culture like that [in the U.S.] had everything. Those high buildings all around. I imagined that I was in heaven." His brief stay in New York ended at the docks when "Someone from the team met me and sent me on the train to Philadelphia where the team was playing."[86]

Fortunately, Pompez found the young Navarro satisfactory, offering him $100 per month. At that moment, he became the first Puerto Rican to play in the Negro Leagues. "When I learned that the Cuban Stars wanted me to play I was very emotional about that," said Millito. "Very, very happy. Very excited. It was a dream for me." He recalled, "Everyone on the [Cuban] Stars spoke Spanish. There were no American blacks on the team. It's unbelievable but we were only Latinos. I did not have any problem adjusting, even though I could not speak English." Navarro roomed with a Dominican teammate, Tetelo Vargas, and fit into his new environment immediately.

Pompez treated his new shortstop like a son, filling his off-days with trips around the city. In 1929 Pompez raised his salary to $125 and Navarro returned the kindness by hitting .337 for the season. Emilio brought many stories back to Puerto Rico after his two years of Negro League play were finished. He would claim that the best players he saw at that time were Martín Dihigo, Alejandro Oms and "Tetelo" Vargas. He remembers occasionally playing white teams, including "the AA class Atlantic City team that had players from the Yankees."

But it was his humorous anecdotes that caught everyone's attention: "We played in the south part of the U.S. in Richmond, Virginia, one time in 1928. We went to a restaurant to eat and they said, 'We don't serve Negro guys.' I told the guy, 'We are Latin people. I am from Puerto Rico.' He said to me, 'Oh, you are white Indians. Come in and eat.'"

Another story he loves to tell involves one of the greatest black ballplayers of the early days of the twentieth century:

> I have story about [John Henry] "Pop" Lloyd. I call this story, A Play in Which the Runner Was Safe and the Fielder Was Out. Lloyd was one of the greatest shortstops at that time. He was playing with the Lincoln Giants and my team the Cuban Stars were playing a game against them in 1928.
>
> I was playing shortstop and Pop Lloyd came sliding into second base and spiked me and injured my toe. And I had to leave the game. You see, the runner was safe and the fielder was out.

Navarro's two years of glory ended with his decision to return home. "It was a dream for me," he said proudly. "I worked hard over there [but] I was eager to come back to back to Puerto Rico. After the [1929] season was over some guy invited me to play in Cuba, but I [declined]."

Navarro was born on September 26, 1905, in the town of Patillas, Puerto Rico. His father, a shoemaker, died unexpectedly when Emillio was five years old, leaving his mother to raise the family of three boys and two girls alone.

Although Emillio had to shoulder some of the family responsibilities at a young age he found his real passion three years later when he learned the fundamentals of baseball. He said, "The first professionals that I saw were a team of Puerto Ricans. They did not belong to a league, but all of the teams were independent and played by invitation." He added, "My hero was Willie Thompson, a man from the Fiji Islands who played here in Puerto Rico."[87]

In high school Navarro set records in track and field in the 100-yard dash, 220-yard low hurdles and the long jump. At the age of 17 Navarro became a baseball professional, playing infield for the Ponce Lions for $25 per week. At that time he would play one game on Saturday and two games on Sunday, with exhibition games during the week.

In 1935, at the age of 30, he married his sweetheart, an 18-year-old high school student. Their love affair lasted for 53 years until she passed away in 1986.

Emilio Navarro started his professional career as a shortstop in 1922 in Puerto Rico. Six years later he came to the United States to play for the controversial figure Alex Pompez, in New York. (Source: Navarro family collection.)

Of his 20-year playing career Navarro cherishes one day in particular:

> The most important moment in my career was when the number-one semipro team in the United States came to Puerto Rico to play the Guyama team in a series. They were a white team and Guyama called me to play this important game.
>
> It was very important to everyone in Puerto Rico. It was a matter of national pride. It was a championship game.
>
> In the ninth inning I was called up to pinch hit and I hit a single that won the game. I was 34 years old and I was in the last years of my career.[88]

Navarro continued to play until he developed knee problems in 1942. Ending his playing career with a lifetime batting average of .300, he was immediately hired as a coach for his Ponce team for the next four years. The team boasted a superstar lineup including Negro League icons Monte Irvin, Leon Day and Josh Gibson.

At the turn of the twenty-first century Navarro is a national treasure in Puerto Rico. He was a pioneer in the original Puerto Rican League and in 1992 was elected to his country's sports hall of fame for achievements in both high school track and field and professional baseball.

When Orlando Cepeda was enshrined at Cooperstown in 1999 he asked Emilio to accompany him to New York.

For Emilio his life continues to be a joyous celebration even as he approaches the age of 100.

Authors note: When I interviewed Navarro in August of 2001 he said, "I have a girl friend who is 55 years old. She gives me a good view of life. I am in good shape and I go to parties and dance. I am very independent." He then proudly admitted, "Last night I went to bed at two A.M. I just enjoy life a lot."

When he turned 98 years old in 2003 he announced, "People ask me why I am so active. I tell them the answer is, the grace of God and good martinis."

Augustín "Tingo" Daviú
The first Puerto Rican...

The first Puerto Rican to play professional ball in the white leagues in the United States was third baseman Augustín "Tingo" Daviú, who joined Allentown in the Eastern League in the mid-twenties.

Emilio Navarro played with Daviú at that time and was not hesitant to praise him. "Tingo Daviu was a wonderful pitcher and he used to play in the infield, too." Navarro added, "He was one of the best third basemen of my time."

Navarro recalled when Daviú was offered a minor league contract. "In those years the Allentown team from the United States came over here [Puerto Rico] to play. They saw him play good and they signed him. He did very well. That happened sometime around 1926."[89]

Although Puerto Rico did not have an organized professional league until 1938, the island had embraced the game nearly four decades earlier, and American teams would travel there for spring training warm-up games.

According to former Puerto Rican star Carlos Santiago, Daviú came from an athletic family. "They were from Ponce and there were three Daviú's— Chelino, Juan and Tingo," said Sanitago.

"All three of them played baseball. Juan played [professionally] for Aguilla and moved to New York. Tingo stayed in Puerto Rico, and Chelino lived in Venezuela. They were spread all over ."[90]

Tingo returned to his native country in the thirties, continuing to play and manage in the Puerto Rican League's historic inaugural season.

Latins Excel at the "Other" Great Sport
The Argentinean clubbed Dempsey through the ropes...

The visibility of talented Latin athletes received an enormous boost on September 14, 1923, when heavyweight boxing champion Jack Dempsey fought the champion of Argentina, Luis Firpo, at the Polo Grounds.

Many boxing historians agree that the bout may have been the most brutal slugfest ever witnessed. Babe Ruth, John McGraw, Alex Pompez and 88,000 other ticket holders watched as the Argentinean clubbed Dempsey through the ropes in the wild first round, and then lost to a knockout in the first minute of the second.

Like Miguel González, Firpo had a true rags-to-riches story and was an inspiration to other Latin athletes. Growing up in a poor section of Buenos Aires, Firpo had worked his way up from being a drug store clerk to being a supremely successful investor. By the time he ventured to New York to fight Dempsey he had already accumulated millions of dollars in wealth.[91]

As more Latinos began to gain fame in America's second-most popular sport, the opportunities for work increased. In 1927 two Chicago promoters, Mickey Lennon and Duke Barry, hatched a plan to sign the top boxers in Cuba and bring them back to the United States. Engaging the services of a Havana promoter named Frank Suarez, they attracted the Cuban light-heavyweight champion, Roleaux Saguero, and the island's flyweight champ, Genaro Piño.

Sounding more like a baseball scout searching for cheap talent, Duke Barry told a reporter, "Several more of the Cuban punchers will be imported to join the troupe now located here."[92]

The first Latin to win a world's championship in boxing was Al Brown of Panama, who won the world bantamweight title in 1929. On July 15, 1931, Cuban-born boxer named Eligio Sardinias won the World Junior Lightweight championship in Philadelphia. Sardinias, who was known as "Kid Chocolate" and the "The Cuban Bon Bon" was the first black Latino boxing champion. Kid Chocolate combined Martin Dihigo's athleticism and flair for the finest tailored suits with Dolf Luque's penchant for mishandling money.

Another Latin boxer, Sixto Escobar from Puerto Rico, won the bantamweight title in August of 1936 and had a stadium named after him.

"Mero" Urena and Juan Vargas
The first Dominican players to take advantage of their talents abroad.

"Mero" Urena is a player so obscure that his name could only be found in one historical publication. However, in 1925 Urena became the first native of the Dominican Republic to play professional baseball in the United States.[93] Two years later a versatile Dominican infielder/outfielder named Juan "Tetelo" Vargas joined Alex Pompez's Cuban Stars.

Vargas played eleven years in the United States, finishing his career in the Mexican League in the 1950s. A native of Santo Domingo, Vargas played throughout the Caribbean and won the Puerto Rican League batting title in 1953 at the age of 46.

If only Urena had known that he was a pioneer of sorts. It would be another 31 years before the trend would catch on, as in 1956 Ossie Virgil, an infielder, became the first Dominican to play in the major leagues. Appropriately, Virgil was also signed by Pompez, then of the New York Giants.

The Dominicans originally caught the baseball bug from Cubans fleeing their island during the war of independence in the 1890s, and the popularity of the game burgeoned after the U.S. Marines invaded the tiny island in 1916. By the 1920s a professional league was in full operation.

In the early twenties a Dominican pitcher named Fellito Guerra was courted by professional scouts from the United States, but he refused to sign a contract.[94] Thus, it was Urena and Vargas who were the first Dominican players to take advantage of their talents abroad.

Negro Leagues Summon the Latin Players

…He put batters in a cocaine-like stupor with his repertoire of pitches.

Nearly three dozen black and white Cubans found jobs in the United States playing for Negro League ball clubs during the decade of the twenties. Among them were such heralded Cuban stars as pitcher Manuel "Cocaina" García, who earned his nickname because he put batters in a "cocaine-like" stupor with his repertoire of pitches.

Also included was Edolfo "Yoyo" Díaz, who was named as one of the great Cuban pitchers by Negro League star Ted "Double Duty" Radcliffe.

Some of the longest-tenured Latinos in the first great Negro League experiment were such unsung heroes as "Yoyo" Díaz (10 years), Silvino Ruiz (7 years), Candor López (12 years), Lázaro Salazar (6 years) , Armando Massip (11 years), Felipe Sierra (12 years) and Luis Arango (15 years).

Buried in the old, obscure biographies are the compelling stories of men like Estaban Montalovo, who was considered one of the great power hitters in the black leagues from 1923 to 1928. Tuberculosis took him when he was approaching 30 years of age and he has since been forgotten.

Julio LeBlanc, a tall, muscular pitcher with the Cuban Stars of Cincinnati, was another player who had a promising career extinguished by tragedy. During the winter league season of 1921–1922 he became embroiled in an argument with another player, Antonio Susini. During the melee Susini attacked LeBlanc with a bat and killed him.

The long-forgotten legend of Cuneo Gálvez is another story worth repeating. Gálvez stood 7' tall and pitched underhand when he was first discovered by "Tinti" Molina in Cuba. The lanky Cuban may have made a good box-office draw, but little else. In 1929 he had a 4–9 record for Molina's Cuban Stars (West) and ended his career after four years on United States soil.[95]

6

The 1930s

In the decade of the thirties only six Latin-born players made their debuts in the major leagues. They included the first two Mexicans, the first Venezuelan and three Cubans. Alejandro "Alex" Carrasquel of Caracas, Venezuela, was the first player from his country to gain that honor. A feature on Alejandro and his nephew Chico appears in the 1940s chapter.

Mel Almada, an outfielder, and Chile Gómez, an infielder, were the first two Mexican nationals to make the big leagues. Gómez debuted on Juy 27, 1935, with the Philadelphia Phillies, playing only 200 games in three seasons. The Mel Almada story is featured later in this chapter.

The three Cubans were Roberto Estalella, an outfielder; Mike Fermín Guerra, a catcher; and René Monteagudo, a left-handed pitcher and outfielder — all signed by the Senators. Monteagudo appeared in 156 games in three seasons and Guerra was primarily a back-up catcher for nine years. The Roberto Estalella story appears later in this chapter.

During this same decade, approximately two dozen Latinos were added to the faltering Negro Leagues. The worst year for the organized black leagues was 1932, with teams and leagues crumbling under the weight of the Great Depression. The domino effect actually began when Rube Foster's famed Negro National League was dismantled in 1931. Afro-American players scattered, desperately trying to find a solvent ball club. There was little room for Latinos until more leagues were created in the late thirties.

One enterprising young Cuban outfielder, Pedro Pagés, made the jump from the United States to the Mexican League and to the Canadian League. Pagés somehow found work from the late thirties through the early fifties by making the right moves at the right times. Another adventurous Cuban, Javier "Blue" Pérez, spent nine years playing infield positions in the Negro National League before he became one of the first Latinos to play in Japan and the Philippines.

Luis Eleuterio Tiant Sr.

"He was better than his son"

Agustín "Tinti" Molina had a great eye for talent. His executive position in the Cuban League offered him a unique chance to evaluate young talent before signing them to play summer ball for his team in the United States. When a slim 19-year-old lefthander named Luis Tiant took the mound for the first time in 1926, everyone, including Molina, took note. Tiant's herky-jerky pitching style and deceptive followthrough earned him respect around the league. After he led the Cienfuegos Elephants to the league championship in 1929 Molina felt that this was the time to take him to America.

From 1930 through 1947 Tiant pitched for three Negro League teams including Molina's Cuban Stars. He suffered through a 4–13 record in his first season, but eventually improved and earned a spot in two Negro League East-West All-Star games.

In 1946 he was selected for both the East-West game and the all-star team in Cuba, and at the age of 41 had posted a 10–0 record. That year he threw three shutouts and helped Alex Pompez's New York Cubans to clinch the Negro National League pennant.[1]

Carlos Santiago played against Tiant for many years and remembers that he combined "a good move to first base and a terrific screw. He used to throw the screwball to right-hand hitters and the ball zipped away." He also noted, "In those days in the colored leagues [he] used to pitch the spitball."[2]

Tiant stuffed his repertoire with junk pitches and had the ability to change speeds while using the same unorthodox delivery style. His famous windup caused hitters to lose their timing and look foolish. Ultimately, it was the basis for several funny stories, including the one that Hall of Fame outfielder Monte Irvin kept circulating for many years. During one particular Negro League game Tiant was trying to keep a base runner from stealing second. He started his trademark windup and suddenly threw to first base to pick off the runner. According to the version that Irvin told, the batter was so confused that he swung for strike three as Tiant threw to first base.[3]

Negro League legend Ted "Double Duty" Radcliffe faced Tiant in the thirties and claimed that he was one of the best Latin pitchers that he had ever seen.[4] In 1935 Tiant pitched an 11-inning masterpiece against the St. Louis Cardinals in Cuba, allowing only one run; and later that year he held Babe Ruth to only one hit in two games during exhibition play.

In the early 1940s Armando Vasquez saw Tiant pitch a full 18-inning game in Cuba and finish with a victory.[5]

At the age of 39 the slender Cuban pitched in 29 games, leading the Cuban League during the 1944–1945 season. As his arm wore down he worked hard on adjusting his pitching repertoire.

Oscar Garmendia played professional ball for 12 years and remembers hitting against Tiant in the late forties in Cuba, just as he was about to retire. Garmendia said, "He threw a lot of slow stuff and he had a nice curve. But every time you hit against him you had to wait for, what we called then, "*garbage.*" He threw slow, then slow, then slow."[6]

Despite his legendary career, Luis Tiant will forever be a footnote to his namesake son, who gained superstar status pitching for 19 years in the major leagues. Tiant Sr. joins another great star from his era, Pedro Perucho Cepeda, standing in the shadows and watching their sons achieve remarkable success.

Both Tiant Sr. and Pedro Cepeda are considered by their contemporaries to have had skills superior to those of their offspring. But it was first their skin color, and then their age, which prevented them from advancing past the Negro Leagues. Ask most ballplayers from the era of the thirties and the forties and they will say the same thing.

Felix Delgado played against the elder Tiant and saw the junior pitch also, and believes "He was better than his son."[7] Armando Vasquez played with Tiant Sr. on the New York Cubans in the forties and states, "[He] was a hell of a pitcher. Maybe I'm wrong but, by my way, the father was a better pitcher."[8]

Although Luis Jr. inherited his father's unorthodox delivery, he rarely saw him pitch, because the son was only seven years old when Tiant Sr. retired from professional baseball in 1948.

In the early 1940s Lefty Gomez of the Yankees had waxed philosophical on aging hurlers when he said, "I'm throwing twice as hard as I ever did. It's just not getting there as fast." Taking the implied advice, Tiant Sr. finally called it quits at the age of forty-two. Scraping together his meager savings he went into business with his brother-in-law. In 1948 they purchased a truck and began a furniture-moving business while Luis's wife, Isabel, took a job as a domestic, cooking meals for middle-class families in their hometown of Nicanor del Campo.

Even though they were cash-strapped Luis and Isabel focused on one goal — the education of their only child, Luis Jr. While sending him to a private school they stressed the importance of an education and a career that involved the intellect, not the back. But when Luis Jr. caught baseball fever they would not attempt to dissuade him from his youthful dreams.

Remembering how he was snubbed by the big leagues and then paid so poorly in the Negro Leagues, the elder Tiant would caution his son against playing professional ball in America. But times had changed. After pitching for the Mexico City Tigers from 1959 through 1961, Luis Jr. was sold to the Cleveland Indians for the then-princely sum of $35,000.

As life was surrendering its richest promises to the son, it was serving a bitter reality to the father. Fidel Castro had taken power in 1959 and over the next two years he had imposed incredible restrictions and penalties on Cubans who sought to emigrate abroad. When Luis Jr. and his new wife Maria wanted to fly to Cuba for a reunion in September of 1961, the elder Tiant told his son not to come. He did not want his only child to see what had happened to him. There was also a real fear that Luis Jr. might not be allowed to leave.

In late 1968 Isabel Tiant was granted a temporary exit visa to visit her son, daughter-in-law and three grandchildren, who were living in Mexico City. Luis Sr. begged his wife to stay in Mexico, but, fearing for the safety of her husband, she returned after the Christmas holidays.

The once-great pitching hero of Cuba was fully prepared to suffer the last years of his life without her, confident she was safe and living in decent conditions. At the age of sixty-nine he was now reduced to working at an auto repair garage, pumping gas.

Acting out of desperation, Luis Jr. was now using his influence as an athlete to free his parents. The year was 1975 and he had been the rotation ace for the Boston Red Sox for the past five seasons. There were powerful politicians in Massachusetts and he had to petition them. He made impassioned pleas to all of his political contacts. Soon, his request had reached the desks of Massachusetts state senator Edward Brooke and former presidential candidate George McGovern.

On May 5, 1975, McGovern arrived in Havana bearing a document which demanded the release of Luis and Isabel. Later that week he was granted a meeting with Castro which lasted nearly twelve hours. When the meeting ended the senator received the guarantee that he had sought. The phone call that Luis and Isabel had been dreaming of became a reality as they sat in their cramped little apartment #9 on Calle 30. They would be granted permission to leave.

It took nearly four months for their papers to be processed, but finally they were free. Carlos Santiago knew some of the details. "Luis (Jr.) called Bobby Avila," said Santiago. "And Avila tried to get his parents into the United States through Mexico to Boston."[9] Roberto Avila was a big-league star with the Indians in the fifties who had returned to Mexico, eventually entering politics. Avila was close to the Tiant family and had been instrumental in getting Luis Jr. his first professional contract in Mexico.

After receiving their visa clearance at the U.S. Embassy in Mexico City, Luis and Isabel boarded an American Airlines plane on August 20, 1975. The reunion at Logan International Airport was caught on camera by hordes of local and national media reporters. It had been fifteen years since Luis Jr. had seen his father. The tears that were shed at the terminal gate were magnified across the country. Tough, hardened teammates of Luis Jr. could not hide their emotion. They wept as the drama was played out on television.

Seven days later Luis Sr. walked to the mound in Fenway Park, holding a baseball in his gnarled left hand. The pregame ceremony was augmented by thirty-two thousand fans leaping to their feet, chanting "Loo-ee, Loo-ee!" His son stood behind him, covered in goose bumps. One day short of his seventieth birthday Luis Tiant threw a pitch in a major league ballpark.

The new life that Tiant had desired for such a long time was not destined to last more than 29 more months. Luis Tiant Sr. died on December 12, 1977, of a heart attack in Boston.

Mel Almada
The first Mexican-born player…

He came from the remote Mexican town of Huatabampo, situated slightly inland from the Gulf of California. Every one of the 16,000 residents had something to be proud of when their native son left to play his first professional ball game in the early 1930s. Later, the entire country of Mexico cheered with pride when he signed with the Boston Red Sox in 1933.

In spite of the grip of the Great Depression there was finally something to rejoice over — Baldomero Melo "Mel" Almada was the first Mexican-born player to make it to the major leagues.

The Red Sox had experimented with Latin-born players twice before. Two Cuban infielders, Eusebio González (1918) and "Mike" Herrera (1925) had short-lived careers; but Almada came out of the gates looking good. The 20-year-old center fielder made a quick adjustment to major league pitching after a short stint in the Pacific Coast League.

Almada made his major league debut on September 8, 1933, in Boston during a doubleheader against the Detroit Tigers. The rookie was thrown into the starting center fielder's position for both games, where he acquitted himself well, going 2 for 8 and scoring one run. By the time the season ended three weeks later he had posted a .341 batting average in 14 games and drew a walk approximately every five at-bats. He completed his freshman year with an admirable on-base percentage of .473.

However, there was no opportunity for him to claim the center field position from Dusty Cooke, who had become a fixture since arriving from the Yankees at the beginning of the season. Opportunities in 1934 didn't improve after the Red Sox received Carl Reynolds in a trade from the Browns. Cooke was given a backup role and Almada saw action in only 23 games.

When the Red Sox finished in fourth place with a .500 winning percentage the ownership decided to clean house at the end of the season. They hired Joe Cronin to be their new skipper — and shortstop — for the upcoming 1935 campaign.

Cooke was moved to right field and Reynolds was consigned to the bench. With the center field position now up for grabs Almada came on like a seasoned pro. Missing only two games all season the Mexican line-drive hitter batted .290 and stole twenty bases in the leadoff position.

His success mirrored that of the entire franchise as the Red Sox broke out of their prolonged funk and enjoyed their first winning campaign in 16 years. Filled with a sense of promise for the next season they nabbed the great Jimmie Foxx and veteran third baseman Bill Werber in winter trades.

Almada was moved to right field for the 1936 season, and his questionable fielding abilities improved immediately. Having made 12 outfield errors during the previous year, Almada committed only two gaffs in 81 games.

Werber was one of Almada's teammates who was entertained by his tenacious fielding exploits. Recalling a play that the Mexican made after the move to right field, Werber exclaimed, "He made one of damnedest catches I had ever seen in my life!"[10]

The play that shines so brightly in his memory occurred in Yankee Stadium where, at that time, the short right-field fence had a high wire screen attached to it so the fans in the bleachers could watch the game. The Yankees' power hitter Bill Dickey smashed a towering fly that seemed destined to clear the wire fence and land solidly in the stands for a home run.

Almada tracked the ball as he sprinted back to the screen, and, in an amazing display of coordination and timing, he leaped onto the screen like a cat, hanging-on for dear life. Werber elaborated, "With his left hand he held himself there until that ball came down. He reached way up in the air at the very top of the wire and caught that ball in his glove as it was going into the bleachers. It was more than amazing. It was the damnedest catch I had seen in 13 years of professional ball."[11]

Another teammate, Stewart Bowers, felt that Almada had developed a reputation in the American League with his defensive play. "He just did his job well," said Bowers. "He had a great arm and I recall him throwing out men at home plate from deep right field. Guys going from first base to third on base hits respected his arm."[12]

Despite all of the cosmetic changes and Almada's acrobatics, the Red Sox slid back into mediocrity with a fifth-place finish and an 74–80 record.

Just before spring training of 1937 began Almada received a call from Eddie Collins, the Red Sox general manager. "I'd like you to meet a rookie we have coming to camp and escort him to Sarasota. It would be a help to the kid," said Collins. "His name is Doerr. Bobby Doerr."

The Los Angeles–born, 19-year-old second baseman had seen Mel pitch during an amateur tournament in southern California during the early 1930s. Doerr had also played against Mel's brother, Luis Almada, in minor league ball in San Francisco.

Doerr would spend the next 14 years as a major league star, but he would always remember the kindness and patience that Almada showed him during his first few months in a Red Sox uniform. He acknowledged, "[Almada] was a real nice person to be with. A class guy."

Doerr was also there when Almada suffered a serious head injury that could have ended his career. "That spring, we were going north to Durham, North Carolina, to play the Cincinnati club [in an exhibition game]," he remembered. Almada was known for his quick reflexes, but he couldn't avoid a high fastball that hit him squarely in the head. Doerr couldn't recall whether Almada was knocked unconscious, but confirmed, "It was a bad hit. They left him in the hospital overnight and we went on [with the tour]. Later he joined us, but it seemed like he was a little plate-shy after that."[13]

In May of 1937 Boston traded Almada to the Senators, who were searching for a full-time center fielder. In 100 games the Mexican slugger hit .309 for Washington and assured a job for himself for the next season. The move back to center field did not help his fielding percentage, however. He made 15 errors.

Although he started the 1938 campaign in a slump, he was traded to the St. Louis Browns in June and his confidence was revived again. Before the trade was announced he contacted his former roommate, Stewart Bowers, who had retired from the major leagues and was residing in Washington. "The last time I saw Mel was in 1938," Bowers acknowledged. "He was with Washington and he called my home and I stopped down to see him and we went out to dinner." According to Bowers, his friend was brimming with enthusiasm and there was no indication that he feared his career was coming to an end. "He was very positive."

The Browns had dealt their long-time star center fielder Sammy West in the move, but they felt that trading an aging 33-year-old for the rising star Almada, who was just 25 at the time, was a rational exchange. For the next 102 games Almada was one of the top hitters in the American League, pounding opposing pitchers for a .342 average.

Something happened to him in the off season, though, because when he returned to the Browns' training camp in 1939 his skills were dramatically diminished. During midseason he was traded to the Brooklyn Dodgers where he completed his major league tenure. In seven big-league seasons Almada batted .284, including a pinch-hitting average of .348.

"Almada was a quiet sort of fellow," said Bill Werber. "He didn't effervesce very much. He just did his job. I remember him as a real outstanding asset to the ball club. He was a very well liked young man in the clubhouse and he was a damned good ball player."[14]

Stewart Bowers recalled, "I roomed with Mel while I was there in the spring of '36 and again in the late summer." Bowers and Almada, who was fluent in English, spent many evenings together, talking about baseball and discussing their future plans. "The only thing he wanted to do," said Stewart, "was to continue to be a major league ballplayer and do the job well. That's all." Unlike many of his teammates Almada was very careful about his personal habits. "He was a clean cut fellow," said Bowers, "and I never saw Mel take a drink."

Almada may have been well liked, but he was not immune to being victimized in an elaborate practical joke. Recalling a time in the early 1930s Werber said, "We all lived at the Sheridan Hotel in Boston and Almada was single. Not long after he arrived he developed a contact with girl. He would call her or she would call him, but he didn't want anybody to know about it. He was very quiet about his personal life."

Along with a couple of accomplices Werber cornered the hotel's telephone operator and plied her with candy and flowers in return for a chance to tap into their teammate's phone conversations. When a call came in for Almada the group rushed into the operator's room and listened as the couple made plans for a clandestine rendezvous.

The next day the conspirators were waiting for Almada at the clubhouse.

"Hi, Mel," said one with a broad grin.

"How did it go with Gloria last night?" asked another.

Astonished and defensive Almada replied, "What Gloria? Who are you talking about?" He couldn't figure out how the entire Boston Red Sox team knew about his private life.

After he left the major leagues Almada eventually returned to Mexico, where he was spotted at his new job by longtime scout and manager Charlie Metro. "I saw him when I played in the Mexican League," said Metro. "I met him in '47 and he was working with a radio station."[15]

Although his celebrity was confined to a limited geographical area, the people of his hometown would continue to honor his accomplishments. Growing up in Mexico, Ruben Amaro Sr. recalled that his father, Santos Amaro, would remind everyone about the historical significance of Almada's career. When he became a teenager Amaro Sr. played in a national amateur tournament in Almada's home state and was impressed by the reverence they showed him. He said, "Every time there was an event in Sornora they always mentioned Mel Almada."[16]

Almada died August 13, 1988, in Mexico with barely a mention in the American newspapers. Melo Almada may not be a household name, but, because of his early success, he made major league owners take notice of other Mexican stars. In his own way he paved the road for Chile Gómez and Bobby Avila in the 1950s.

New Ports Are Opened

…Uncharted waters to the Dominican Republic.

The Depression forced hungry ballplayers to find work in the Latin countries that were just beginning to construct their own professional leagues. The decade of the thirties saw professional ball players from the United States venture across uncharted waters to the Dominican Republic. The port of Santo Domingo drew the stars of the Negro League circuit in the early part of the decade while the Cincinnati

Reds became the first major league team to schedule exhibition games there in 1935. This was also the decade when Satchel Paige, Josh Gibson and other famous Negro Leaguers began exhibition tours to another untested port, Puerto Rico.

Rodolfo Fernández

No one knew that the 73-year-old black
man had shut out the Brooklyn Dodgers.

Every morning at 7 A.M. the old man would leave his apartment building at 200 West 108th Street in New York and walk the four blocks to his job at St. Luke's Hospital. Along the way he would see kids playing baseball in the park and his mind would wander back to those days in the late 1920s when he would try to earn money by pitching in the villages that dotted the countryside in Cuba.

"How lucky those kids are," he would tell interested friends. "We used rocks for bases. We would make a bat out of any tree limb. We put together a glove anyway we could, using cardboard or cloth."[17] Even poor kids have regulation bats, balls and gloves today.

His knees were bad from six decades of baseball and so the walk took progressively longer each year. But the walk this day was particularly sweet. It was the last time he would have to make it.

Wearing a Almandares Blues uniform, Rodolfo Fernández poses for a photograph in the 1940s. (Source: Fernández family collection.)

Children would race past him on their way to school and middle-aged adults would pass by without a second look. No one knew that the 73-year-old black man had shut out the Brooklyn Dodgers in 1937 and held the Cincinnati Reds to one run later that spring. His once magical arm was now arthritic and crooked at an awkward angle. His back was out of plumb. But perhaps if his neighbors had known he was a great pitcher long ago in the Cuban and Negro Leagues, they might have stopped to shake his hand this special day.

If they had paused to meet him they could have boasted to friends that they knew a man who had pitched a four-hit shutout against the National League–champion New York Giants forty-seven years before. But in 1984 no one knew.

Rodolfo Fernández, the man who could inspire awe with his sinker and curve in front of 20,000 fans, was a forgotten hero to the following generations. Athletic heroism was in the distant past and today was special, because he and his wife Matilde had saved up enough money from their humble jobs to finally allow him to retire. Playing, managing and coaching baseball in nine countries for nearly half a century had left him with a lean bank account.

When he took the hospital job in 1973, he was starting a new career when most men his age were retiring. For the next eleven years he would walk the corridors and climb the stairs of the hospital complex delivering packages in an effort to create a nest egg. After retirement he spent his first few years meeting with other friends in the Cuban community, talking about the old days and cursing the destructive regime of Fidel Castro.

But just as it seemed that his legacy would die on the barbed fences of segregation and public indifference, he was rediscovered. Suddenly, the phone started ringing and strangers were asking him to tell his life story. In 1993 George Steinbrenner invited him to Yankee Stadium to be honored along with other forgotten Negro League players. In 1997 he was honored in Atlanta and in June of 1998 he was summoned to Milwaukee County Stadium. Now adults and children respectfully handed him a scorecard or a ball to autograph as he stood on the cinder strip inside a major league park. He was pitched back in time to the days when he was a strong, young man, sought by promoters and anxious fans.

Fernández was born on June 27, 1911, in a dilapidated village on the outskirts of Havana. His father was a laborer and Rodolfo, along with his ten brothers and sisters, scrambled to put food on the table each day. At an early age he sought refuge on the rock-strewn playing field near his home. When he was old enough to pitch in the well-funded amateur leagues in Havana he was stunned to find that he was not welcome. He recalled, "Maybe you don't believe it, but in Cuba there were things that were wrong. [They] did not like the colored ballplayer in their amateur leagues. So, we played around the small towns hoping to make a little money."

The decision to become a paid athlete was easy, but making the plan workable was more difficult. "When I was 16 and 17 I tried to make a living with the other boys, playing ball in the other towns. Sometimes we would take one dollar a week. It was a difficult time," he explained.

Despite the roadblocks, his confidence was strongly rooted in his God-given abilities. Also, his brother José had been earning a living playing summer ball as a catcher with black teams in the United States since 1916.

In the winter of 1925 José was playing for the Cuban team Almandares, and he invited his younger brother to come to Havana and see his first professional game. Recalling it, Rodolfo chuckled, "Even though it cost [only] five cents to go from my home town to Havana I couldn't afford it." So José paid the fare.

As Rodolfo stood against the Almandares dugout, awestruck by the size of La Tropical Stadium, José nudged him. He wanted to introduce him to another player — the immortal Martín Dihigo. From that moment Rodolfo would never want to do anything else but play the game of baseball. Although his relationship with Dihigo would endure for another thirty years, the first introduction was the one which would remain with him forever.

In 1930 Rodolfo was noticed by scouts. Later he would characterize them as "Guys who were also looking for boxing prospects." José Cardenal, a black Cuban who made it to the big leagues in the 1960s, explained why those professional scouts were so popular. "There were only two ways to get off the island back then," he said, "and that was baseball and boxing."[18]

Signed to a professional contract, Rodolfo pitched for the Almandares team for the next two years and, because of his brother's influence, came to New York in 1932 to play for Alex Pompez and the Cuban Stars. His arrival in the United States was exciting but disappointing. Expecting to see streets lined with gold, he saw instead the grief and hopelessness inflicted by the Great Depression. "I was coming from Miami to New York on a bus," he remembered, "and we saw many, many people [lined up] outside the capital [in Washington DC]. I asked somebody, what is happening? They said they are waiting in line for food. I couldn't believe it."[19]

But he was not disappointed by the level of talent that he witnessed in the Negro Leagues. "I found that it was really high quality baseball. Very extraordinary. We would actually make enough to pay for our meals and then earn a salary too!" he said excitedly. "They gave me one dollar a day for food, but I remember everything was so cheap. In New York if you go to the restaurant you eat for 25 cents."

Although he earned a salary which exceeded the $125 per month he made in Cuba, his life was not comfortable by any means: "Sometimes we traveled 200 miles after a game because we would have to play in another state the next day and sometimes we didn't have a chance to eat. It was a lot of tough work and sacrifice, but we loved the game so much."

For the next 41 years Fernandez would remain in baseball, traveling to more countries than he could count and meeting the greatest black players in the game.

Reminiscing about his life Fernandez was circumspect. When someone would ask him to describe the most treasured possessions he had collected after such a long career he would sadly say, "Everything that I say to you is in my memory. I spent many years in baseball and I traveled a lot but I don't have any newspaper [clippings] or magazines [articles]. When I played ball there were no records [maintained]. We didn't have anything. I played all over South America and the Caribbean and America, but I don't have a book or a record of my accomplishments. Everything I say to you is in my memory, believe it or not."[20]

Although he always said the most memorable event in his long career was the day he shut out Leo Durocher and the Brooklyn Dodgers in an exhibition game in 1937, he couldn't help feeling vindicated after his experience at Yankee Stadium in 1993. "We had the opportunity to live those few moments [in a major league park]," he declared. "But we were not able to demonstrate who we were, or what talents we had, in a big-league ballpark when we were young. Now after all these years we have been recognized."[21]

During the last months of his life he was bedridden with arthritis, but somehow struggled to the phone to answer one more question from a writer or to acknowledge an admirer. This gentle and patient man played his final inning of life on September 5, 2000.

Roberto Estalella

"I can't imagine what he went through."

It was a typically crisp spring afternoon in San Francisco, April 28, 2001. The outfield at Pac Bell Park became a dense forest of ticket holders, clutching their cameras, waiting for the beginning of the annual "Fan Photo Day." As several thousand people strained against the rope barriers, a handful of Giants players approached the screaming throng with a look of resignation. Suddenly, as if on cue, the alto shriek of hundreds of young women filled the air.

"Its him! Its Bobby Estalella," they shouted.

One girl leaned forward to get the attention of Giants manager Dusty Baker. "Can you let Bobby come home with me?" she pleaded.

Six decades earlier Bobby's grandfather had a much different experience, because many of the fans reaching over the barriers had a less inviting message. The younger Estalella began his professional career in 1993 after being selected as a catcher in the twenty-third round by the Philadelphia Phillies. His rugged good looks and muscular build made him a female-fan favorite, whether he was playing for the Phillies, the Giants, the Yankees or the Colorado Rockies.

His grandfather, Roberto Méndez Estalella, a Cuban native, started in the major leagues in 1935 with the Washington Senators as a third baseman/outfielder. Like his grandson, he was an imposing physical presence at two hundred pounds of muscle. Because of his powerful build he was nicknamed *El Tarzán* and scouts throughout Cuba thought he would become a power-hitting threat in the United States.

Mickey Vernon, a player and manager for over four decades in major league baseball, was very impressed with the young Cuban's strength when he saw him for the first time in 1935. "He was a big kid," said Vernon. "Short and squatty with broad shoulders and very strong." Roberto proved his power during his second season, when Vernon saw him hit "one of the longest balls I ever saw a right-hander hit to the opposite field."[22]

Walter Masterson heard about his prowess before the Cuban strong man ever became a big-leaguer. Masterson, who would eventually spend eleven years pitching for the Senators, explained, "[Roberto] Estalella was the principal home-run hitter for the Senators' minor league team, but back then we only had three or four [teams] at the time. He came up from Charlotte and he did hit the long ball."[23]

When Clark Griffith brought him to the majors everyone knew that there would be challenges from the press and the public regarding his skin color and ethnic background. The younger Estalella said, "My grandfather didn't have it extremely easy by any means because he was from Cuba, and being from a different descent. Also he had a language barrier. He didn't speak the language at all. I know he had a lot of rough times. I can't imagine what he went through, but he never really talked about that."[24]

Legendary writer Bob Considine gave us a glimpse of the hurdles Roberto faced in 1940. He revealed that the Cuban endured an "alarming number " of fastballs aimed at his head, not just to keep him from digging in at the plate, but also to send him a message. According to Considine, "Others who 'dusted' Estalella were of that peculiar big-league mold which is almost psychopathically opposed to Roberto and his coffee-colored colleagues."[25]

For decades there has been a legend swirling around the community of old-time scouts regarding Roberto. This story was told to me by a respected scout who had been in baseball for nearly half a century.

It relates to the time in the late 1930s when Roberto had invited his father to

Washington to see him play major league ball for the first time. Clark Griffith was at the train station to greet the old man, who had made the arduous journey from Cuba. As he stepped off the train Griffith immediately intervened. Before the press could see Estalella's dark- skinned father, he was put back on the train and returned to Cuba.

While this story cannot be verified, given the climate of the times it is not improbable.

Despite the obstacles that his grandfather had to overcome, Bobby Estalella saw no sign of regret in him. "He was a guy who never dwelt on negatives or talked about negative stuff," said Bobby. "The only thing he did tell me was to always work hard and not look back, but to work harder than the guy next to you. Because you are different you are going to have to work harder than the next guy."[26]

Roberto Estalella established himself as a power hitter during the 1936–1937 winter season, when he led the Cuban League in home runs.[27] Manny Mota, once major league baseball's pinch-hitting champion, was a child in the Dominican Republic when he first started hearing of Estalella's exploits. "I remember listening to Cuban baseball on the radio in the 1940s," said Mota. "and Roberto Estalella was the greatest slugger in Cuba."[28]

With the Senators Roberto played in only 110 games during the 1935, '36 and '39 seasons combined, hitting a respectable .279. He returned to the majors in 1941 with the St. Louis Browns and was sent back to Washington in the following year. In 1942 he played in a career-high 133 games and hit .277, including one double for each 5.5 official at-bats.

His finest seasons were 1944 and 1945 with the Philadelphia A's when he hit .298 and .299 respectively. In 1945 he hit a double for every five official at-bats, but Estalella never became the power hitter his scouts had envisioned. He did hit well for average, however, and he ended his nine-year career with a decent average of .282. Opposing pitchers must have respected his physical strength because he drew a base on balls every third time at bat.

Although Estalella hit only 44 homeruns in his career, Mickey Vernon saw one he will never forget. "For a right-handed hitter he hit one of the longest balls to right center in Griffith Stadium," declared Vernon. "It went over the scoreboard and the fence, which was about thirty feet high. Today it's not unusual for power hitters to hit opposite-field home runs. But it was then."[29]

Estelella attempted to join the cross-border exodus to the Mexican League in 1946 and was suspended by Commissioner of Baseball Happy Chandler for five seasons. Although he hit over .300 in Mexico he was excluded from winter ball in the Cuban League because of pressure exercised by big-league owners on Havana officials. There were others who suffered because of this ban, including Dolf Luque and Mike González.

In 1949 he was re-admitted to baseball after Chandler lifted the ban, but he played in only eight games for the A's. Although he had a marvelous display of power in the Cuban League, he never returned to the big leagues.

Young Bobby Estalella would never have heard about his grandfather's exploits if it hadn't been for the houseful of friends who often came to show their respect. "I heard it all secondhand from other parties," his grandson confessed. "I respected him a lot for it because he never bragged about his accomplishments or how he went about his business. I heard plenty of stories from everybody else."[30]

Born in Cárdenas, Cuba, in 1911, Roberto began his professional career as a teenager with a semipro team in Matanzas Province. Signed to a minor league contract by the Senators' scout Joe Cambria, his first assignment was with the Albany Senators in the International League in 1934.

Whereever he played minor league ball he seemed to easily break the .300 level, including a .378 average at Charlotte.[31] Stewart Bowers was a minor league pitcher in the Red Sox farm system when he faced Estallela at Charlotte. "He was a great ballplayer," said Bowers with a chuckle. "He was leading the league in hitting, and our manager told us to walk him all the time."[32]

Estallela was an average infielder, and, although he made as many errors as he did home runs, neither amounted to a substantial number. According to Vernon he was an aggressive defenseman, and one fielding incident in 1942 led to a rather surprising ending.

The Senators were playing the first game of a doubleheader in Yankee Stadium with Sid Hudson on the mound and Estalella manning third base for Washington. With the score tied in the bottom of the ninth the Yankees had a runner on third and one out.

Hudson recalled that the Yankees catcher, "Bill Dickey was (at the plate), and he was a left-handed hitter so the infield was swung around toward right field. Estalella was playing toward second base."

On the first pitch Dickey did something that no one had expected him to do. He bunted. As the ball rolled down the third-base line Hudson thought to himself, "The only chance we have is to let the ball go foul."

Out of the corner of his eye, he saw Estalella charging the ball. He yelled, "Let it go! Let it go!" but it was too late. Estalella gloved the ball just as Dickey crossed first base and the runner scored to win the game.

Hudson remembered, "I was yelling at him and got on him about it, and gave him a good going-over on the field." Hudson respected Roberto and his tirade wasn't personal. Everyone knew it, except one fan in the grandstand.

After the game Hudson had showered and found a seat behind home plate so he could watch the second contest. His hopes of enjoying a peaceful late afternoon watching his teammates play were quickly shattered when an angry woman approached him.

"What did you say to that Cuban?" she demanded.

"Ma'am?"

Apparently worried that Hudson had hurt Estalella's feelings, she repeated her question: "What did you say to that Cuban?"

It didn't take long for Hudson to realize that his inquisitor was the famous Broadway singer and actress Ethel Merman. Needless to say, it was a moment that he would never forget.[33]

Roberto Estalella spent the final years of his life in Florida, watching baseball games on TV, entertaining his many friends and teaching his grandson the fundamentals of the game. Bobby recalls, "I was seven years old and we would be playing in the front yard. He taught me how to swing and just showed me some of the basics. He'd always be watching baseball games so we'd be sitting down together. He would say, 'Watch how they play. Watch how they go about their business. Watch the catcher and how he sets up and what he does. You can learn from it.'"

Bobby knows that his grandfather could have taken the easy way out and returned to Cuba when the prejudice became too intense. He knows that his debt to Roberto will never be repaid. "He is the reason that I got into baseball. He was my inspiration," he said.[34] When Roberto died on January 6, 1991, his grandson Bobby was sixteen.

A Writer's Holiday

Rodríguez had appeared at camp and requested a tryout.

During the 1930s the fraternity of baseball writers in Philadelphia were a sad lot. Connie Mack had sold off his most valuable players on a once-great Athletics' team and the Phillies had developed the worst pitching staff in baseball since 1920. Some of the writers had resigned themselves to mediocrity and had lost interest in their assignments.

During a spring training camp for the Athletics in the mid-thirties a writer for the *Philadelphia Evening Ledger* named Al Horwits decided to play a joke on a lazy colleague from the *Philadelphia Bulletin*. The laggard, named Cy, would spend his afternoons playing golf and then return to the hotel to quiz his competitors on the day's events so he could file a report.

One day Horwits, who was fed up with this journalistic welfare, told the reporter that a Cuban player named Rodríguez had appeared at camp and requested a try out. He said, "Connie [Mack] put him on second base, and it looks like he's going to start the season there."

This was a story worth reporting, because neither the A's or the Phillies had a Latino on their squads. For the next few days Cy filed numerous reports based on Horwits' testimony.

"Rodríguez had two hits in the game camp," declared Horwits one evening. And another glowing story was filed by Cy.

When Cy decided to see this Latin phenomenon for himself, he approached Connie Mack and asked for a quote.

"Rodríguez?" Mack responded. Turning to his son Earle, Mack asked if there was anyone in their camp named Rodríguez.

"No," came the prompt answer.

Realizing he had been "snookered," Cy immediately filed a report stating that Rodríguez was given a sudden and unconditional release.

The joke backfired, however: The next day Horwits received a telegram from his boss at the *Evening Ledger* demanding to know why he hadn't bothered to do a story on the young star named Rodríguez.[35]

Santos Amaro

"Amaro was one of the great men from
Matanzas who shined above all the others."

Santos Amaro never achieved stardom playing in the Negro Leagues; however, his direction and inspiration led the next two generations of Amaro men into the major leagues.

Santos was born in Cuba around 1908 and began his professional career sometime in the late twenties. He was following in the footsteps of his father, who played at the turn of the century. When I interviewed Santos at the age of 92 he could not remember whether his father had confined himself to pitching or had played many positions as was customary in those early days.

But there were many things about his own career which he could recall with clarity. He looked back seventy years and said, "My most exciting moment in baseball was when I played in the championship in Cuba in 1930. I was an outfielder."[36]

Amaro and the man he admired most, Martín Dihigo, would represent the first black Cubans to eventually settle in Mexico and help build their fledgling leagues. He twice found a measure of fortune in Mexico. Not only did he fashion a solid career, but he also met the love of his life.

Prior to a game in Mexico in 1931 he was introduced to a member of the Vera Cruz Women's Professional Baseball Club named Josefina Mora. They would eventually marry and spend the next seven decades together.

As he gained a reputation as a hard-hitting hard-throwing left fielder, the 6'3", 225-pound Amaro was courted by promoters in the United States. In 1932 he was invited to play on a barnstorming team in America, but like so many players who were not accustomed to racism, he refused to return the following year.

Along the way he earned the nickname *El Canguro,* the Kangaroo, for the impressive vertical leap he had developed. For the next 35 years he would play and manage for teams in Mexico in the summer and in Cuba during the winter.

His son, Rubén Amaro Sr., remembered, "Dad played in Mexico until 1957, where he was a player/manager. Off and on he was the manager there for another ten years, until 1967."

Nearing the age of 50, Santos Amaro took his last professional at-bat. His son said, "[In 1957] he was the manager of the Vera Cruz Eagles and he was more of a pinch hitter than an everyday player. His last time at bat [as a pinch hitter] he hit a home run."[37]

Ultiminio Ramos was raised on a steady diet of rice, beans and baseball. Since he was from Matanzas Province his dreams were fueled by the successes of Martín Dihigo and others, who proved that black men could be national heroes. Somewhere along the way his athletic pursuits moved from the diamond to the ring because, as he likes to say, "boxing is a faster sport."[38]

After Castro took power, Ramos, now a struggling fighter, moved to Mexico, where he met another expatriate. He was introduced to Santos Amaro, one of those black heroes of Matanzas that he had heard so much about in his youth.

"Amaro was one of the great men from Matanzas who shined above all the others," Ramos said with enthusiasm. "He brought a great glory to us because he was such a great baseball player."[39]

Amaro encouraged the young pugilist and followed his career closely. On March 31, 1963, "Sugar" Ramos won the World Featherweight championship in Los Angeles. Three years later, when he captured the world lightweight title, Santo Amaro cheered as loudly as anyone.

Santos was respected as much for his attitude as he was for his playing abilities.

"He was a very kind and gentle man. He never hurt anyone," explained Cuban legend Minnie Miñoso, who played for Amaro early in his career.[40] Ramos echoed those sentiments when he declared, "He attracted people and liked to engage them. He was a guy who liked to have a good time."

Despite all the years that he sacrificed for the game, it would be the influence and guidance he passed down to his son and grandson which kept Amaro's legacy alive. In the mid-1950s his teenage son, Rubén Amaro (Sr.), was harboring dreams of becoming a professional baseball player, but now he had a formidable task. He would have to convince his father to allow him to leave college and accept an offer to play ball in the United States.

Santos, who was forced to abandon school in the fifth grade, had stressed education above anything else. But his son was convincing and Santos reluctantly agreed.

Rubén's career nearly came to a premature end, however, after he arrived in the United States and encountered the scourge of racism. "After the first year in the Texas League I told my dad, 'Look, when I came to you to let me play professional baseball I said that I would emulate Bobby Avila, who came from our hometown of Vera Cruz. But now I want to go back to school and work at the bank. I do not want to play in the states because its really too tough to live isolated. I cannot go to theatres, to public places, and use the same facilities as the other teammates.'"

Rubén was surprised at the answer he received. "My father was smart. My father told me, 'Fine, you can come back and forget about baseball.'" This was not the answer that he expected from a man who had spent his entire life in the game and he soon found that the lesson was not over.

"But," Santos continued, "I thought that your goal was not to play in the Texas League. I thought your goal was to eventually play in the big leagues." Rubén confessed, "That statement made me react and decide to stay."[41]

In fact Rubén stayed a total of 11 years as a player in the major leagues (1958–1969), mastering all infield and outfield positions. On June 8, 1991, his son, Rubén Jr., became the third generation of Amaro professional ballplayers when he made his debut in a California Angels uniform. The youngest Amaro sustained a major league career for eight years as a versatile infielder/outfielder.

As they approached their ninth decade of life, Santos and Josephina moved into the La Paz Retirement Home in Vera Cruz—reveling in the knowledge that both their son and grandson had achieved something that they would never have dreamed of.

After retiring as an active player in 1998 Rubén Jr. became the assistant to the general manager of the Philadelphia Phillies. Rubén Sr. is currently managing in their minor league organization, having amassed over 46 years in professional baseball.

In June of 2001 the three Amaro men were about to be honored at Veteran's Stadium in Philadelphia and presented with the Al Dia Latino Legends Award when Santos died, just two weeks short of the celebration.

Roberto Ortiz

*Johnson removed his jacket and tie
and began to warm up alongside Ortiz.*

The story goes like this. In 1938 the Senators' masterful scout, Joe Cambria, found a big, muscular cane cutter by the name of Roberto González Ortiz playing for a sugar mill team called Central Senado, in the backwaters of Cuba.

He salivated at the vision of Ortiz pitching in the major leagues, despite the fact that he seemed to be a natural power hitter. The Senators nicknamed their new discovery the "*Giant from Camaguey*" and debuted him during the spring training camp of 1939.

Teammate Mickey Vernon was shocked when he first saw the 6'4", 200-pound specimen. Vernon thought to himself, "He was like Paul Bunyan, like he just came out of the woods."[42] The Senators' pitcher Walter Masterson remarked, "He was one of the most perfectly developed men you'd ever look at in your life."[43]

One day soon after spring training commenced, the Senators' coaching staff stood in awe as Ortiz found an unoccupied corner of the field and started throwing one fastball after another. Soon, however, they noticed a flaw. Masterson recalled, "He could throw the ball with astounding speed but he had an unfortunate habit. He would throw the ball straight. And of course if you throw it straight, [major leaguers] will hit it. If you shoot it out of a cannon they will hit it."

Despite the apparent concerns, everyone wanted to see the new kid from Cuba. It wasn't long before the radio broadcaster for the Senators caught sight of this exhibition. Walter Johnson was almost 53 years old, and although he had resigned himself to sitting behind a microphone, he could not resist staring at the dark-complected Cuban.

Without question, Walter Johnson was one of the greatest pitchers in the history of baseball, dominating the American League with his whip-like delivery for over 20 years. Now he felt compelled to match himself up against the young stallion. Summoning a catcher from a practice field, Johnson removed his jacket and tie and began to warm up alongside Ortiz.

Johnson started gaining speed on his pitches until he was timing his windup and release with Ortiz. They were soon locked in a surrealistic duel of speed — the ancient hero versus the cocky rookie. Now Johnson's pitches were popping into the catcher's mitt long before those of his junior. Finally, realizing that he had been beaten, Ortiz stood back and just watched the old master continue with the lesson.

As with any legend there are bits of fantasy and hyperbole mixed with the truth. Masterson claims that Johnson would never have tried to humiliate Ortiz. "Johnson was a complete gentleman," said Masterson, "and he would never put a bad mark onto a young man who was trying to get along with the team."[44]

But Masterson did admit that it wasn't unusual to see Johnson take his turn with the ball. "We had some hard throwers on the ball club and someone asked [Johnson] to start turning the ball loose. They got him to fool around for a week or two and throw batting practice." Masterson added, "After a couple of weeks and he could throw harder than anybody we had on the ball club."

Johnson's biographer, Henry W. Thomas, concludes that the famous contest is exaggerated, but noted in his book *Walter Johnson: Baseball's Big Train* that Ortiz idolized him and Johnson was mystified that Ortiz was not a member of the pitching staff. Truth or not, it is a great story.

After more critical analysis the Washington brain trust thought that Ortiz would be more valuable elsewhere on the field. As one writer put it, "Cagey Joe [Cambria] brought [Ortiz] with a half-dozen others to Washington Senators' camp ... disguised as a pitcher. He had swift and lots of it but had difficulty keeping the ball within bounds of the batting area. Presently since the Old Fox, Clark Griffith, liked his swing, Roberto, a big handsome fellow, was chased to the outfield and told to start swinging...."[45]

Bob Considine noted that Ortiz was hustled down to the Senators' minor league club in Charlotte, "where he is undergoing the rigors of forgetting how to pitch and learning how to be an outfielder."[46]

During the 1940 season Ortiz was maintaining a .300 batting average when his skull was fractured by a thrown ball as he was racing towards second base in the midst of a double play. Fortunately he recovered, and in the fall of 1941 he was summoned from Charlotte and played his first major league game on September 6.

At the ripe old age of 26, Ortiz had an impressive rookie year with Washington by hitting .329 and driving in 17 runs in 22 games. This was, however, his most effective year, because in the following five major league seasons the "Giant from Camaguey" hovered between .167 and .279.

But like his friend Roberto Estallela, Ortiz could occasionally shock his contemporaries with his power. Masterson recalled one game in particular. "I remember he came up to bat in Philadelphia in Shibe Park," said Masterson. "He didn't realize that, when he picked up a bat off the rack in front of the dugout, he got Cecil Travis' batting practice bat, which was about 38 oz. and was about 36" long. It was a bludgeon. He hit a line drive that went out of the ballpark underneath the stands and hit a brick wall and bounced all the way back into the infield. I never saw a prodigious blast like that in my life. It was a rocket."[47]

Although Ortiz was considered a friendly competitor, he wasn't likely to shy away from a challenge. Former St. Louis Browns catcher Myron Hayworth likes to retell the story about a scuffle that occurred during a winter league game in Cuba. As Hayworth recalled, "Homer Gibson was pitching for us, and Homer has a knuckleball. Ortiz would lunge in on the plate. Of course, the ball hit him in the shoulder and [Ortiz] charged the mound. Well, when he charged the mound I went in right behind him and of course I wouldn't let him hit Homer."

Hayworth was a big man himself, but still gave away nearly four inches to Ortiz. So he decided he would bring some protection along: "I had the mask in my hand and you know catchers have the advantage. You hold on to that mask don't throw it away, 'cause that's the best weapon you can have. But we got it broken up and he was friendly later."[48]

But his self-confident attitude was sometimes mistaken for cockiness, which then led to other incidents. While Ortiz was playing in Mexico in 1946 he found himself embroiled in a conflict with an equally intimidating individual, Sal Maglie. A washout in the majors, Maglie had followed Dolf Luque to the Mexican League in an effort to rehabilitate his pitching career. Within one year Luque had molded his protégé into a hardnosed pitcher who was not reluctant to hurt a batter with an inside pitch.

Maglie recalled his first experience with Ortiz for *Sports Illustrated*. "[Ortiz] hit a homer off me. I was always embarrassed when that happened, but Ortiz annoyed me because he was laughing as he ran around the bases." Maglie shouted at the Cuban and vowed that he would never let him humiliate him again in public. "I kept my promise," said Maglie.

"Every time I pitched against him I flattened him."

Ortiz wasn't about to be humiliated either, because the verbal conflict continued, with Maglie responding, "If he said anything he went down again."[49] The two never came to physical blows, but the rivalry was legendary in Cuba.

In 1944 Roberto's younger brother, Olivrio "Baby" Ortiz, was given a brief audition with the Senators. The 6', 200-pound pitcher was sent packing after two starts, two losses and an ERA of 6.23. From 1945 through 1948 Roberto Ortiz bounced back and forth among the minor leagues, the Cuban League and the Mexican League. He did stay south of the border long enough to win the Mexican League home-run crown in 1945, 1946, 1947 and 1948. Because of his prodigious numbers, he was inducted into the Mexican Hall of Fame after his retirement.[50]

In 1949 Ortiz was brought back to Washington and played in 40 games, hitting .279. Remarkably, he and pitcher Julio Gonzáles were the only Latin-born players on the team. It seemed as if the great Latin experiment had been abandoned altogether. After spring training had finished, the *New York Times* columnist Arthur Daley correctly speculated, "Browns, White Sox and Senators are going through the motions of pretending to be major league ball clubs...."[51]

At the conclusion of the 1949 season Ortiz and Gonzáles were mere accessories and the Senators finished in last place with a record of 50–104. After 39 games of the 1950 season Washington traded Ortiz to Connie Mack's Philadelphia A's. This would prove to be the last year that either man was employed in the major leagues. Ortiz played in six games, striking out three times and managing only one hit.

In the 1950s he returned to the United States, playing for the Havana Sugar Kings in the International League for a short period of time. Despite an athletic career spanning three decades Roberto Ortiz died at the young age of 56 in Miami.

7

The 1940s

The sputtering evolution of Latin players in the United States changed gears and reached a momentous surge in 1942. The manpower drain on professional baseball during World War II presented an opportunity both for both Latin players and for cash-strapped owners of major league clubs.

During the decade of the forties 27 Latin-born ballplayers made their debuts in the major leagues. Amazingly, this number exceeds the total number of Latin rookies for the previous four decades combined. Out of the total of 27 new recruits, 13 were products of the Washington Senators' farm system.

The big-league owners, desperate for bodies, not only scoured the islands for good white players, they even tried to resurrect the careers of retired veterans. Washington's owner Clark Griffith unsuccessfully tried to persuade 42-year-old Ossie Bluege to come out of retirement and play third base.[1] Clyde Sukeforth was 43 years old and nearly blind in his right eye when he caught 18 games for Brooklyn in 1945. "I could tell night from day," he said, "but that's all."[2]

Johnny Cooney, a pitcher and outfielder whose career began in 1921, played for the Braves, Dodgers and Giants during the war years. Paul Schreiber thought his career was over when he retired in 1923, but when the Yankees asked him to pitch out of the bullpen in 1945 he could not refuse.

The search was not limited to old warhorses, either. In 1944 a 15-year-old left-hander from Hamilton, Ohio, named Joe Nuxhall was brought up to start a game for the Cincinnati Reds. He recalled, "Two weeks prior to my first big-league game I was pitching against 13-and 14-year-old kids in junior high school and all of a sudden you look up and you're pitching against the to-be world champion St. Louis Cardinals and Stan Musial. I really realized where I was standing, and it wasn't in the middle of the Wilson Junior High baseball field. It was at Crosley Field."[3]

On September 6, 1943, Carl Scheib took the mound for the Philadelphia A's at the age of 16 years. In 1945 Pete Gray played outfield for the Browns with only one arm, and Bert Shepherd was brought up to the Senators missing his right leg.

Between 1943 and 1945 conscription, enlistment and defense-related jobs took 86 Afro-American players out of the Negro Leagues.[4] Roughly 30 Latin-born players filled those ranks.[5]

The manpower shortage for American industry was so severe that the owner of the Mexican League, Jorge Pasquel, made an unusual offer. According to historian Peter Bjarkman, Pascuel had wanted to sign several Negro League stars in 1943, so

144

he offered the U.S. State Department 80,000 Mexican laborers if they would allow draft deferments for the players he coveted.

But when the war ended the welcome mat was quickly removed. Few people realize that, by 1948, there was only one Latin playing regularly in the major leagues. The lone survivor was Mike Guerra, a 35-year-old Cuban-born catcher with the Philadelphia Athletics.

While the major leagues were scaling back on the Latin invitees, the struggling Negro Leagues were actively scouting the Caribbean for them. After Jackie Robinson's heroic advancement in 1947, many of the talented Afro-Americans were signed to the white minor leagues and eventually the majors. With the Negro Leagues severely depleted and teetering on the verge of economic collapse, there was a wealth of dark-skinned Latino players to fill the void.

From 1940 through 1949 more than 60 Latin ballplayers played in the Negro Leagues.[6] In 1946 a Caribbean-based team was admitted to an accredited league in the United States. The Havana Cubans, owned by Clark Griffith and Roberto Maduro, joined five teams from Florida to create the Florida International League, then recognized as a Class C league. The team had a 35,000 seat stadium in Havana, and led the league in attendance, while winning four championships.

In 1947 the New York Cubans won the Negro National League pennant and beat the Negro American League champs, the Cleveland Buckeyes, four games to one in the World Series. The Cubans included players from the Dominican Republic, Panama, Puerto Rico and Cuba.

Hiram Bithorn

Bithorn held the Reds to one run through seven innings.

The Brooklyn Eagles came to Puerto Rico just days ahead of the Cincinnati Reds. The Negro League team was faltering financially, but they were planning on a successful series of exhibition games on the island to prepare them for the 1936 season. The series would begin in late February with several contests against local Puerto Rican teams, culminating in the big box-office draw—a set of games pitting the Eagles against the Reds. An 11-year-old fan named Eduardo Valero was so impressed by the visiting ballplayers that he still remembers the Eagles lineup, almost seventy years later.

"Listen to this," he said recently. "The Eagles had Buck Leonard, first base; Ray Dandridge, third base; Frank Duncan, catcher. Leon Day was the pitcher. They had a hell of a team. These were great players."[7]

During their series against a Puerto Rican team, the Eagle's players were so impressed by a muscular right-hander named Hiram Gabriel Bithorn that they asked him to join their team. They needed him for one of the upcoming games against the Reds. On March 1, 1936, the 20-year-old Bithorn took the mound against a major league club which was powered by future hall of famer Kiki Cuyler. Valero said, "They didn't have enough pitchers so they had to pick a Puerto Rican to complete the team."

Bithorn held the Reds to one run through seven innings, but was pulled for a relief pitcher in the eighth when three Cincinnati runs scored. The Eagles salvaged the game in the bottom of the ninth, and Bithorn was offered a minor league contract to play in the United States.

The youthful fan, Eduardo Valero, eventually became an award-winning journalist and chronicled the Bithorn saga through three countries. Valero claims that the turning point in Bithorn's young career was his relationship with the Eagle's catcher Frank Duncan, who "polished Bithorn's pitching" during his short stay in Puerto Rico.

In 1937, at the age of 21, Bithorn began his professional career by pitching for the Norfolk Tars in the Piedmont League. Although he pitched well enough to earn a mid-season promotion to Binghamton in the Eastern League, there was one 24-hour period with Norfolk that stands out in the annals of minor league trivia.

Bithorn had won the first game of a doubleheader on a Thursday evening and decided to watch the second game from the stands, still in his uniform. As the game dragged into extra innings the Norfolk manager, Johnny Neun, had depleted his entire pitching corps and had to summon Bithorn from the grandstand. At two A.M. on Friday morning, Norfolk batters finally ended the game by driving in two runs to win the game in the fifteenth inning. Bithorn had won back-to-back games on two different days without removing his uniform.

After signing a contract with the Yankees in 1938 he was moved from Binghamton to the Newark Bears to Oakland and then to Hollywood in the Pacific Coast League.[8]

Success on the sporting field was nothing new for the 6'1", 200-pound athlete. Before becoming a celebrity pitcher, Bithorn gained national prominence when he represented Puerto Rico in the 1935 Central American Games in El Salvador, participating in volleyball and basketball.

The first few years in the United States were relatively calm for the olive-skinned native of Old San Juan. In 1939 he became the Oakland Oaks' rookie workhorse, earning a record of 13–14 with an ERA of 3.64 in 35 games. The Oaks had enjoyed a working agreement with the powerhouse New York Yankees, but their relationship collapsed by the end of that season. Wanting to keep a few premiere players in their farm system, the Yankees organized a trade that sent Bithorn and three others to the Hollywood Stars, another team with which they had an informal agreement.

Bithorn endured a lackluster 10–17 record with the Stars in 1940 because of a growth on his pitching elbow and an ailing back. In 1941 he began the season by piecing together a ten-game winning streak, however, allowing an average of only five hits and one run per game.[9] His comeback was hailed by local sportswriters and noticed by major league scouts. In August one writer declared that Bithorn "owns the fastest ball on the Pacific slope."[10] When the season ended he had amassed a record of 17–15 and an ERA of 3.59.

Back in Puerto Rico he was named that nation's most popular athlete by a panel of 53 sportswriters. It was apparent that Bithorn was destined to be the first Puerto Rican to make it into the major leagues.

Believing in his potential, and desperate for help on their beleaguered pitching staff, the Cubs drafted Bithorn after the Pacific Coast League season had ended. In 1941 the Cubs had finished in sixth place. Mired in mediocrity they had accumulated the fifth-worst record in strikeouts and the fourth-worst ERA in the league. With only nine saves recorded all season the Cubs needed help both in their rotation and in the bullpen.

As soon as the 1942 season began Bithorn provided the firewall that the Cubs needed. He started 16 games and came out of the bullpen 22 times, finishing his rookie season with nine wins, two saves and an ERA of 3.68.

Success on the field was tempered by cheap gossip behind the scenes, however. Hall of Fame journalist Fred Lieb noted that during Bithorn's rookie year there was a rumor, "among baseball writers and in clubhouses," that he was a mulatto.[11] This was cause for alarm. The Cubs sought to quell the controversy by noting in the team biography that Bithorn was of Danish and Spanish parentage.[12]

Fred Lieb, in his 1977 autobiography, disclosed an incident that would re-ignite the controversy about Bithorn's heritage. After the 1946 major league season Lieb attended a dance performance at a theatre in St. Louis and met a black dancer during the intermission. After learning that Lieb was a famous baseball writer the young lady told him that she was Bithorn's first cousin, explaining that her mother and Bithorn's mother were sisters. When Jackie Robinson debuted with the Dodgers during the following season Lieb considered the possibility that Bithorn might have been "entitled to be called the first black player to appear in a big league uniform."[13]

After pitching in Puerto Rico during the off-season, and working over the Christmas holiday in the sporting goods department at Macy's in Manhattan, Bithorn set his sights on returning to Chicago for the 1943 season. Proving his value in spring training, he earned a starting slot in the rotation and launched the most productive season of his career.

In 30 starts he won 18 games and finished the campaign with an ERA of 2.60. This was a remarkable achievement for a sophomore, because he led his team in practically every pitching category and had recorded more shutouts (seven) than any hurler in either league. He also had four one-run games and three two-run games.

His sixth victory was on June 20, when he defeated the reigning world champion St. Louis Cardinals—for the third time that season. The likes of Stan Musial (.357), Whitey Kurowski (.287) and Harry Walker (.294) didn't seem to faze him. On June 25 he returned for a fourth time, blanking the Cardinals on seven hits. In four games he allowed the defending champions (they would win the pennant again that season,) only two runs in 32 innings.

Chicago's legendary first baseman Phil Cavarretta acknowledged, "If he had been on a better ball club he would have won 17 to 20 ball games, because he had exceptionally good stuff and was a hard worker and very dedicated. He was one of my favorite guys."[14]

Like many of his dark-skinned contemporaries, Bithorn was also the subject of ridicule and harassment from opposing players. Cavarretta remembers that Bithorn was "very quiet. If you talked to him he'd be fine but in the clubhouse he was very quiet." But that changed on July 16 during a game against the Brooklyn Dodgers.

Cavarretta was at first base and could hear the venomous commentary coming out of the Dodgers' dugout just a few yards behind him. "Leo Durocher was managing Brooklyn and Leo was always yakking and yakking and getting on guys and calling them dirty names," said Cavarretta. "And he started to get on Bithorn because he was pitching really well."

After the fifth inning Bithorn stormed off the mound in frustration. In the dugout he kept repeating, "I'm going to get him. I'm going to get him." Cavarretta stepped in to calm him down. "Forget about it," he said.

Getting the Puerto Rican hurler frustrated and angry was exactly what Durocher wanted. In the sixth inning the diatribe reached a new level as Bithorn called timeout. Thinking that he was going to signal for the catcher and discuss the next sequence of pitches, Cavarretta moved out of his crouch position and watched. There was no gesture. Just Bithorn staring at the batter. Suddenly he turned towards the Dodgers' bench and fired the ball directly at Durocher, who dove to his knees.

Everyone thought it was funny except Durocher and the commissioner of baseball, Ford Frick, who issued a well-publicized warning and a $25 fine.[15]

Bithorn's reaction was indeed out of character, because everyone had seen him as a very serious student of the game. Cavarretta said, "In the clubhouse meetings we would go over the opposing hitters. [Bithorn] was always observing what the manager had to say to the pitcher who had to pitch that day, so when he got his chance to pitch he was ready."

As he became more comfortable with his teammates Bithorn also started to develop a reputation as a prankster. As Columnist Ed Burns observed early in the 1943 season, "He has been full of fun and wisecracks all spring even before he won 60 per cent of the team's first five victories."[16] Burns described one incident in which Bithorn approached Wrigley Field's "hardboiled" groundskeeper, Harry Hazlewood, just before a game he was scheduled to pitch. "Is there any special treatment or molding you want me to do on the mound?" Hazlewood asked a serious tone.

Looking equally serious, Bithorn replied, "There certainly is. Just move the rubber about two feet closer to the plate."

It seemed that just as he was about to scale heights that hadn't been reached by a Latin pitcher since Dolf Luque, his career made a dramatic change of course. After the attack on Pearl Harbor in December of 1941 Bithorn applied for and received a draft deferment, claiming that he was the principal support for his mother and invalid father. But, on October 6, 1943, he was reclassified by the War Department to 1-A status and was eventually inducted into the U.S. Navy in Puerto Rico on December 1.[17]

For most of 1944 Bithorn served at the Naval Air Station at San Juan while trying to maintain his skills on the military post's baseball team. The games would attract 8,000 fans with proceeds directed towards the Red Cross and war-relief efforts. On the military base he had a 7–1 record in 60 innings of pitching and recorded a .375 batting average.[18]

In September of 1945 Bithorn was discharged and immediately boarded a train to report for duty with the Cubs. Although he did not play the final months of the '45 season, his name did appear in the Cubs' World Series program when they faced the Tigers.

When he returned to spring training in 1946 he was faced with the challenge of cracking a rotation with five pitchers who had recorded double-digit victories the previous year. It also appeared as if the war had taken away more than the brief two years of his career. After faltering as a starter he spent most of the season in the bullpen, completing a 6–5 record and an ERA of 3.84.

He hadn't completely lost the magic, however; especially when it came to humiliating would-be base stealers. As Cavarretta explained, "He was an exceptionally big man and the majority of runners thought that his move [to first base] would be slow. But it was just the opposite. He was just like a cat. He had a very good pick-off move."[19]

The following season would be Bithorn's last in major league baseball. He had been traded to the White Sox in 1947, and because of nagging arm problems he appeared in only two games, pitching one inning each game.

Despite the premature end to his budding major league career, the baseball fans of Puerto Rico never forgot Bithorn's meteoric rise to the majors and the phenomenal season of 1942. When his playing career in the United States had ended he continued to live in Chicago, residing with his wife, Virginia, at 4613 Beacon Street. After a futile attempt to resurrect his pitching career in Mexico he became a minor league umpire in the Class C Pioneer League on the Pacific Coast.

The sleepy little town of El Mante straddles one of the major north-south roads running through Mexico, called Federal Highway 85. It was just another place that Hiram Bithorn had to pass through on his way to visit his 68 year-old mother in Mexico City for a New Year's celebration, 1951. It would be another 600 miles before his journey would end, so perhaps he stopped in that strange village to rest for the evening.

But within an hour Hiram Bithorn, the hero of Puerto Rico, was lying beside his car with a single 45-caliber bullet lodged in his stomach. Standing over his body was police Corporal Ambrosio Castillo Cano. This is all we know as the truth.

According to Cano, Bithorn had attempted to secure a hotel room for the evening but did not have any money to pay for the accommodations. When Bithorn suggested that he would sell his car to raise the money, Cano intervened.

The corporal asked for the registration papers, but when Bithorn could not produce them Cano decided to detain him for questioning. Ordering Bithorn to drive his car to the local police station, Cano climbed into the passenger seat for the short ride. Suddenly Bithorn became violent and Cano was struck in the face. While Bithorn was attempting to push the car door open, Cano reached for his revolver and fired.

An ambulance rushed him to a hospital in Victoria, 84 miles to the north, but within an hour of his arrival at Hospital Civil the 35-year-old Bithorn was dead. The coroner fixed the time of death at 11:30 P.M. December 30, 1951. Cause — Internal hemorrhage.

When Mexican officials began to ask questions officer Cano could not provide legitimate answers, and his account of the incident did not make sense. Why would Bithorn attempt to sell his car when he had ten more hours of driving ahead of him? Why did Cano abandon his police car to ride with his prisoner?

Suddenly his testimony took a strange turn: Cano contended that "Mr. Bithorn had said in his dying breath that he was a member of the Communist party," and that he was "on an important mission."

Bithorn's mother, Maria, and brother, Fernando, charged the Mexican government with covering up the details and asked the F.B.I. to intervene.[20] On January 2 Cano was arrested, and nine days later he was indicted on charges of homicide.

Even today, over fifty years after the incident occurred, people in Puerto Rico still discuss it. His death remains a national controversy, fattened by conjecture and multiple conspiracy theories. Eduardo Valero sadly noted, "I don't think anyone knows why he was killed. It is still a mystery." His remains (first buried in Victoria, Mexico, and then reclaimed by his family) were brought to Puerto Rico and placed in Sixto Escobar Stadium for public viewing.

The respect and admiration that his countrymen carried for him solidified in 1962 when the city of San Juan constructed a new baseball park, naming it after their fallen hero. Hiram Bithorn Stadium gained national recognition in the United States in 2001 when the Texas Rangers and the Toronto Blue Jays played their season opener there. Its reputation was further enhanced when the Montreal Expos played many of their home games at the stadium in 2003 and 2004.

Felix Delgado

"No, Papa, they are Puerto Rican Indians
and they are here to play baseball."

Felix Delgado was in a strange little town in Alabama and he was hungry.

He wanted to believe that there was at least one restaurant in this shabby stain on the map that would serve a man of color who had a few bucks to spend. He and his teammates on the New York Cubans had a game scheduled at 4:30 against a local team of factory workers and now he had several hours and a growling stomach to fill.

As he and outfielder Francisco Coimbre began wandering Main Street they noticed a trailer sitting on the corner. The roughly scribbled cardboard sign indicated it was a diner, but the dilapidated exterior seemed as inviting as a case of the stomach flu. But hunger was the more urgent demon, and they decided to limit their intake to cake and milk. Their animated debate continued as they entered the ramshackle, little structure.

A boy of about 17 stood behind the counter, watching them with keen interest, while the shadowy figure of an older man sat motionless at the far end.

"Where are you from?" the young man asked.

"Puerto Rico," they answered hesitantly.

He smiled and they relaxed. "Oh, you're from Puerto Rico! I'm taking Spanish in high school. Will you order in Spanish?"

"*Me gustaría pastel de piña, café y un vaso de leche, por favor,*" declared Delgado. They shared a laugh and helped the young man with his diction.

Suddenly, the enigmatic figure at the corner of the trailer stood up and shouted, "We don't want any Negroes in this restaurant or I'll lose my business! No one will ever eat in here again if they catch me."

"No, papa! They are Puerto Rican Indians and they are here to play baseball. They are not real Negroes like we have here."

The old man calmed down and grudgingly returned to his seat to sulk while the boy went into the kitchen to prepare the food.

Again the father rose from his seat, however, shouting through the serving window, "Listen to me, those guys are too dark!"

Outside, two Afro-Americans from the team were passing by and saw the Latinos in the restaurant. They entered, thinking that the forbidding-looking diner would welcome black patrons. As the boy emerged from the kitchen carrying a tray laden with cups, glasses and plates, the father bolted from his seat, screaming obscenities. He grabbed the tray and violently shoved its contents into a trash can.

"We don't serve Negroes! Get out of here or I will call the police and you will be sent to the chain gang breaking rocks for six months!"

Felix Delgado at the age of 20, playing for the San Juan club. (Source: Wayne Stivers collection.)

It now became a showdown between the old man and Delgado's black American teammates. Delgado's reaction was immediate: "I left the place in a hurry, because the American Negroes were angry and it looked like there was going to be a fight. [All this time] the owner kept yelling."[21]

That 1941 incident forced Delgado to dramatically change the course of his career, because it was the first time he had ever experienced the raw racism that he had been warned about.

When he was barnstorming on a team five years earlier, in 1936, he had been geographically insulated.

"When I was in the northern part of the U.S. that sort of thing did not happen," he said.

And this day he promised himself that it would not happen again. He decided never to return as a ballplayer.

"The next year (Alex) Pompez sent me tickets to New York," he recalled. "But I sent them back saying 'Sorry, but here in Puerto Rico I'm living like a king and nobody is bothering me.'"

Pompez persisted but Delgado was not swayed: "Pompez called me about three or four times to go back but I said no."

Felix Rafael Delgado was born March 31, 1915, near San Juan, and played his first professional game during the Puerto Rican winter league season of 1935–1936. That season he spent the summer barnstorming in the United States for the Havana-based Cuban Stars. In 1941 he returned, playing the outfield and first base for Pompez's New York Cubans.

Knowing the limitations of segregated baseball Delgado was impressed that a black man like Pompez could command the rental of Ebbets Field, Yankee Stadium and the Polo Grounds for Negro League contests. However, he sadly reflected, "Mr. Pompez paid to use the stadiums even though we could not use the facilities in the clubhouse. We would have to run to the bus outside (where) we had empty gas cans. We would go to the bathroom there."[22]

Delgado was a superb defenseman, playing first and second base, plus any outfield position. Returning to Puerto Rico in 1942 he went to work full-time for the local bus line and played and coached for another 29 years in the winter league on weekends.

In 1951 he was assigned to manage Licey in the Dominican Republic's first summer league season. The team finished in first place and won the championship.

In 1970 he was hired as a bird dog for a succession of major league teams, ending his career with the Milwaukee Brewers as a part-time scout. During his scouting career he signed 31 boys who made it to the professional leagues.

Delgado was never angry or disillusioned about his experiences in the United States. In fact he was a frequent visitor to New York, where he had relatives.

When he died in June of 2001 he had just celebrated his sixty-fifth year in professional baseball.

The Unsung Heroes of the Forties
"He would tell you, 'I'm the greatest,' just like [Mohammed] Ali."

There were dozens of Latinos who found work in the U.S. major leagues and Negro Leagues between 1940 and 1945. Major league clubs debuted 22 Cubans, two Puerto Ricans, one Venezuelan and two Mexicans. Most of their names have been forgotten, but their achievements cannot be dismissed.

One of the greatest hitters to ever come out of Puerto Rico was outfielder Francisco Coímbre, who made his American debut in 1940 with the New York Cubans. Hall of fame pitcher Satchel Paige once called Coímbre the greatest hitter he had ever faced. Roberto Clemente always maintained that Coímbre was a better hitter than he (Clemente) was.

He played professionally from 1926 through 1951 in seven countries, and then scouted for the Pittsburgh Pirates for 25 years. In his freshman and sophomore seasons with the Negro League he batted .330 and .353 respectively.[23] He stayed in the United States for only five years, departing, like so many Latin players, after World War II had ended.

Cuban outfielder Pedro Formental was another well-known star in his native country when he was recruited by the Memphis Red Sox in 1947. Formental prospered in the Negro and Mexican Leagues before being picked up by the Havana Sugar Kings in the International League for a two-year stint.

Julio Bécquer played with Formental before starting his own major league career in the mid-fifties. He asserted:

> I saw a guy who would compare to [Cristóbal] Torriente and that was Pedro Formental. Oh, man. This guy was incredible. "Pedro 300" we called him.
> He knew it and he would tell you, "I'm the greatest," just like [Mohammed] Ali. He would tell you, "Maybe I'll get three [hits] today," and he'd do it.
> I played with Formental and he was a character. He was 5'11" but well built just like a rock. He would say, "I don't feel well today. Maybe I'll only get two hits. Maybe I'll take just one out [home run]."
> Guys like him just live for baseball.[24]

Formental was nearly forty years old when he joined the Havana Sugar Kings in 1954. Although several Latin players graduated from the International League to the majors in the 1950s Formental was too old to be given a second look. Former Sugar Kings' executive Jose Montiel recalled that Formental took advantage of his first opportunity in the integrated minor leagues. He explained, "He took a twelve-hour flight from Cuba to Richmond, Virginia, to join the Sugar Kings for a double header that afternoon. And he went 5 for 7 at the plate."[25]

More and more players were coming from locations other than Cuba. Left-handed pitcher Vibert Clarke may have been the first Panamanian to play in the Negro Leagues when he signed with the Cleveland Buckeyes in 1946. It was not until 1955 that Humberto Robinson would be the first Panamanian to make it into the major leagues.

Luís Olmo was the first Puerto Rican on the Dodgers ball club in 1943 and outfielder Jesus Ramos was the first Venezuelan on the Reds team in 1944. In 1942 Pitcher Jesse Flores was only the third Mexican to make the bigtime, and the first debuted by the Cubs.

The Carrasquels in America

The Vice President of the United States, Henry A. Wallace, made a gesture that no one expected.

First came Alejandro "Alex" Carrasquel of Caracas, Venezuela. The dark-skinned, right-handed hurler slipped under the color line and made his debut with the Washington Senators in 1939. Clark Griffith and his charismatic scout, Joe Cambria, had done it again.

Bob Considine introduced him in print by exclaiming, "And a more forbidding-looking character than Carrasquel never climbed over the rail of a Spanish galleon with a dagger in his teeth. His fierce, saddle-colored face makes him look forty, but through interpreters he has said that he is 27, 28 and 29."[26]

When the aging Red Sox hurler Lefty Grove saw Carrasquel for the first time he remarked, "If that guy's a rookie, I'm Paderoosky. I betcha a hat I pitched against him in an exhibition game in Cuba in 1924."[27] (According to official records Alejandro Alexander Aparicio Elroy Carrasquel was born on July 24, 1912, in Caracas.)

Back home, Carrasquel had already been hailed for his performance in the Venezuelan League, but he was now a national hero for being the first native to make it to the American big leagues. In seven seasons with the Senators Alex was used primarily out of the bullpen, but managed to secure an admirable 50–39 record with an career ERA of 3.73. Despite having a good fastball, he averaged more walks than strikeouts (347 vs 252) and Griffith never trusted him to start more than 64 games in his 255 appearances.

Alex was playing in Havana when he was discovered by Washington Senators' scout Joe Cambria during the 1938–1939 winter league season. Like his contemporaries, he endured the routine indignities that befell dark-hued men who joined a major league club. And consistent with the times, he was also labeled "moody and temperamental" when he protested.

There were plenty of highlights during his short tenure, however. In his first big-league game he was matched against the New York Yankees, and after loading the bases with two outs he faced a tall, powerful hitter he had never heard of before — Joe DiMaggio. Working the corners, he got the Yankee Clipper to hit a harmless pop-up to end the rally.

During his rookie year of 1939 he also stopped the Tigers (four hits), the St. Louis Browns (five hits) and the Philadelphia A's (four hits) as a starter.[28] In 1943 he went 11–7 with 13 starts and 26 relief appearances.

On Opening Day 1944, the Vice President of the United States, Henry A. Wallace, made a gesture that no one expected. Pointing to a group of players, he singled out the dark-skinned Carrasquel and invited him into his Griffith Stadium box. Wallace had learned a bit of Spanish earlier in life and wanted to express his appreciation. With Alex at his side he addressed the newspaper writers, saying, "For this year, thanks to United States manpower troubles, there are more Latin Americans in the major leagues than ever before."

The writers reported that "the Iowan (Wallace) and the Venezuelan chatted briefly in Spanish and when Wallace threw out the first ball of the season he aimed it at Carrasquel, who caught it."[29]

During his last season with Washington, in 1945, he went 7–5 with an ERA of 2.71, registering two shutouts and five complete games.

Back in Venezuela the family legacy was continuing, with a nephew named Chico who could suck the air out of a stadium with his defensive ballet. Standing anxiously in the wings, the young Carrasquel was mesmerized by the respect Alex commanded when he returned home each fall. But there was more than the public adulation to inspire the nephew.

"When he used to come to Venezuela with his uniform, that's what impressed me a lot," Chico confessed. "I wanted to get a uniform like his. He was like a guide and role model for me and for many people in Venezuela."[30]

By the age of 15 Chico, the second of ten children, had quit school to follow his baseball dreams. He accepted a job working at the General Tire Company and played shortstop for their ball club. With his major league career seemingly ended, Alex returned to Venezuela in 1945 and became a mentor to the young prodigy.

Late in 1945 Alex and Chico had a chance to attend an exhibition game in Caracas between a local club and a black all-star team from the United States. There was particular interest in watching the moves of the Americans' gifted shortstop, Jackie Robinson. At that time no one knew that Robinson had secretly agreed to sign a minor league contract with Branch Rickey and the Brooklyn Dodgers only weeks earlier. (Chico would be destined to follow Robinson's career path several times over the next few years.)

Before Robinson left Venezuela, Rickey made the historic announcement to the public. Now Chico thought he would not have to try to hide his familial heritage.

In 1946 Chico made it to the Venezuelan winter league and in his first professional contest slugged a game-winning home run. Because of his timely hitting and slick fielding he was named Rookie of the Year. At the end of the season he was approached by both the Detroit Tigers and the Brooklyn Dodgers. The Tigers offered him a new baseball mitt and the Dodgers offered him $1,000.[31]

When Chico finally agreed to a minor league contract with the Dodgers, in 1949, he would proudly tell everyone, "The most important influence in baseball for me was my uncle Alejandro, the first Venezuelan to play in the big leagues."

The summer season of 1946 was a time of frustration for Alex, however. On February 27 he signed a hefty contract for $8,000 with Jorge and Bernardo Pasquel, to pitch in their Mexican League. But the "atmosphere of sweetness and light" was soon drenched with acrimony and accusations when his salary was cut in half and he was then transferred to another team.

The feud was covered by Milton Bracker, who wrote, "Pasquel sent word that under the circumstances [Alex] wouldn't be paid his original contract sum." Pasquel claimed that Alex had guaranteed 25 victories, and when he finished the season with a 13–10 record, they withheld $4,000. According to Bracker, emotions reached a boiling point at the end of the season. He wrote, "The night before leaving for Cuba, Carrasquel let fly at the Pasquels, Jorge in particular."[32]

As Uncle Alex found a job pitching in the outlaw Provincial League in Canada in 1949, Chico was heading for Vero Beach, Florida, and the Dodgers' spring training headquarters.

Out of the limelight, but not out of dreams, Alex was searching for a way to make a comeback to the big leagues. Enter Frank "Trader" Lane. In 1948 Charles Comiskey II had recruited the brash young president of the American Association to be his new General Manager for the Chicago White Sox. Lane was aggressive, and within one year had snatched future hall of famer Nellie Fox from the A's.

Turning his attention to the Caribbean and Latin America, the Spanish-speaking GM approached Alex Carrasquel with an offer to pitch out of the bullpen for the 1949 season. Now both Carrasquels were earning a living, playing ball in the United States.

By the time the 1949 season was finished, however, Alex was wearing a yoke of disappointment. At 37 years old, the elder Carrasquel flamed out after three games. In a mere 3.2 innings he allowed eight hits, four walks and six earned runs.

Chico, now 21 years old, found success early. After spring training concluded, the speedy shortstop was transferred to Ft. Worth, where he hit .315 and was second in the Texas League for fielding average.

But the language barrier kept dogging him and the cultural differences were equally frustrating. He couldn't understand why he didn't receive the full amount of his salary ($600 per month). When it was explained that $90 was taken out for Uncle Sam he exclaimed, "Uncle Sam?! I don't have any uncle in the States."

His roommate, Cal Abrams, spoke Spanish and gladly introduced the young Venezuelan to the new culture. Most of it was positive until Abrams had to translate a sign outside a restaurant — "We serve no Mexicans, no Negroes, no dogs." Chico would brush off these incredible injustices with the final line, "Still, I had a good time."[33]

Towards the end of the 1949 season the Dodgers began to shop Chico Carrasquel to other teams. Dave García, a veteran of over 65 years of professional baseball, was a manager in the Giants system when he heard the details of Chico's departure from a first-hand source.

As García explained it, Frank Lane, the general manager of the White Sox, wanted [Chico] Carrasquel and he said to Branch Rickey, "'You told me you would sell me Carrasquel whenever I wanted him.'" And Rickey said, "'Did I say that? I don't remember that.'" After a few minutes Rickey said, "'Well, if I said that I'll sell him to you for $35,000.'"

According to García, the Dodgers' general manager had nothing to lose. "Rickey also had Chico Fernández and Don Zimmer in their farm system and they were all behind Pee Wee Reese."[34](Maury Wills was two years away from being signed.)

Frank Lane jumped on the offer, because he envisioned Chico replacing their aging shortstop, future hall of famer Luke Appling. He snatched Chico for a reported $25,000 in cash and two marginal players.

As the negotiations were underway Chico was heading home to see his family and begin preparations for the winter league season. When he stepped off the plane at the Caracas Airport a sportswriter cornered him in the terminal and told him that he had been traded.

To bolster his ragged bullpen (and give Chico an interpreter), Lane arranged to sign Cuban-born Luis Aloma and then released one of his relievers — Uncle Alex Carrasquel. (Despite the fact that Alex had pitched for the Sox the previous year, Aloma is recognized as the first Latin-born player to begin his career with the club.)

To complement the two new Latin players, Lane acquired Minnie Miñoso from the Indians in 1951 and signed Cuban third baseman Héctor Rodríguez in 1952.

By the end of his rookie season in 1950, Chico had proved that Lane was a shrewd judge of talent by having his career-best season at the plate, hitting .282. In 1951 Chico beat out Phil Rizzuto to become the first Latin to appear in an All-Star game.

From 1952 through 1955 Chico bounced back and forth between a decent .279 batting average and a modest .248. But his specialty was always defense. In 1951 he led the league in fielding percentage (.975) and assists (477) and in 1953 he regained the fielding title (.976).

In 1954 he led in fielding percentage (.975), games played (155) and double plays (102), but with a young sensation named Luís Aparicio waiting in the wings, Carrasquel was traded before the 1956 season. His final four years were spent between Cleveland, Kansas City and Baltimore, and an operation on his left leg in 1959 effectively ended his major league career.

After ten long years in the major leagues, Chico retired and returned to

Venezuela. Refusing to become inactive, he threw himself into the local amateur and professional leagues and, following in his uncle's footsteps, Chico now became the mentor. But, while he was reveling in his newfound role as teacher, his uncle Alex died at the age of 57 in August of 1969.

Venezuela was beginning to produce some very gifted players in the 1970s and 80s including Davey Concepción, Ozzie Guillén and Tony Armas, and Chico touched them all, in one way or another. One of his disciples was a chubby but powerful teen-ager named Andrés Galarraga. The raw rookie remembers that he first met Carrasquel at an amateur championship tournament.

"When I was 16 we played for the Carrasquel trophy," Andres said. "When he saw me play that year he helped me sign a professional contract with the Caracas team."

Galarraga, known as *The Big Cat*, enjoyed a major league career that spanned three decades, while earning several hitting and fielding titles. And he credits Chico with much of his early success. "He helped me especially in my rookie year and my first couple of years," Galarraga said. "He taught me a lot of stuff. He was a big man and a great player. He is a great friend to me and all the way around is a great person."[35]

As a manager, Chico led the Leones de Caracas team to the championship of the Caribbean Series in 1982.

Toward the end of his life Chico could be seen frequently at Comiskey Park, enjoying the game he loved. Asked to identify his greatest moment, Chico replied, "When I arrived to big league baseball." Chico died of a heart attack in May, 2005.

Despite all the accolades he received in his professional career Chico understood that he had little hope of ever making the majors back in the mid-forties. It was fortuitous that the Negro League shortstop named Robinson, who played in Caracas that October day in 1945, would open the door for him just as his talents were beginning to blossom.

(*Author's note.* Although he was not given his nickname "Chico" until he came to the United States to play, I have used it to simplify the story. His birth name is Alfonso.)

Salvador "Chico" Hernández

Student strikes had disrupted classes at the university and
Cuban leader Fulgencio Batista ordered the closure of the institution.

In 1936 Chico Hernández was a 20-year-old freshman at the University of Havana, secretly dreaming that someday he would be a catcher in the Cuban League. These were the days when Cuban catchers with major league tenure would return to the island for a season of winter league ball. With Mike González, Ricardo Torres and Mike Guerra acting as rolemodels for aspiring Cuban boys, Hernandez had a rich pool of experience on which to draw.

Those were also the days of political upheaval. Late in the year several student strikes had disrupted classes at the university and Cuban leader Fulgencio Batista ordered the closure of the institution in December.[36] With his life suddenly thrown into turmoil, Hernández traded in his books and slide rule for a catcher's mask and glove.

After gaining experience in the Cuban League, the muscular 6' 195-pound Hernández was courted by the Chicago Cubs and in 1938 he was sent to the United States to catch for Bloomington in the Three-I League. His first year of professional ball in America gave him the opportunity to prove that he was a workhorse. Blending good offensive numbers with the ability to handle pitchers, Hernández caught all but one game that season.[37]

After toiling in the minor leagues for the next five years, Hernández got his big break just after World War II began. Called up to the Cubs for the 1942 season along with Puerto Rican pitching sensation Hiram Bithorn, Hernández caught in 43 games, but batted an anemic .229. In 1943 he was Bithorn's primary battery-mate but still caught in only 41 games. Improving at the plate, he boosted his batting average to a respectable .270.

But no matter how much he had improved, it seemed evident that he would always be in the shadow of Chicago's first-string catcher, Clyde McCullough. When McCullough broke his leg prior to Opening Day 1944, Hernández was not there to claim his position. Instead he had gambled on a full-time position in Jorge Pasquel's Mexican League. Hernández may have been the first big-leaguer to make the switch, a full two years before a group of renegade major leaguers defied the Commissioner of Baseball and made the same move.

In December of 1944 McCullough was drafted into the military and Hernández signed another contract in Mexico. Several years later Hernández returned to Cuba and caught professionally until 1950.[38]

If Hernández had not taken a larger payday south of the border, would he have become the Cubs' number-one catcher in 1943 and 1944? If statistics are any indication, the answer may have been yes, because he and McCullough had career batting averages in the .250 range and similar fielding percentages.

Phil Cavarretta was the Cubs' first baseman during that period and he remembers that Hernández could have been a very good catcher if he had not been in competition against a seasoned veteran. "Chico never got a chance to catch very much because of Clyde McCullough, who was their number one," Cavarretta explained. "Hernández was a good catcher and pretty good hitter. He had a good head on him and called for the right pitch. But McCullough was a real good catcher too and had a super arm."[39]

For the next five years the Cubs scrambled to replace both men with a variety of catchers who fared no better at the plate.

Hernández did leave the major leagues with one legacy. He and Hiram Bithorn represented the first Latin-born battery in major league history.

Americans in Paradise

Durocher's friends ran the gamut from
tough-guy actor George Raft to gangster Bugsy Siegel.

As more American-born players swarmed to the Caribbean and Latin America for the winter leagues, the scandals and juicy gossip increased accordingly. Dodgers' manager Leo Durocher was spotted in the company of some known gamblers at Havana's Gran Stadium during an exhibition game in 1947. Fearing rumors of fixed games, Commissioner Happy Chandler suspended him.

Durocher's friends ran the gamut from tough-guy actor George Raft to gangster Bugsy Siegel. His infamous tirades against umpires reached a crescendo in 1941, when Cuban police were summoned onto the field. The President of Cuba, Fulgencio Batista, thought Durocher was play acting and believed his wild display was part of the Dodgers' exhibition. Enjoying the performance, Batista requested that Durocher repeat his routine for the next game.[40]

During spring training in Havana in 1941, Brooklyn's ace hurler Van Lingle Mungo had to be spirited off the island when he became an unwelcome third party in a relationship between a bullfighter and a woman.[41]

One of the most avid sporting fans in Cuba in the '40s was novelist Ernest Hemingway. While living in Havana the middle-aged author would invite American ballplayers to join him in dove-shooting contests during the day and carousing the casinos at night. After a few drinks he would challenge his guests to boxing matches. Only the intervention of his wife prevented serious injury. However, on one occasion in 1948, Hemingway challenged Dodgers relief pitcher Hugh Casey to a boxing match in his living room. Casey promptly hit the author, who spun backwards and fell through a glass table.[42]

Silvio García

*"I think Branch Rickey considered
Silvio García first, before Jackie Robinson"*

It's a story that every former ballplayer from Latin America knows, but the rest of the baseball world hasn't caught onto yet.

To start this story let's go back to the mid 1940s when the visionary leader of the Brooklyn Dodgers, Branch Rickey, sent out a group of scouts to find a single talented black ballplayer who could break down the doors of the segregated major leagues.

Ray Hayworth was one of the scouts who was assigned the secret duty. "After 1945 I went into scouting with the Brooklyn club [with] George Sisler [and] Wid Mathews," Hayworth said. "We traveled as a team and we scouted all the colored clubs, and that's how Mr. Rickey got the cream of the crop over all the others."[43]

One of the popular rumors that surfaced was that Rickey's secret spies wore disguises when they went to Negro League parks, to keep his ultimate intentions a secret.

The most famous of all the Rickey scouts was Clyde Sukeforth, who was credited with luring Jackie Robinson to the Brooklyn team in August of 1945. Sukeforth admitted that after the war there were many undercover agents in the bushes: "At that time everyone was scouting the colored leagues, but they didn't advertise it."[44]

The former scout added that this widespread activity stopped after the club owners took a secret vote to maintain the color barrier. The vote, according to Sukeforth, was 15 to 1 in favor of segregation, with the one dissenting vote coming from the Brooklyn club.

While it is true that Sukeforth, Hayworth, Mathews and Sisler spread out across the country to find the ultimate athlete who could break the color line, it is not well known that for a brief moment in time a man of black African heritage from the Caribbean was considered for the honor.

Although Hayworth could not remember Rickey referring to a "black Cuban or Puerto Rican," there are other witnesses who claim that scouts were secretly sent to investigate the talent of one Silvio García of Cuba. Preston Gómez, a former player and manager, knows the story from a firsthand source: "This is a story that Leo Durocher told me," Gómez said.

"In 1941 when the Dodgers went to play an exhibition game against a group of Cuban players, Silvio was playing shortstop. When Durocher went back he told Mr. Rickey, 'I saw a player and if we had brought him back he would have the chance to play in the big leagues.'"

According to Gómez, Rickey was intrigued by Durocher's claims and sent two trusted aides to see him. "So they went to see him in Cuba and then sent a guy named Clyde Sukeforth to see him play in Mexico."[45] And, he continued, "...then the late Walter O'Malley Sr., who at that time was a lawyer for the Brooklyn Dodgers, went to Cuba to take a look at him, also."

There are several men who played with García in the 1930s and 1940s who remember that time well. Armando Vasquez, a veteran of the Negro and Caribbean leagues, said, "Leo Durocher was the manager of the Brooklyn Dodgers and they were doing their spring training in Cuba. He saw Silvio García playing a game and he said, 'If they ever let the black people play in the big leagues right now, I would sign that fellow. He would be the shortstop for the Brooklyn Dodgers.'"[46]

Two close friends of García tell of his auditions for Rickey in Havana and Brooklyn several years before Jackie Robinson was signed. During Minnie Miñoso's rookie season with the New York Cubans he roomed with García and one event stands out in particular. Miñoso recalled, "We played a game in Cuba and later I heard Rickey had come to Cuba and said, if we could mix the black players in the white league, he would pay Garcia $100,000." But Miñoso admits that he dismissed the rumor that day because "I don't think anyone had any idea that black people would ever play in the big leagues."[47]

Felix Delgado was a teammate of García's in the Puerto Rican winter league when he heard that scouts had followed him to New York. Delgado claimed, "The Dodgers wanted to see Silvio García pitch (in the United States) and the owner of the Cuban Stars, (Alex) Pompez had rented Ebbets Field when the Dodgers were away."

One day Delgado went to the ball park and saw the scouts clamoring to see García play.

He recounted the event:

I was in New York on personal business and I went to Ebbets Field to see Silvio pitch [in a Pompez-sponsored Negro League game]. I heard that the president [of the Dodgers] and three other guys were looking at him. They were sitting in the front row paying attention to what he was doing. He won the game 1–0. Yes, I think Branch Rickey considered Silvio García first before Jackie Robinson because he was a great pitcher and a great hitter.[48]

Rumors still linger that Rickey was prepared to sign Garcia in 1943 for $25,000, because he led the Cuban League in batting average (.351), homeruns (4), base hits (69), and runs scored (24) in the winter season of 1941–1942.[49]

Just who was Silvio García, and, ultimately, why wasn't he signed before Robinson?

Born in Limonar, Cuba, on October 11, 1914, García began his professional career as a pitcher with the Cienfuegos ball club in 1931. Over the next 23 years he collected a battalion of admirers as he established himself as a solid hitter, a respectable pitcher and a defensive whiz at shortstop, third base, second base and outfield.

His career batting average in the Cuban League during nineteen years of action was .282, while his average after six years in the Mexican League was .335. Pitching in the 1936–1937 winter league season in Cuba, he had a 10–2 record. He played the 1939–1940 winter season in Puerto Rico, where he batted .298 while posting a 10–6 record with an ERA of 1.32.[50]

Former major league hurler Adrian Zabala said, "I started in 1936 and Silvio García was one of the best pitchers in the professional league in Cuba. And he was one of the best shortstops in the league, too. He weighed about 200 pounds or more and he was a good runner and a good infielder and he could throw the ball like a bullet."[51]

While playing in Puerto Rico, Felix Delgado remembered, "He was one of the greatest pitchers we had. He could throw hard and he was a line drive hitter." Outside of the stadium Delgado was struck by Garcia's introspection. "He was a quiet man, but he was always reading a newspaper or book all the time. He was very intelligent."[52]

Julio Becquer, a seven-year veteran of the American League, exclaimed, "Oh god, I don't even know who to compare him to. He was a big guy for a shortstop, 6'2" or 6'3" and he weighed around 200 some pounds. He was so agile it was incredible." Comparing the great players that he had seen during his career, Bequer was not shy to admit, "García was the kind of hitter that [Rod] Carew was. He hit the ball all over the place. Silvio could have been a star in the big leagues, because at that time he was one of the best hitters in the Negro leagues."[53]

García was very nearly the perfect fit that Rickey was looking for, exhibiting a wealth of brains and talent and experience. He nearly had everything. Very nearly.

José Montiel held front office-positions with the Cienfuegos club for many years and he was privy to the interest that the Americans had in García. "The Dodgers wanted to sign him," said Montiel, "but the only problem was his age. He was almost 30 years old and Durocher wanted to sign a young guy."

Besides the issue of age, Rickey demanded that his final choice be a man who possessed the ability to control his temper in the face of incredible abuse. Montiel acknowledged, "Silvio also was a temperamental guy. He had a lot of pride. Maybe he wouldn't resist the American fans. If they would say something against the blacks he would fight back."[54]

Miñoso added, "He was one tough ballplayer in Cuba." And, in his 1995 autobiography, Buck Leonard noted Garcia's aggressiveness on the field.

He wrote, "[He] was kind of mean. What we call mean is, he stayed evil all the time."[55]

Because the first black player would be under constant media scrutiny, Rickey also had to consider García's ability to express himself in English. The Latin players who preceded García were mocked in the press for their heavy accents and mispronunciations. Rickey had to find a candidate who could articulate without flaws.

Preston Gómez said, "The story I hear is that he could probably have been the first one but there was the language barrier. I think Mr. Rickey studied it real well and the language was a problem and only a man like Jackie Robinson could have taken all that abuse."

Baseball patriarch Don Zimmer saw García play during the forties. "When I played (in Cuba) it was before the majors brought in the first black players," explained Zimmer. "Silvio García was a great, great player but he had some age on him even then. This guy was a surefire major leaguer if the black situation started earlier. But when Jackie Robinson started in the big leagues, Silvio was over the hill."[56]

García eventually came to the United States, playing infield positions for the New York Cubans (with Miñoso) in 1946 and 1947, Sherbrooke in the Provincial League from 1949 to 1951, and with the Havana club in the Florida International League in 1952.

According to his former teammate Carlos Santiago, García's career took a near tragic turn in the 1940s. "He played here in Puerto Rico on the Ponce team and he used to be our pitcher," said Santiago in a somber tone. "One day he threw a pitch to a player from the Mayaguez team and he hit him on the head. The guy almost died. So he quit pitching [that day]."[57]

Felix Delgado could never forget the last time he saw García alive. The Castro regime had already established itself and García had to return to Havana and settle his personal affairs. As Delgado was driving him to the airport in San Juan, Puerto Rico, Silvio expressed his deep concerns. "He told me confidentially, 'Felix, I think I will only return here by boat because things are changing in my country. Things are not good.'" Taking his friend to the airport was a tough assignment, but this is what García wanted.

In subsequent phone conversations with García, Delgado learned that the trip was a terrible mistake: "He wanted to leave Cuba but he could not." Denied entrance to the major leagues and denied exit by the new Cuban regime, Silvio García lived his last years in obscurity. He died in 1978 in Cuba.

Tomas de la Cruz
"Hell, [he] was as black as they came."

In 1944 Tommy de la Cruz had a bright future ahead of him. He had just completed a magnificent season with the Syracuse Chiefs, an affiliate of the Cincinnati Reds in the International League. A writer for *Newsweek* saw no outward sign of discontent when de la Cruz appeared at his first training camp. The scribe noted, "Tomas de la Cruz, Havana-born right handed pitcher, helped his fellow Reds in spring training by teaching them the rumba and conga."[58]

Midway through the 1944 season he received his big chance, having been promoted to the majors at the age of 29. However, he did not enjoy the acceptance that seemed to follow his lighter-skinned colleagues.

De la Cruz has frequently been mentioned by historians and fellow ballplayers as being one of the half-dozen or more Latinos who slid under the color barrier despite having black African heritage. He notched a 9–9 record with a 3.25 ERA in his rookie year, but he was literally run out of the league because of dissent within the league and from the stands. One Pittsburgh scout proclaimed to a bystander, "Hell, [he] was as black as they came."[59]

Major league and minor league records reveal that he would probably have been a very capable pitcher if his career had been allowed to continue. During his short freshman year in the big leagues (34 games) he averaged about two walks per nine innings and completed nine of the 20 games he started.

De la Cruz was born in Marianao, Cuba, in 1914 and reached the ranks of professional baseball while still a teenager. At the age of nineteen he led the Cuban League in complete games pitched (7), followed by total games pitched (23) the next season.[60] By 1940 he was being courted by minor league scouts.

Despite his troubled tenure in Cincinnati, de la Cruz seemed to thrive in the racially tolerant northeastern part of the United States. As a starter for Wilkes-Barre in the Eastern League in 1941, he had a record of 17–6 with an ERA of 2.52.[61] The Street & Smith's Year Book analysts predicted he would be wearing a Reds uniform for the 1942 season, but he was not called up.

In 1942 he was the #4 starter in the rotation for Syracuse, winning 13 games and helping the Chiefs win the league championship, four games to none over Jersey City. In 1943 he returned to be their best hurler, completing a phenomenal 21 –11 record with an ERA of 1.96.[62]

After his brief and humiliating experience with the Reds in 1944, de la Cruz headed south to play in Jorge Pasquel's renegade Mexican league, where he won 17 games.[63] On January 3, 1945, he pitched a no-hitter for Almandares in the Cuban winter league.

Success in gambling, real estate investments and the Cuban lottery earned de la Cruz a sizable nest egg; however, he died young, only twelve days before his 47th birthday.

Pedro Preston Gómez

*Throughout his seven-year, three-team
managerial career he accepted "suicide" jobs.*

There was baseball fever in the city of San Diego during the spring and summer of 1968. On May 27 the city was awarded its first major league franchise after a series of marathon meetings in Chicago.

Three months and two days later the ownership group announced their decision for the team's first manager. They had selected Preston Gómez — a white Cuban who had only played in eight big-league games, but had established his credentials as a coach for the Los Angeles Dodgers.

Born on April 20, 1923, in the small Cuban village of Central Preston, the young Pedro Gómez could never have imagined that he would make history as the first

Latino to be signed to a managerial contract in the major leagues. (Although Mike González served as a temporary manager in 1938 and 1940, Gómez was the first Latin to be hired in a permanent position.)

After sifting through a mountain of qualified applicants, Gómez assembled a coaching staff which included veterans Wally Moon, Roger Craig, and a former minor league skipper with a career destined for immortality, Sparky Anderson.

On opening day, April 8, 1969, the San Diego Padres introduced a patchwork team of raw rookies and a few seasoned veterans. Pitchers Johnny Padres and Al McBean provided experience and direction to the youngsters, Joe Niekro and Clay Kirby. At 32 years old, two infielders, Tony González and Roberto Peña were ancient warriors compared to Cito Gaston at age 25 and Fred Kendall at 20.

By the end of their inaugural season Gómez's team had lost 110 games. But the disappointment was mitigated when the other National League expansion club, the Montreal Expos, finished with the same record. Gomez's tenure with the Padres lasted from opening day 1969 until mid–April 1972.

At the beginning of the 1974 season he was hired as the fourth manager in three years to pilot the faltering Houston Astros. Greg Gross was one of the players who remembers Gómez and his rise from coach to manager of the Houston club. "When I first came up he was coaching third base," said Gross. "[Gómez] had different signs for different people. The outfielders had a set of signs. Also signs for the infielders, the catchers, or even individuals. That was his way of disguising signs and I have not seen that since. He was always an inning or more ahead, into the game."[64]

When Gómez took over the helm in Houston he was able to blend his unique on-field strategies with a form of clubhouse compassion. Gross explained, "I had just turned 21 and he threw me out there as pretty much the everyday right fielder. In an era when young players didn't get treated as well as they do now, he encouraged me. He didn't get down on me because I was young and a rookie. It was a pretty veteran ball club so I have to give him a lot of credit for helping me relax in that initial few months of the season. He set me down against certain left handers to make me as comfortable as he could and I'll always thank him for that."

After his seventeen-year playing career ended, Gross used the lessons he had learned from Gómez to fashion a successful career as a manager and coach in the Rockies and Phillies organizations.

Gómez remained with the Astros until the 127th game of the 1975 season, when he was replaced by Bill Virdon. He returned to the Dodgers as a coach and was a part of their 1977 and 1978 pennant championships.

In 1980 he led the Chicago Cubs for 90 games before being replaced by Joey Amalfitano, who had been their interim manager during the previous season. Again, Gómez had been caught in a revolving-door organization: From 1979 through 1984 the Cubs changed managers seven times.

Throughout his seven-year, three-team, managerial career he accepted "suicide" jobs with clubs that had limited talent and short budgets. When he ended his final season of management in 1980 he had recorded 346 wins and 529 losses.

From the beginning of his adult life Gómez refused to back away from daunting challenges, whether they were on the field or in the clubhouse. At the age of nine

Preston Gómez, age 81, is surrounded by the field staff of the Anaheim Angels. Left to right — first-base coach Alfredo Griffin, Gómez, manager Mike Scioscia and bench coach Joe Maddon. (Source: Nick Wilson collection.)

he was playing organized ball in Cuba and by the age of 21 he was signed as an infielder to a professional contract by Joe Cambria of the Washington Senators.

Recalling his first visit to the United States in 1944, Gómez said, "When we first arrived in the U.S., in Miami [a Senators' representative] put us on the train. If the player didn't speak English he gave us a letter: 'To whom it may concern, this man should go to such and such a place.' When we arrived, the team was waiting for us and we went to College Park, Maryland, because that's where we were training during the war."[65]

Although he was dropped off in the frigid Northeast he found that he was not alone. "Luckily we had Gil Torres and Mike Guerra who spoke English and they helped us," said Gómez. "Also they had a Cuban barber who was more like a counselor. He was more like a father to us. Clark Griffith [hired] him and he used to come and explain to us what to do, not to do, and how to order food, and help us find a place to live. That was the only way we could learn."

The expression "cup of coffee" seems an appropriate description for the seven at-bats Gómez had in a Senators uniform. The next year he was sent to the minor league club in Chattanooga and never returned to the big leagues as a player. Feeling that his destiny lay on the other side of the chalk line, he listened, learned and took notes from some of the great tactical minds of his generation. Playing for the fiery manager Dolf Luque in the winter league, he learned his first lessons as a leader.

Gómez explained, "Since Luque played under [John] McGraw he was very strict and very demanding. And when I became a professional I was very glad to play for a man like that. In those days you respect the manager. Whatever he says, goes. And he taught me to be disciplined and to be organized and to respect people. He was strict. When he said something you had better be there. I was very fortunate when I broke in my first year in Cuba to play for Dolf Luque."

As his playing and coaching career developed he spent more time listening to the veterans he met. "I had the opportunity to have close to me the great manager Walter Austin and great baseball people like Leo Durocher and Charlie Dressen and Frank Crossetti. So by the time I had the opportunity to manage in the major leagues I learned a lot from those people and my job wasn't so difficult."

His debut as a major league manager was preceded by championship years with other organizations. In 1959 Gómez piloted the Havana Sugar Kings to the International League "Little World Series" championship. The following year he was hired as a coach for the Los Angeles Dodgers and was a part of their World Series victory in 1965 and the 1966 pennant championship.

He has continued to contribute to the national pastime by accepting a position as Special Assistant to the General Manager of the Anaheim Angels, where he remains today. Baseball's first Latin-born manager now has two World Series championship rings (one each from the Dodgers and Angels) and three pennant rings. Not bad for a kid who came from a small village in Cuba.

Although the "Latin Revolution" in the 1950s opened the door to opportunities for players, the process has been much slower for managers, coaches and front-office personnel. After Gómez accepted his position with the Padres it was 23 before another Latin was hired as a manager in the National League. In 1992 Felipe Alou was hired by the Expos and Tony Pérez followed the next year with the Reds.

Conclusion

"The march of the new conquistadores has just begun."

The routine of "hot and cold" recruiting strategies for Latin players in the major leagues would end forever at the dawn of the fifties. The period known as the "Latin Revolution" had its humble beginnings with the limited introduction of Bobby Avila and Minnie Miñoso in 1949.

Cultural currents were shifting, but stereotypes were hard to change as Ruben Amaro Sr. explained: "Back in my [early] days when they were talking about "good field–no hit" they were talking about [Latin] infielders," he said. "It was a stigma. But remember, I came up in the Fifties with an awful lot of hitters. I grew up with Tony Perez, Orlando Cepeda and Felipe Alou. Those guys were very, very good hitters. Remember, Bobby Avila was an infielder but he was always a hitter."[1]

Although players like Miñoso, Avila, Cepeda and Roberto Clemente would soon prove that the "good field–no hit" label was pure myth, big-league teams were slow to open the door completely. Opportunities in the minor leagues grew at a greater rate, however. By the end of the decade organized baseball had set a record for the number of salaried players and functioning teams which has never been equaled. In 1949 there were 448 teams and 59 leagues. Today there are 176 teams and 15 leagues.

Looking back at that period, Amaro explained, "The blacks and Latinos could not be fill-ins or platoon players. More so through the '50s until the early '70s. There was no room on the roster for any of them, unless they were starters." He continued, "During the years I played, the twenty-third through twenty-fifth place on the roster were not black or Latin American. The guys who were black or Latin had to be so good that they were starters."

By 1960 Latin players were still burdened by stereotypes, but they were making their presence felt. *Sports Illustrated* celebrated the naming of eight Latin players to the 1965 All-Star game by printing a five-page feature article titled "THE LATINS STORM LAS GRANDES LIGAS." The final paragraph ended on a prophetic note: "The march of the new conquistadores has just begun."[2]

It certainly appeared that McGraw had the power, the influence and the tenacity to tear down the racial barrier, but the forces that kept the wall intact were too strong. There are countless stories about McGraw openly showing interest in players of color, including the time he hired a black pitcher, Rube Foster, to teach Giants' ace Christy Mathewson the art of the screwball.

Longtime Negro League player Bobby Robinson loved to tell his personal McGraw story. After making a brilliant, unassisted triple play in a Negro League championship game in the 1920s Robinson was stunned to learn that McGraw and the entire Giants team were watching the game. When McGraw summoned Robinson to his box he said, "Bobby, if things were right today, you'd be my third baseman for the New York Giants."[2]

In 1915 McGraw told *The Indianapolis Freeman* that he would sign a black pitcher named John Donaldson, "If [he] were a white man." As usual, to add emphasis, he estimated the hurler's worth. "I would give $50,000 for him — and think I was getting a bargain."[3] As a last resort it was suggested that Donaldson move to Cuba for a short time and return under the guise of a Spanish-sounding name.[4]

McGraw was especially fond of Havana. He fell in love with the island when he first arrived for a barnstorming tour in 1891, and was impressed with the caliber of play that the Cubans exhibited. In 1905 he called Luis Bustamante a "perfect shortstop" and failed in an attempt to sign a dark-skinned Cuban by the name of Antonio María García as early as 1889. When Pelayo Chacón hit .350 in 1911 and .364 in 1920 against his Giants in exhibition games, he openly declared that another future major league star lay just out of reach. In 1911 he publicly announced that "José Méndez is better than any pitcher except Mordecai Brown and Christy Mathewson."

He considered hiring the Cuban slugger Cristóbal Torriente in the early 1920s, but reluctantly rejected the idea because he didn't think Torriente's complexion or kinky hair would pass the censors. Articulating her husband's frustration with the color barrier, Blanche McGraw once wrote, "John bemoaned the failure of baseball to cast aside custom or unwritten law ... and sign a player on ability alone."[5]

As his love affair with the island continued, so did his personal investments there. He and Blanche wintered frequently in Havana and in 1919 he made a sizable business investment. McGraw and the Giants' owner, Charles Stoneham, had tendered a bid for the city's gambling and racetrack mecca, Oriental Park. Stoneham secured 90 percent of the partnership while McGraw purchased the final 10 percent.

The duo would have kept their cherished investment if it hadn't been for that pesky scandal back in Chicago about the White Sox and the fixed World Series of 1919. Baseball Commissioner Judge Kenesaw Mountain Landis ignited a holy war against fraternization with gamblers of any ilk, and eventually forced McGraw and Stoneham to divest themselves of the Havana property.

Despite all his well-published efforts to sign a talented Latin ballplayer, he was beaten to the punch by the Reds (1911), Braves (1912), Senators (1913) and Yankees (1914). It wasn't until 1915 that McGraw finally landed a Cuban pitcher, Emilio Palmero.

His fierce personality was depicted by the last surviving ballplayer to play for the Giants in the 1920s. The former infielder granted me several interviews in 1999, but asked not to be identified.

> McGraw was a driver and lot of people couldn't play for him. But he could really spot talent and he had a big heart for his older ballplayers. He would do anything to win and he was most profane. But I had to accept the opportunity I had. McGraw was a little, short guy and he was very stern. He would look down the bench at us rookies after a particular play on the field and quiz us. "What would you have done in a situation like that? You'd better be awake." In other words the bench was under his control. Very orderly. In the clubhouse there was nothing played but Dominos before the game. McGraw was not a leader. He was a driver. He was pretty strict. The ballplayers had a private car on the railroad when we traveled and in the car behind us were the newspapermen. "Don't be talking to one of them!" Nobody could talk to the press but John McGraw. I was a young boy and I was pretty afraid of him.

In comparing the career of McGraw against that of the Philadelphia A's skipper, Connie Mack, *Little Napolean* has the edge. Although Mack had more victories, (3776 vs 2840) he also had 22 more seasons to achieve that record. McGraw was a genius at manipulating talent. He led the Giants to the World Series nine times (one more than Mack) and retired with a .589 winning percentage (vs Mack's .484).

McGraw died in 1934 knowing that despite his aspirations, he had never succeeded in bringing a talented player across the color line. Thirteen years after McGraw's death, Jackie Robinson pushed open the floodgates, and gifted black Latin players with the names of Clemente, Marichal, Miñoso and Cepeda vindicated the old man's foresight.

Clark Calvin Griffith

Griffith's fingerprints are found throughout the first half of the twentieth century.

When it comes to the evolution of the Latin ballplayer in America, Clark Griffith's fingerprints are found throughout the first half of the twentieth century. He made every effort to covertly include dark-skinned Cubans on his major league teams from 1911 through the 1940s. He gave jobs to players who would not be considered by other teams, and sometimes launched fabricated public relations campaigns to prove their lineage.

Griffith discovered one flaw that John McGraw could not. The major league color barrier was porous. But historians caution us not to interpret Griffith's actions as entirely altruistic.

The son of a Missouri fur trapper, Griffith successfully moved his way up the baseball ladder to become one of the most powerful men in the game. Initially a successful turn-of-the-century pitcher in the old American Association, he eventually became the player/manager for the Cincinnati Reds from 1908 to 1911. When he was lured to the ever-impoverished Washington Senators in 1912 he purchased 10 percent of the team's stock for the princely sum of $27,000. By 1920 he had become the majority partner.

If there is one brand that has been permanently affixed to Griffith's legacy it is that of a penny-pincher. While he was with the Reds he made history by signing two gifted but inexpensive Cubans, Rafael Almeida and Armando Marsans. After he moved to the Senators he again turned his eyes to the Caribbean. During his first eight years with Washington he introduced four Cuban players to the big leagues, but shifted into high gear during the Great Depression and the war years of the forties.

In 1934, during the depths of the Depression, Griffith began an ambitious crusade of scouring Cuba for the least expensive talent he could find. Dispatching Joe Cambria, a former laundryman turned big-league scout, to the island, he built a reliable and seemingly inexhaustible pipeline of ballplayers to stock his six-team minor league system.

During World War II he signed dozens of Latin ballplayers and had nine Cuban players rotate through the Senators' roster. As other major league teams were drained of their top players because of the war, the cellar-dwelling Senators caught fire. Because of their investment in draft-deferred, foreign nationals they found themselves fielding a team of young, healthy and talented players. In 1943 and 1945 the Senators were contenders for the pennant, but took a dive back into obscurity after the American superstars returned from military service in 1946.

Although some of his decisions were made in the name of fiscal strategy during the Depression, they could be questioned for their lack of sentiment. In 1934 he sold his team's best hitter (and his own son-in-law), Joe Cronin, to the Red Sox for cash. And in the winter of 1934, Griffith saw the box-office potential in signing 40-year-old Babe Ruth to manage the Senators. Despite the fact that Ruth had made $30,000 with the Yankees during the previous year, Griffith offered him a mere $15,000. Ruth declined the offer.[6]

According to Joe Culinane, a sports broadcaster and author with seven decades of professional experience, Griffith could be excused for his parsimonious ways. "Clark was known as a cheapskate, but he just didn't have the money," said Culinane. "Jacob Ruppert (the owner of the Yankees) had his fortune from his brewery and many other owners got their money far removed from baseball. But baseball was all Clark had."[7]

In terms of taking a public stand on integrating his ball club, Griffith was one of the last. Although he certainly brought Cubans with black African origins into the major leagues decades before Jackie Robinson, when the racial barriers were finally breached in 1947 it was seven years before Griffith allowed a black man to appear in a regular season game.

Writing for the 2002 issue of *The National Pastime*, historian David Evans concludes that Griffith was reluctant to hire black players after Jackie Robinson's debut in 1947. He quotes Griffith as stating, "Nobody is going to stampede me into signing Negro players...." When the pressure became too overwhelming he introduced outfielder Carlos Paula, a black Cuban, in a "halfhearted manner." According to Evans, "Griffith did not want a lot of press attention."[8] And he succeeded, because even the black press gave Paula's debut little notice.

Griffith was finally forced to comply when protesters demonstrated at his stadium and *Washington Post* columnist Shirley Povich criticized the fact that there were no blacks on the team in the nation's capital. Considered to be only a mediocre ballplayer, Paula hit .290 in his last minor league assignment; during his three-year, 157 game major league career he scratched out a .271 batting average.

Although the muscular Paula stood 6'3" and weighed close to 200 pounds he hit only nine big-league home runs. After hitting .183 in 1956 the Cuban was not offered a contract for the following year. At the age of 28 Paula returned to play in his homeland, where he failed to lead the Cuban League in any hitting categories.

It is curious that Griffith would pass up so many talented African American and Cuban blacks in favor of someone he knew would not stand out.

After Griffith died in 1955 his adopted son Calvin assumed the leadership role in the Senators' front office and moved the team to Minnesota five years later. Calvin began assembling a team of very talented Latin players, culminating in 1965 when the Minnesota Twins won the American League pennant.

Rube Foster

"He had a big head, big neck, big shoulders, big arms, a big body and big legs."

Prior to 1920 African American and black Cubans were consigned to playing ball for barnstorming teams or disorganized associations. When salaries were paid they were sadly meager; travel was over long distances and scheduling was often play-as-you-go.

On February 13, 1920, a group of black entrepreneurs met at the YMCA in Kansas City in an attempt to form a major league circuit for black baseball players. Led by a former pitching star named Andrew "Rube" Foster, the businessmen decided to organize the eight baseball teams that they individually owned into the Negro National League. Foster, the owner of the Chicago American Giants, was the driving force behind the organization and operation of the league for the next six years.

Ten years earlier Foster had fired a public shot across the bow when he challenged investors to provide funds for an organized league for black men. He wrote an editorial in the black-owned newspaper, *The Indianapolis Freeman* saying "The time is now at hand when the formation of colored leagues should receive much consideration."[9]

His dream for a league of black players received a boost when olive-skinned Cubans began to be admitted to the big leagues. From 1919 through January of 1920 he barraged black newspapers with scathing editorials, demanding that black entrepreneurs follow his vision. By Christmas 1919 he had received only one commitment.[10]

Arguing that an organized league would mean profits for every team, he contrasted the economies of the Cuban Stars who "have never had a dime invested beyond their uniforms and advance money," with black, home town "clubs that are burdened with heavy overhead expense." Out of frustration he penned an ultimatum on New Year's day. "This will be the last time I will ever try and interest Colored club owners to get together on some working basis."[11]

He did not limit his attack to the club owners, either. "[Black] Ballplayers have had no respect for their word, contracts or moral obligations," he wrote later in January of 1920.[12] He argued that unless the owners united and formed a constitution (instituting a form of the reserve clause) they would forever be hampered by players who jumped from one team to another.

The prodding and threatening finally paid off when the articles of incorporation of the Negro National League were drawn up on February 14.

The Chicago Defender hailed the agreement and prophesied, "His great effort will be handed down to posterity long after he is dead. His work will stand as a tribute to athletics, the crowning efforts of a life in promoting a game that from the beginning has been a task few men would undertake."[13] The Negro National League was to become the first safe place for talented players who were not welcome in the major leagues.

Rube Foster also brought a semblance of order to the barnstorming circuit. For example, Bobby Robinson started playing in the Negro Leagues with the Indianapolis ABC's in 1925 at a lean but secure monthly salary of $125. After the Negro League was organized the total expenditures for black players' salaries jumped from $30,000 per year to $275,000.[14]

Foster was born in 1879 in Calvert, Texas, and began his pitching career shortly after graduating from the eighth grade. Bobby Robinson said, "I knew Rube Foster and I played against his team for I don't know how many years. He was a big guy. He had a big head, big neck, big shoulders, big arms, a big body and big legs. He was a great pitcher once."[15]

Employing his famous screw ball Foster won 51 games in 1902, 54 games in 1903 and 51 games in 1905. He also began pitching in the Cuban winter league as early as 1903.

Proving himself to be as proficient a businessman as he was an athlete, Foster started his own team in 1910, eventually renaming it the Chicago American Giants and bringing it into his Negro National League.

Foster's entire world was snuggled into a small area on the south side of Chicago, within a short driving distance of Comiskey Park. Foster resided at 39th Street and Wentworth Avenue, just across the street from the stadium he leased, named the 39th Street Grounds. His Negro National League headquarters were on 32nd street at 3242 Vernon.

Foster was selfless in his pursuit of his dream, often laboring through 18-hour days. He created teams, moved franchises and supported the league with his own money. Realizing the box-office draw of Cuban players, he aggressively pursued them, regardless of skin shade.

One of the early franchises in the new league was the Cuban Stars (West), owned by Agustín "Tinti" Molina and based in Cincinnati. Facing challenges from the U.S. Immigration Service, Foster personally posted a $10,000 bond with the Department of Labor so the Stars could join the league.[16] In addition, Foster helped negotiate a lease with the owners of the Cincinnati Reds that allowed the Cuban Stars to play the entire season of 1921 in Redland Field. The historic rental agreement, costing $4,000 annually, was the first time that a black ball club was allowed to become a full-season tenant of a major league park.[17] The first Latinos to play in his new league were José Méndez, Bartolo Portuondo, José Rodríguez and Cristóbal Torriente.

There is little doubt that Foster's main objective was more than the establishment of a black league. He desperately wanted to prove to the major league owners that blacks were capable of playing on a professional level. His dream was to force open the doors of segregation and secure a big-league franchise, fielding a team of all-star players from his league.

His aspirations received a boost when Almeida and Marsans were signed by the Cincinnati Reds. In 1914 he told a sportswriter from Seattle, "They're taking in Cubans now, you notice. And they'll let us in soon." Through a thin veil of humor he then intimated that the two Cubans were black.[18]

Foster had inspired other visionaries to build their own circuits. By the mid–1920s the Texas Negro League was formed and included clubs from Austin, San Antonio and Galveston. They played in the white Texas League parks when the hometown teams were traveling.

Teams in Mexico frequently invited the clubs from the Texas Negro League to come south of the border to play exhibition games. Although little has been written about the short-lived Texas Negro League, it is assumed that clubs shopped for talented players when they ventured into Mexico.

Other leagues which followed Foster's lead included the Texas-Oklahoma-Louisiana League (1929–1931) and the Negro Southern League (1920–1950s). The Eastern Colored League (1923–1928) was created after a squabble between Foster and the owner of the Hilldale Daisies, Ed Bolden.

In 1921 a Caucasian entrepreneur named Andy Lawson thought he could blend a little of Foster's imagination and still challenge the color line. His dream was to create the Continental League, which included eight teams, four white and four black, to play against each other in a full summer schedule.

Lawson's revolutionary idea was promoted by *Baseball Magazine*, which noted, "We cannot but sympathize, however, with the attempt of the Continental League to give the colored ballplayer a show. He has never had a decent chance before."[19]

To the optimist it certainly appeared that a new era was approaching. Foster had created a stable league for blacks, Lawson was proposing interracial play, and the most influential magazine in baseball seemed to endorse integration on the ball field. Players like Méndez, Dihigo and Torriente must have sensed that changes were possible.

But their optimism did not last long. Foster was admitted to a mental institution in 1926 and died there four years later. His beloved Negro National League disbanded during the Great Depression, to be replaced by other struggling and ill-funded circuits. Lawson's idea never made it past the drawing board, and although *Baseball Magazine* continued to occasionally call for equality and justice, the cry was never taken seriously.

Joe Cambria

"Cambria literally *pirated* them off the gunboat"

The idea of crowding hundreds of young Cuban boys in to a stadium and attempting to find a white diamond in this mass of humanity wasn't conceived overnight. Clark Griffith and John McGraw had tested individual Latin players based on the advice of scouts since the turn of the century and Branch Rickey devised the first large-scale major league try out camp in 1919 in St. Louis. But it was Joe Cambria, a laundryman from Baltimore, who re-engineered the art of scouting.

Many players called him a godsend, while his critics described him as a heartless vulture. Cambria, who was born in Italy, and raised in United States, had achieved limited success as a minor league baseball player prior to the First World War. Searching for a new career, he bought the Bugle Apron and Laundry Company in Baltimore, but deep inside he never lost his love for the game. Gambling against the effects of the Great Depression, he purchased the Baltimore Black Sox in the Negro National League after the 1932 season, and was eventually exposed to the enormous talent pool that was available in Cuba.

When Cambria was introduced to the owner of the Washington Senators, Clark Griffith, the two entrepreneurs became friends. By 1934 Griffith asked Cambria to be his eyes and ears in Cuba and to follow a simple strategy: open the Cuban pipeline and sign ballplayers to cheap contracts.

Former major league manager Preston Gómez explained the system that Cambria employed:

> He had former players who they called bird dogs and they used to call him and say, "Papa Joe there is a guy in Camaguey that you should take a look at." In those days he had the advantage (because) he used to follow the players that were playing in the leagues in Havana and other places on the island. He used to go himself and watch them play a regular game. And that's how he signed Tony Oliva and other players.[20]

Using his large network of agents he found hundreds of players, including many of mixed Afro-Spanish blood. Ironically, he discovered players who could pass the "whiteness" test in the U.S. major leagues but could not play in the Cuban amateur league because of their black heritage.

Cambria employed Branch Rickey's method of identifying a few good players in a quantity of candidates. The tryouts, sometimes involving hundreds of young men, would include a battery of tests, usually starting with the sixty-yard dash. The best of the lot would then compete in the throwing contest and the winners would then advance to the next stage — hitting. It was a form of Darwinism at warp speed.

Adrian Zabala was contacted by one of Cambria's bird dogs in his remote village of San Antonio de los Banos. After a long bus trip to Havana, Zabala, an accomplished left-handed hurler, was auditioned by Cambria in a private session. Zabala recalled:

> It was 1936 when I first met Joe Cambria and my life changed. A friend of mine asked me to go to Tropical Stadium, because Cambria had heard of me and he wanted to see how I throw the ball. So I got out there and started warming up. I threw the ball about six or seven times and I was throwing pretty good. I had good speed. Suddenly he said, "Hey, hey," and he walked in front of me and I almost hit him.
>
> Cambria said, "You don't have to throw anymore. You can go." That's what he said to me.
>
> He said, "Do you want to go to the United States?"

And I said, "But, I don't speak English! Besides that I have to speak to my daddy."
"You know," he said, "They pay you money to play."
He wanted me to call him Papa Joe and he explained the situation to me.
When Cambria asked me to play I was glad. I wanted to get away from Havana and go someplace new.
So I went to my Dad and he said, "If you go play ball how are you going to make a living?"
I said, "Daddy, they'll pay me to play baseball!"
He couldn't believe it.
So he said, "Oh, Oh." And he changed his mind and he let me go.[21]

During the next 25 years Cambria signed about 400 Cubans to professional contracts. One of his first signups was Roberto Estalella, in 1934, and one of his last was Hall of Famer Tony Oliva, in 1960.

Ray Hayworth began scouting in Latin America for Brooklyn's Branch Rickey in the 1940s and learned to appreciate the challenges and satisfaction that Cambria experienced:

In Cuba they were strong young boys, many who grew up cutting the sugar cane for making molasses and sugar.
    They were strong, healthy boys and I suppose I gave many of them the break of their lives. It meant everything in the world to them. They'd give their right arm to come over here for just the opportunity to come and play. There was plenty of poverty. That's all you'd see in some of those countries.[22]

In an effort to become more efficient with his factory-style recruiting, Cambria moved to Havana. During this period he invested in a café, a restaurant, and several apartment buildings and bars.[23] In addition, he entered into a partnership with Roberto Maduro after World War II to create the Havana Cubans Baseball Club.

Cambria adapted to his new environment rapidly. Carlos Pascual, a pitcher Cambria signed in 1949, remembered, "Joe Cambria spoke Spanish and wore a Panama hat and a guayabera (a traditional long white shirt). He was just like a Cuban and the people there just loved him."[24]

Julio Becquer, a major league shortstop with Washington/Minnesota for seven years, added, "Joe Cambria, the greatest scout that ever lived. Joe Cambria spoke Spanish very well. In fact I never spoke English to Joe. When we spoke he never used a translator." Becquer joked, "He was like a native of Cuba. He was a very jovial individual and was very likable. Even the dogs said hi to him."

He continued, "When I remember him, it is almost like a member of my family. Not just a scout. You know most of us came from poor families and when we'd have a problem we'd go to Joe. He was our godfather."[25]

Out of the Cambria legend came erroneous and downright unbelievable myths. According to a story appearing in a national publication in 1944, Cambria's Spanish was limited to "*Firme aqui*"—"Sign here."[26] A story printed in *Sports Illustrated* in 1965 noted, without detail, that the Cuban leader, Fulgencio Batista, had ordered three young baseball prospects to a training camp in Tampa when Cambria literally "pirated" them off the gunboat they were traveling on.[27]

Cambria is the central figure in the persistent myth about Fidel Castro nearly signing a professional contract with the Washington Senators. Castro, in fact, distinguished himself only briefly as a basketball player in high school in 1944. Although Cambria never showed any interest in him as a pitcher, Castro encouraged the lie by telling Mike Wallace of "60 Minutes" that President George H.W. Bush might have played baseball in college, but he had never been offered a professional contract with the Senators.

Along with the glory and legend-building there also came stiff criticism. It was rumored that Cambria signed some players, using a single baseball as bonus.[28] Several Cuban and American writers scalded him for enticing naïve young players into contracts and then throwing them into an environment in the United States that included meager pay and rampant racism.

As exposed in the groundbreaking book *Dollar Sign on the Muscle*, unethical methods were used by many major league scouts in the process of signing Latin players. A popular way to attract the quantity of applicants after the 1930s was to issue undated contracts or to write them in such a way as to render them unbinding. Another method was the "tentative contract" which benefited only the ball club. The contracts would remain worthless until the player proved his worth under fire.[29]

Some critics argued that players who failed their minor league opportunities would be stranded in some bush-league city with no fare home. One magazine claimed that Griffith would farm out failed major league Latin players by depositing them on the train platform at the Washington station and tying a sign around their neck with their minor league destination scrawled across the front.[30]

On balance, however, Cambria's supporters far outnumber his critics.

Former outfielder Tony Oliva was delivered to Cambria by one of his bird dogs in the village of Pinar del Rio in 1960. Although he was signed for bus fare, Oliva said, "Joe Cambria was great. A lot of ballplayers were released from different organizations and he gave them another chance to come back."

Just as he was having concerns about the obstacles he would encounter in the minors, Cambria took him aside. Oliva recalled, "I remember seeing him in Charlotte back in 1961 and he gave me some advice. He told me, 'Tony, you keep working hard and you'll have a the chance in the big leagues. Get along with the coaches and make sure who you marry.' He was like a father to me."[31]

In his autobiography, Felipe Alou called Cambria "A caring and reliable friend to all Latins he signed."[32]

World Champion skipper Jack McKeon began his six-decade managerial career with the Washington Senators' organization in 1955. When he was promoted to Missoula, Montana, in the Pioneer League the following season he became acquainted with Cambria and his unique eccentricities. One day, early in the 1956 season, he received a surprise phone call from the station manager at the Missoula bus depot.

"Hey we've got some guys down here. We've a got all these players down here from Cuba."

McKeon responded with frustration, "We don't know anything about it."

After driving to the depot in downtown Missoula, McKeon soon discovered the truth. He recalled, " Joe would put them on a bus in Miami and ship them (out) and we didn't even know they were showing up." McKeon confessed that after a while it became comical. "I'd get guys showing up at the ballpark with letters. Some of them were good and some of them were not too good, but we took a look at them."

He also recalled the unusual way that Cambria would format his scouting notes. "He wouldn't tell me these guys are coming. He'd just give them a letter. He'd [put] letter inside the envelope and when he filled [the first page] of the letter he would write the rest of [the scouting report] on the outside of the envelope. He wouldn't get another piece of paper, he just put it on the envelope."

Despite the constant surprises Cambria was well liked and respected by the minor league managers within the Senators' system. His untempered enthusiasm and paternal instincts for the players were expressed in each letter. "He was always promoting his players," McKeon explained. "He'd say they were all great players and he'd tell me all about them. He used to send them over by the busloads and if he sent you ten, three could play. But he kept throwing enough against you that you'd get some good ones."[33]

Fidel Castro's revolution, and subsequent dissolution of the Cuban professional league, changed the good life that Cambria had enjoyed in Havana. Accepting a position of scouting in south Florida and Latin America for the Minnesota Twins, he relocated his residence to Miami. Carlos Pascual was one of the last of his colleagues to see him alive.

"I took him to the airport one day [in 1962] and he looked pretty good," said Pascual.

"He went to Baltimore because he had some family there. And after a week or so he died suddenly. After two or three months the Twins gave me his job."

In retrospect it seems amazing that a former laundry owner would eventually be known as one of the greatest scouts in baseball history.

Appendix B: Washington Senators' Spring Training

"In my first year in 1939 we had fifty-some pitchers in camp and we were going to wind up with ten."

The Washington Senators' spring training camps from 1939 through the war years were unique to baseball because of the rapid influx of Latin-born players signed into their system. As an addendum to the Joe Cambria story this appendix includes the recollections of several ballplayers who played on the Senators during those years.

The addition of this section to the book has particular significance because this period was the first time that Latinos represented a significant percentage of recruits on a spring training roster. Today we take for granted that perhaps 25 to 30 percent of a ball club's minor and major league system is made up of Latin-born players, but in 1939 it was unheard of.

Mickey Vernon appeared at his first Senators training camp in 1939 and remembered:

> Our head scout in Washington [Cambria] did all his scouting in Cuba and that's why we had so many coming and going. At one point in spring training we had more Latins than any other group. I saw a lot of them coming through. Sandy Consuegra, Julio Moreno, Gil Torres. Mike Guerra the catcher and Frank Campos at first base. Quite a few didn't make it, though.[1]

Walter Masterson was a rookie pitcher in 1939 when he noticed a different flavor to the game:

> The first Latin ballplayers [that] I remember Cambria brought in were Bobby Estalella who was at Charlotte. He was an outfielder. The first pitcher was Roberto Ortiz that I remember. And he was a cane cutter from Cuba. And of course Alejandro Carrasquel came in, but he was from Venezuela. Subsequently there was Gil Torres who was a shortstop/pitcher who came through Charlotte. René Monteagudo was another left-handed pitcher. Then there was a succession of two, three or four pitchers plus infielders and outfielders who would be coming in each year in spring training. But they were not regulars on the ball club. They didn't stay too long at that time, [until] the war years. There was more of a Cuban contingency during the war years. They blended in very well with the other players although few of them could speak English. Gil Torres was the only one who could speak English fluently and of

course everyone leaned toward him. Say for instance there was a vote or conversation in the clubhouse, he spoke for them collectively.[2]

Writer Bob Considine found that some of the players had become a curious novelty. "The Washington club also embraced the Mutt and Jeff of Cuban pitching — 6 feet–4 inch Roberto Ortiz and runty, fattish René Monteagudo. They made a curious knot in the center of the predominately Southern ball club."[4]

Masterson, who enjoyed a pitching career that spanned three decades, remembers that it was a very challenging environment:

> I was just trying to make the ball club as a young player myself, so it was a highly competitive situation. Normally you would have 20 – 30 pitchers in camp, but in my first year in 1939 we had fifty-some pitchers in camp and we were going to wind up with ten. Consequently it was very competitive. As a matter of fact Mr. Griffith went to another ball club and got Al Lopez to help out with the selection of the pitchers, because we didn't have enough catchers. We went to spring training around January the 6th at that time, because of the number of pitchers; it took a longer time to weed them out.[4]

Sid Hudson was a tall, gangly 25-year-old pitcher from the small mining town of Coalfield, Tennessee, when he was first introduced to foreign-born ballplayers on the Senators' training grounds:

> The first year I went to spring training was in 1940 and they had us new guys, and all the Latins, in a rooming house in Orlando, Florida. None of them could speak English and of course all of us took our meals there. We had a lot of fun with them trying to learn our language and we trying to learn theirs. Especially when we were eating. One of them could only say 'ham and eggs,' and he'd order ham and eggs every meal.[5] Anyway we had a lot of fun with them.

Clark Griffith had established an unorthodox way of letting a player know that he was destined for the big-league roster. As Masterson explained it,

> In spring training you had to graduate from a rooming house to the hotel. This was part of the process to make the team. At first all of the pitchers and catchers went to two rooming houses in Orlando. If you were weeded out and destined for a minor league club you stayed [in the rooming house]. The survivors moved into the Angibilt Hotel. We started playing games and if you did well then you were moved to the hotel with all the big players. After about ten days or two weeks I was moved to the hotel. And so I didn't see much of the Latins except out on the field. Cambria brought a lot of them to camp but few of them made it immediately.[6]

Herb Plews, a prospective second baseman during that period, felt that the Senators did a good job of forging a cohesive environment among the players: "There wasn't any segregation. It might have happened a few years before, I guess, but that passed. I think the main reason is because all of them were just good fellows and they were good ballplayers. And that had a lot to do with it."[7]
Masterson concurred that there was no discrimination.

However, Bob Considine penned an article for *Collier's* claiming that there was one ugly incident at the 1939 training camp. Considine wrote about a scuffle at the boardinghouse: "...several Washington rookies began to toss the bewildered Cubans around. Above the din of crashing furniture and the howls of the landlady the Cubans learned that they were being slugged because [Roberto] Ortiz had 'forgotten his place.'"

He also quoted a Havana-based story suggesting that in 1940 a Cuban prospect was on the field without socks because "the Washington club would not trust the rookie with the socks until he could raise the fifty cents."[8]

Not all sportswriters were sympathetic to the changes taking place in the clubhouse. In 1940 Vincent X. Flaherty called the new arrivals, "a sideshow of geographical freaks."[9]

In 1943, Hall of Fame writer Shirley Povich revealed that, years earlier, the Latinos had been treated with disdain by a couple of the veteran players and the clubhouse attendants. The hostility seemed to abate after executives from the Senators' front office demanded that the American players change their attitude for the sake of the team.

One other event that seemed to close the gap between the two sides occurred in 1941, when Roberto Ortiz physically pummeled a St. Louis Browns player who was threatening a Washington teammate. As writer noted, "...the attitude of certain American players toward the Cuban element underwent a marked change."[10]

Several other interesting stories came out of those early spring training camps, including the purported "pitching showdown" between Roberto Ortiz and baseball icon Walter Johnson, as described in Chapter 6. After the 1941 season there were several baseball writers who enthused over the future possibilities for the Senators. One writer noted:

> Roberto [Estelella]'s performance with the Nats during the fag end of the [last] season would indicate that the Senators have the best hitting outfielder in almost a decade.
>   Estalella might give [Senators' manager] Bucky Harris two thirds of a Cuban outfield if he and Ortiz make the grade. Neither is eligible to US army draft as both are citizens of Cuba.... Bucky Harris is convinced [Ortiz] can hit.[11]

Washington did indeed recover from three consecutive seventh-place finishes to make a run for the pennant in 1943 and 1945.

Chapter Notes

Introduction

1. Personal interview, 1998.
2. Personal interview.
3. Minnie Miñoso, *Just Call Me Minnie.*

Chapter 1

1. *Harper's Weekly,* May 19, 1900.
2. Mark Rucker and Peter Bjarkman, *Smoke.*
3. John B. Holway, *Blackball Stars.*
4. Holway, *Blackball Stars.*
5. James A. Riley, *Biographical Encyclopedia.*
6. *Baseball Magazine,* March 1913.
7. Peter C. Bjarkman, *Baseball with a Latin Beat.*
8. Charles C. Alexander, *John McGraw.*
9. Alexander, *John McGraw.*
10. Riley, *Biographical Encyclopedia.*
11. *Baseball Magazine,* December 1918.
12. *Baseball Magazine,* July 1913.
13. Personal interview.
14. *Baseball Magazine,* March 1913.
15. Bjarkman, *Baseball with a Latin Beat.*
16. National Baseball Hall of Fame (HOF), Méndez file.
17. Janet Bruce, *The Kansas City Monarchs.*
18. Riley, *Biographical Encyclopedia.*
19. *Chicago Defender,* February 28, 1920.
20. *Chicago Defender,* February 20, 1920.
21. *Chicago Defender,* April 24, 1920.
22. *Chicago Defender,* May 15, 1920.
23. *Chicago Defender,* June 7, 1920.
24. Robert Peterson, *Only the Ball Was White.*
25. Riley, *Biographical Encyclopedia.*
26. Holway, *Blackball Stars.*
27. Bruce, *The Kansas City Monarchs.*
28. Peterson, *Only the Ball Was White.*
29. Bjarkman, *Baseball with a Latin Beat.*
30. Riley, *Biographical Encyclopedia.*
31. Bruce, *The Kansas City Monarchs.*
32. Riley, *Biographical Encyclopedia.*
33. Bjarkman, *Baseball with a Latin Beat.*
34. Rucker and Bjarkman, *Smoke.*
35. Bjarkman, *Baseball with a Latin Beat.*
36. Bob Considine, "Ivory from Cuba."

37. Riley, *Biographical Encyclopedia.*
38. Personal interview.
39. Personal interview.
40. Roberto González Echevarría, *The Pride of Havana.*
41. Echevarría, *The Pride of Havana.*
42. Samuel O. Regalado, *Viva Baseball.*
43. *Baseball Magazine,* December 1918.
44. *Baseball Magazine,* March 1913.
45. Holway, *Blackball Stars.*
46. Robert Ripley, untitled article, September 1912.
47. Peterson, *Only the Ball Was White.*
48. Peterson, *Only the Ball Was White.*
49. Personal interview, January 10, 1999.
50. Fred Dartnell, *"Seconds Out!"*
51. Rucker and Bjarkman, *Smoke.*
52. HOF, Marsans file.
53. Peter Toot, *Armando Marsans.*
54. Society for American Baseball Research (SABR), Negro League Researchers/Authors Group.
55. Toot, *Armando Marsans.*
56. HOF, Marsans file.
57. Louis Heilbroner, memo to Garry Herrmann, December 30, 1910, and January 4, 1911.
58. *Baseball Magazine,* June 1914.
59. Echevarría, *The Pride of Havana.*

Chapter 2

1. Peter Toot, *Armando Marsans.*
2. *Philadelphia Inquirer,* story copyrighted 1912.
3. *Philadelphia Inquirer.*
4. Peter C. Bjarkman, *Baseball with a Latin Beat.*
5. *Detroit News Tribune,* January 1912.
6. *Philadelphia Inquirer.*
7. *Philadelphia Inquirer.*
8. *Detroit News Tribune.*
9. Mike Shatzkin, *The Ballplayers.*
10. Personal interview, 1999.
11. Felipe Alou, *My Life and Baseball.*
12. Louis Heilbroner, memos to Garry Herrmann, December 30, 1910, and January 4, 1911.
13. Lyle K. Wilson, "Mr. Foster Comes to Washington."

14. National Baseball Hall of Fame (HOF), Marsans file.

15. Riley, *Biographical Encyclopedia.*

16. Riley, *Biographical Encyclopedia.*

17. *Philadelphia Inquirer,* 1912.

18. Bob Considine, "Ivory from Cuba."

19. HOF, Marsans file.

20. HOF, Marsans file.

21. HOF, Marsans file.

22. Heilbroner memo, 1910.

23. Toot, *Armando Marsans.*

24. HOF, Marsans file.

25. Heilbroner memo, 1910.

26. *Philadelphia Inquirer,* 1912.

27. Heilbroner memo, 1910.

28. HOF, Marsans file.

29. Stewart Bowers, personal interview, January 24, 2004.

30. Toot, *Armando Marsans.*

31. Negro Leagues Museum, undated article.

32. *Philadelphia Inquirer,* 1912.

33. *Newsweek,* May 29, 1944.

34. Bjarkman, *Baseball with a Latin Beat.*

35. HOF, Marsans file.

36. Personal interview.

37. *Baseball Magazine,* September 1914.

38. *Detroit News Tribune,* January 1912.

39. Robert Ripley, untitled article, September 1912.

40. HOF, Marsans file.

41. *Baseball Magazine,* September 1914.

42. *Baseball Magazine,* July 1913.

43. *Baseball Magazine,* July 1913.

44. W.G. Hirsig, telegram to August Herrmann, July 18, 1913.

45. *Baseball Magazine,* Oct. 1913, and HOF, Marsans file.

46. Samuel O. Regalado, *Viva Baseball.*

47. Armando Marsans, letter to August Herrmann, March 2, 1913.

48. HOF, Marsans file.

49. *Baseball Magazine,* June 1914.

50. *Baseball Magazine,* September 1914.

51. *Baseball Magazine,* September 1914.

52. HOF, Marsans file.

53. HOF, Marsans file.

54. HOF, Marsans file.

55. HOF, Marsans file.

56. *Baseball Magazine,* September 1914.

57. HOF, Marsans file.

58. HOF, Marsans file, June 4, 1914.

59. *Baseball Magazine,* June 1914.

60. HOF, Marsans file.

61. HOF, Marsans file.

62. HOF, Marsans file.

63. HOF, Marsans file.

64. HOF, Marsans file.

65. HOF, Marsans file.

66. *Baseball Magazine,* July 1918.

67. HOF, Marsans file.

68. *New York Times,* July 19, 1917.

69. *New York Times,* August 10, 1917.

70. *New York Times,* August 11, 1917.

71. *New York Times,* August 18, 1917

72. *New York Times,* February 19, 1920.

73. *New York Times,* February 19, 1920.

74. *New York Times,* February 20, 1920.

75. *New York Times,* February 20, 1920.

76. HOF, Marsans file.

77. Syndicated article, August 9, 1923.

78. Fred Lieb, "Casual Comment."

79. Echevarría, *The Pride of Havana.*

80. Bjarkman, *Baseball with a Latin Beat.*

81. Personal interview.

82. Robert Creamer, *Babe.*

83. Personal interview.

Chapter 3

1. Personal interview.

2. John B. Holway, *Blackball Stars.*

3. Michael and Mary-Adams Oleksak, *Beisbol.*

4. Holway, *Blackball Stars.*

5. James A. Riley, *Biographical Encyclopedia.*

6. Holway, *Blackball Stars.*

7. Riley, *Biographical Encyclopedia.*

8. Peter C. Bjarkman, *Baseball with a Latin Beat.*

9. Negro League Researchers/Authors Group, SABR.

10. *Chicago Defender,* April 17, 1920.

11. *Chicago Defender,* May 6, 1920.

12. *Chicago Defender,* May 1, 1920.

13. *Chicago Defender,* May 15, 1920.

14. *Chicago Defender,* June 12, 1920.

15. Holway, *Blackball Stars.*

16. Riley, *Biographical Encyclopedia.*

17. Holway, *Blackball Stars.*

18. Robert Peterson, *Only the Ball Was White.*

19. Holway, *Blackball Stars.*

20. Bjarkman, *Baseball with a Latin Beat.*

21. Mark Rucker and Peter C. Bjarkman, *Smoke.*

22. Holway, *Blackball Stars.*

23. *Baseball Magazine,* July 1917.

24. Bjarkman, *Baseball with a Latin Beat.*

25. Holway, *Blackball Stars.*

26. Robert W. Creamer, *Babe.*

27. *Baseball Magazine,* July 1917.

28. *Baseball Magazine,* July 1917.

29. Personal interview.

30. Personal interview.

31. Bjarkman, *Baseball with a Latin Beat.*

32. *Baseball Magazine,* June 1916.

33. HOF, Palmero file, March 9, 1915.

34. HOF, Palmero file, October 1913.

35. HOF, Palmero file, October 1913.

36. HOF, Palmero file, December 1913.

37. HOF, Palmero file, March 25, 1914.

38. HOF, Palmero file, March 25, 1914.

39. HOF, Palmero file, March 9, 1915.

40. HOF, Palmero file, October 1913.

41. HOF, Palmero file, March 25, 1914.
42. *Baseball Magazine,* September 1914.
43. HOF, Palmero file, March 9, 1915.
44. *New York Times,* September 25, 1915.
45. *Baseball Magazine,* July 1916.
46. *New York Times,* September 30, 1915.
47. *Baseball Magazine,* June 1916.
48. American Association League archive records.
49. Bill O'Neal, *The Texas League.*
50. Bill O'Neal, *The Texas League.*
51. *Baseball Magazine,* July 1918.
52. HOF, March 27, 1915.
53. Echevarría, *The Pride of Havana.*
54. *Baseball Magazine,* May 1914.
55. Bjarkman, *Baseball with a Latin Beat.*
56. Echevarría, *The Pride of Havana.*
57. Echevarría, *The Pride of Havana.*
58. *Baseball Magazine,* July 1917.
59. *Baseball Magazine,* July 1917.
60. *Baseball Magazine,* February 1912.
61. Echevarría, *The Pride of Havana.*
62. Holway, *Blackball Stars.*
63. David Cataneo, *Peanuts and Crackerjack.*
64. SABR, Negro League Researchers/Authors Group
65. *Baseball Magazine,* December 1918.
66. *Baseball Magazine,* May 1917.
67. *New York Times,* October 5, 1916.
68. *Sporting News,* March 8, 1917, and *New York Sun,* March 15, 1917.
69. *Baseball Magazine,* May 1914.
70. Personal interview.
71. Personal interview.
72. *Baseball Magazine,* September 1914.
73. Rucker and Bjarkman, *Smoke.*
74. O'Neal, *The Texas League.*

Chapter 4

1. Roberto González Echevarría, *The Pride of Havana.*
2. John B. Holway, *Blackball Stars.*
3. HOF, Luque file, July 8, 1957.
4. HOF, Luque file, July 14, 1957.
5. Echevarría, *The Pride of Havana.*
6. Fred Lieb, "Casual Comment," July 3, 1930.
7. Personal interview, September 25, 1998.
8. HOF, Luque file, July 1913.
9. Personal interview, October 18, 1998.
10. Angel Torres, *La Historia del Beisbol Cubano.*
11. Lieb, "Casual Comment."
12. HOF, Luque file, May 4, 1933.
13. HOF, Luque file, July 1913.
14. HOF, Luque file, July 1913.
15. Wes Singletary, *Al Lopez.*
16. Lieb, "Casual Comment."
17. Bill James and Mary A. Wirth, *The Bill James Historical Baseball Abstract.*
18. HOF, Luque file, July 1913

19. Mike Shatzkin, *The Ballplayers.*
20. Lieb, "Casual Comment."
21. Lieb, "Casual Comment."
22. *New York Times,* May 21, 1914.
23. *Baseball Magazine,* September 1926.
24. Felipe Alou, *My Life and Baseball,* and HOF, Luque file, May 4, 1933.
25. *Baseball Magazine,* September 1926.
26. HOF, Luque file, March 13, 1915.
27. *Baseball Magazine,* September 1926.
28. *Baseball Magazine,* September 1926.
29. HOF, Luque file, July 8, 1957.
30. *New York Times,* July 4, 1957.
31. Shatzkin, *The Ballplayers.*
32. Bjarkman, *Baseball with a Latin Beat.*
33. *Baseball Magazine,* June 1919.
34. Lieb, "Casual Comment."
35. HOF, Lague file, January 21, 1923.
36. Bjarkman, *Baseball with a Latin Beat.*
37. Echevarría, *The Pride of Havana.*
38. HOF, Luque file, December 29, 1923.
39. Torres, *La Historia del Beisbol Cubano.*
40. HOF, Lague file, February 17, 1922.
41. Newspaper column dated November 15, 1923.
42. Bob Considine, "Ivory from Cuba.
43. Bob Graham, "Graham's Corner."
44. Robert W. Creamer, *Stengel: His Life and Times.*
45. Creamer, *Stengel.*
46. Arthur Daley, *New York Times,* July 14, 1957.
47. HOF, Luque file, May 4, 1933.
48. Graham, "Graham's Corner."
49. HOF, Luque file.
50. Charles Alexander, *Rogers Hornsby.*
51. HOF, Luque file, November 29, 1928.
52. Torres, *La Historia del Beisbol Cubano.*
53. Dan Gutman, *Baseball Babylon.*
54. *Baseball Magazine,* November 1920.
55. Donald Honig, *Baseball When the Grass Was Real.*
56. Honig, *Baseball When the Grass Was Real.*
57. HOF, Luque file, February 4, 1926.
58. Cullen Cain, HOF Luque file, 1926.
59. *Baseball Magazine,* September 1926.
60. Cain, HOF Luque file.
61. Personal interview September 25, 1998.
62. Personal interview.
63. Personal interview.
64. Personal interview.
65. Personal interview.
66. Cain, HOF Luque file.
67. HOF, Luque file, October 28, 1926.
68. HOF, Luque file, November 1926.
69. William J. Klem, "My Last Big Game."
70. Mitchell V. Charnley, *Secrets of Baseball.*
71. HOF, Luque file, May 4, 1933.
72. Anthony J. Connor, *Voices from Cooperstown.*
73. HOF, Luque file, July 31, 1930.
74. Jack Kavanagh and Norman Macht, *Uncle Robbie.*

75. Alexander, *Rogers Hornsby.*
76. Charles Alexander, *John McGraw.*
77. Personal interview, December 14, 2003.
78. Daley, *New York Times.*
79. Personal interview, October 18, 2003.
80. Personal interview.
81. Personal interview.
82. Personal interview.
83. Personal interview.
84. *New York Times,* October 8, 1933.
85. Oleksak, *Beisbol.*
86. *New York Times,* July 14, 1957.
87. *New York Times,* July 14, 1957.
88. *New York Times,* October 8, 1933.
89. Considine, "Ivory from Cuba."
90. HOF, Luque file, July 3, 1957.
91. Danning, personal interview.
92. HOF, Luque file.
93. Personal interview.
94. Personal interview, August 31, 2000.
95. Personal interview.
96. Personal interview.
97. Personal interview.
98. Personal interview.
99. Personal interview.
100. *Life,* October 1, 1956.
101. *Life,* October 1, 1956.
102. *Sports Illustrated,* April 22, 1968.
103. *Life,* October 1, 1956.
104. *Life,* October 1, 1956.
105. *Saturday Evening Post,* March 8, 1947.
106. HOF, Luque file, June 7, 1949.
107. Personal interview.
108. Personal interview.
109. Author's collection, newspaper column by Martino Martínez, n.d.
110. Bjarkman, *Baseball with a Latin Beat.*
111. Personal interview.
112. Personal interview.
113. Personal interview, August 18, 2000.
114. Echevarría, *The Pride of Havana.*
115. Bill Werber and Paul Rogers, *Memories of a Ballplayer.*
116. Personal interview.
117. Personal interview.
118. Personal interview.
119. HOF, Luque file, March 28, 1940.
120. Personal interview.
121. HOF, Luque file, March 28, 1940.
122. George Kirksey, UP story, HOF Luque file.
123. Torres, *La Historia del Beisbol Cubano.*
124. Personal interview.
125. Echevarría, *The Pride of Havana.*
126. HOF, Luque file, March 10, 1938.
127. Personal interview.
128. Personal interview.
129. Echevarría, *The Pride of Havana.*
130. Personal interview, August 21, 2002.
131. HOF, Luque file, July 3, 1957.
132. Personal interview, August 17, 2001.
133. HOF, Luque file, July 8, 1957.
134. Bjarkman, *Baseball with a Latin Beat.*
135. Rucker and Bjarkman, *Smoke.*

Chapter 5

1. *Baseball Magazine,* May 1928.
2. *Baseball Magazine,* April 1912.
3. Personal interview.
4. Personal interview, October 18, 1998.
5. Personal interview.
6. Peter C. Bjarkman, "Peter Bjarkman's Revised Statistics."
7. Personal interview.
8. Personal interview.
9. Personal interview.
10. Personal interview.
11. Personal interview.
12. Personal interview.
13. Personal interview, December 10, 2000.
14. Personal interview.
15. Personal interview.
16. Personal interview.
17. "Bjarkman's Revised Statistics."
18. "Bjarkman's Revised Statistics."
19. Personal interview.
20. Buck Leonard, *The Black Lou Gehrig.*
21. Personal interview.
22. Emilio Navarro, personal interview.
23. Personal interview, July 18, 2001.
24. Personal interview.
25. Personal interview.
26. Personal interview, July 18, 2001.
27. Personal interview, August 18, 2000.
28. Personal interview.
29. Garcia, personal interview.
30. Personal interview.
31. Personal interview, August 17, 2001.
32. *Baseball Magazine,* July 1927.
33. Roberto González Echevarría, *The Pride of Havana.*
34. *Baseball Magazine.*
35. Walter Maranville, *Run, Rabbit, Run.*
36. Lieb, "Casual Comment."
37. *Baseball Magazine.*
38. *Newsweek,* May 29, 1944.
39. *Baseball Magazine,* July 1913.
40. Personal interview.
41. Bjarkman, *Baseball with a Latin Beat.*
42. Charles Alexander, *John McGraw.*
43. *Baseball Magazine,* July 1927.
44. Cataneo, *Peanuts and Crackerjack.*
45. Rucker and Bjarkman, *Smoke.*
46. Personal interview, November 8, 2003.
47. Personal interview.
48. Personal interview, January 23, 2004.
49. Okrent and Lewine, *The Ultimate Baseball Book.*
50. Echevarría, *The Pride of Havana.*

51. Rucker and Bjarkman.
52. Personal interview.
53. Personal interview.
54. Personal interview.
55. Regalado, *Viva Baseball.*
56. Personal interview.
57. Personal interview.
58. Personal interview.
59. Personal interview, January 10, 1999.
60. John Dreifort, *Baseball History from Outside the Lines.*
61. Riley, *Biographical Encyclopedia.*
62. Lawrence Ritter, *East Side West Side.*
63. Personal interview.
64. Oleksak, *Beisbol,* and HOF, Pompez file.
65. *Sports Illustrated,* August 9, 1965.
66. Personal interview.
67. Oleksak, *Beisbol.*
68. *Chicago Defender,* June 12, 1920.
69. Personal interview.
70. Personal interview.
71. Personal interview, January 13, 2001.
72. Personal interview.
73. Buck Leonard, *The Black Lou Gehrig.*
74. Personal interview.
75. Personal interview.
76. Riley, *Biographical Encyclopedia.*
77. *Sports Illustrated,* March 21, 1960.
78. *Sports Illustrated.*
79. *Sports Illustrated.*
80. Personal interview.
81. Personal interview.
82. Personal interview, May 21, 2001.
83. Personal interview, April 9, 2001.
84. HOF, Pompez file.
85. Personal interview.
86. Personal interview.
87. Personal interview.
88. Personal interview.
89. Personal interview.
90. Personal interview.
91. Roger Kahn, *A Flame of Pure Fire.*
92. *Ring Magazine,* February 1928.
93. Allen Klein, *Sugarball.*
94. Regalado, *Viva Baseball.*
95. Riley, *Biographical Encyclopedia.*

Chapter 6

1. James Riley, *Biographical Encyclopedia.*
2. Personal interview.
3. Luis Tiant and Joe Fitzgerald, *El Tiante.*
4. Personal interview.
5. Personal interview, February 2, 2001.
6. Personal interview.
7. Personal interview, January 13, 2001.
8. Personal interview.
9. Personal interview.
10. Personal interview.
11. Personal interview.
12. Personal interview, January 24, 2004.
13. Personal interview, November 11, 2003.
14. Personal interview.
15. Personal interview.
16. Personal interview.
17. Personal interview.
18. Personal interview.
19. Personal interview.
20. Personal interview.
21. Personal interview.
22. Personal interview.
23. Personal interview, July 7, 2001.
24. Personal interview, July 3, 2001.
25. Bob Considine, "Ivory from Cuba."
26. Personal interview.
27. Mark Rucker and Peter Bjarkman, *Smoke.*
28. Personal interview, May 21, 2001.
29. Personal interview.
30. Personal interview.
31. Roberto González Echevarría, *The Pride of Havana.*
32. Personal interview.
33. Personal interview, July 7, 2001.
34. Personal interview, July 3, 2001.
35. Holtzman, *No Cheering in the Press Box.*
36. Personal interview, December 10, 2000.
37. Personal interview.
38. Personal interview, December 18, 2003.
39. Personal interview.
40. Personal interview.
41. Personal interview.
42. Personal interview.
43. Personal interview.
44. Personal interview.
45. *Pictorial Yearbook, 1942.*
46. Considine, "Ivory from Cuba."
47. Personal interview.
48. Personal interview.
49. *Sports Illustrated,* April 22, 1968.
50. Bjarkman, *Baseball with a Latin Beat.*
51. *New York Times,* April 19, 1949.

Chapter 7

1. *Pictorial Yearbook, 1942.*
2. Personal interview, September 25, 1998.
3. Personal interview, August 7, 2002.
4. SABR, Negro League Researchers/Authors Group.
5. Riley, *Biographical Encyclopedia.*
6. Riley.
7. Personal interview, June 5, 2003.
8. HOF, Bithorn file.
9. *Pictorial Yearbook, 1942.*
10. HOF, Bithorn file.
11. Fred Lieb, *Baseball as I Have Known It.*
12. *Pictorial Yearbook, 1942.*
13. Lieb.

14. Personal interview, November 6, 2003.
15. HOF, Bithorn file.
16. "Bouncing Around with Ed Burns," May 13, 1943.
17. HOF, Bithorn file.
18. HOF, Bithorn file.
19. Personal interview.
20. HOF, Bithorn file.
21. Personal interview, January 13, 2001.
22. Personal interview.
23. Riley.
24. Personal interview, December 5, 2001.
25. Personal interview, July 2000.
26. "Ivory from Cuba."
27. "Ivory from Cuba."
28. "Ivory from Cuba."
29. *Newsweek,* May 29, 1944.
30. Personal interview, July 18, 2001.
31. Marcos Bretón and Luis Villegas, *Away Games.*
32. *The Saturday Evening Post,* March 8, 1947.
33. Danny Peary, *We Played the Game.*
34. Personal interview.
35. Personal interview, September 7, 2001.
36. *Pictorial Yearbook 1942.*
37. *Pictorial Yearbook 1942.*
38. Roberto González Echevarría, *The Pride of Havana.*
39. Personal interview.
40. Echevarría.
41. John Thorn and Pete Palmer, *Total Baseball.*
42. Kahn, *A Flame of Pure Fire.*
43. Personal interview.
44. Personal interview.
45. Personal interview.
46. Personal interview, February 2, 2001.
47. Personal interview.
48. Personal interview.
49. Rucker and Bjarkman, *Smoke.*
50. Riley.
51. Personal interview.
52. Personal interview.
53. Personal interview.
54. Personal interview.
55. Buck Leonard, *The Black Lou Gehrig.*
56. Personal interview, June 19, 2002.
57. Personal interview.
58. *Newsweek,* May 29, 1944.
59. Bjarkman, *Baseball with a Latin Beat.*
60. Rucker and Bjarkman.
61. *Pictorial Year Book 1942.*
62. O'Neal, *The International League.*
63. Echevarría.
64. Personal interview, July 6, 2003.
65. Personal interview.

Conclusion

1. Personal interview.
2. *Sports Illustrated,* August 9, 1965.

Appendix A

1. *Detroit News Tribune,* January (date unknown), 1912.
2. Personal interview, October 18, 1998.
3. Robert Cottrell, *Baseball, the Black Sox, and the Babe,* p. 66.
4. *Chicago Defender,* February 23, 1917.
5. John Holway, *Blackball Stars.*
6. Robert W. Creamer, *Babe: The Legend Comes to Life.*
7. Personal interview, December 14, 2003.
8. *The National Pastime 2002.*
9. *The Indianapolis Freeman,* April 16, 1910.
10. *Chicago Defender,* January 10, 1920.
11. *Chicago Defender,* January 3, 1920.
12. *Chicago Defender,* January 17, 1920.
13. *Chicago Defender,* March 13, 1920.
14. Lowell Reidenbaugh, *Baseball's Hall of Fame.*
15. Personal interview.
16. Janet Bruce, *The Kansas City Monarchs.*
17. Robert Peterson, *Only the Ball Was White.*
18. Lyle Wilson, "Mr. Foster Goes to Washington."
19. *Baseball Magazine,* June 1921.
20. Personal interview.
21. Personal interview.
22. Personal interview.
23. Roberto González Echevarría, *The Pride of Havana.*
24. Personal interview.
25. Personal interview, December 5, 2001.
26. *Newsweek,* May 29, 1944.
27. *Sports Illustrated,* August 9, 1965.
28. Kevin Kerrane, *Dollar Sign on the Muscle.*
29. Kerrane.
30. *Sports Illustrated,* August 9, 1965.
31. Personal interview, December 20, 2001.
32. Felipe Alou, *My Life in Baseball.*
33. Personal interview, August 19, 2003.

Appendix B

1. Personal interview.
2. Personal interview, July 7, 2001.
3. "Ivory from Cuba."
4. Personal interview, July 7, 2001.
5. Personal interview, July 7, 2001.
6. Personal interview.
7. Personal interview, December 10, 2001.
8. "Ivory from Cuba."
9. Marcos Bréton and José Villegas, *Away Games.*
10. Bréton and Villegas.
11. *Baseball Pictorial Yearbook 1942.*

Bibliography

Books and Periodicals

Alexander, Charles C. *John McGraw*. New York: Penguin, 1989.

_____. *Rogers Hornsby: A Biography*. New York: Henry Holt, 1995.

Alou, Felipe, with Herm Weiskopf. *My Life and Baseball*. Waco, Texas: Word Books, 1967.

Baseball Magazine. Feb. 1912, Apr. 1912, Mar. 1913, July 1913, Oct. 1913, May 1914, June 1914, Sept. 1914, June 1916, July 1916, May 1917, July 1917, July 1918, Dec. 1918, June 1919, Nov., 1920, June 1921, Sept. 1926, July 1927, May 1928.

Bjarkman, Peter C. *Baseball with a Latin Beat*. Jefferson, N.C.: McFarland, 1994.

_____. "Peter Bjarkman's Revised Statistics," *Elysian Fields Quarterly*, vol. 18, no. 2, 2001.

Bréton, Marcos, and José Luis Villegas. *Away Games: The Life and Times of a Latin Ballplayer*. New York: Simon & Schuster, 1999.

Bruce, Janet. *The Kansas City Monarchs: Champions of Black Baseball*. Lawrence: Univ. Press of Kansas, 1985.

Burns, Ed. "Bouncing Around with Ed Burns" column, May 13, 1943.

Cain, Cullen. Untitled article, 1926. (HOF files.)

Cataneo, David. *Peanuts and Crackerjack: A Treasury of Baseball Legends and Lore*. Nashville: Rutledge Hill, 1991.

Charnley, Mitchell V., ed. *Secrets of Baseball Told by Big League Players*. New York: D. Appleton, 1927.

Chicago Defender, Feb. 23, 1917; Jan. 3, 10, 17, 1920; Feb. 20, 28, 1920; Mar. 13, 1920; Apr. 17, 24, 1920; May 1, 6, 15, 1920; June 5, 12, 1920; Oct. 25, 1924;

Connor, Anthony J. *Voices from Cooperstown: Baseball's Hall of Famers Tell It Like It Was*. New York: Collier, 1984.

Considine, Bob. "Ivory from Cuba," *Collier's*, Aug. 3, 1940.

Cottrell, Robert C. *Blackball, The Black Sox, and The Babe: Baseball's Crucial 1920 Season*. Jefferson, N.C.: McFarland, 2002.

Creamer, Robert W. *Babe: The Legend Comes to Life*. New York: Penguin, 1974.

_____. *Stengel: His Life and Times*. New York: Simon & Schuster, 1984.

Daley, Arthur. Columns, *The New York Times*, Apr. 19, 1949; July 14, 1957. (The latter in Luque file, HOF.)

Dartnell, Fred. *"Seconds Out!": Chats About Boxers*. London: T.W. Laurie, 1924.

The Detroit News Tribune, January 1912.

Dreifort, John, ed. *Baseball History from Outside the Lines*. Lincoln: Bison/Univ. of Nebraska Press, 2001.

Echevarría, Roberto González. *The Pride of Havana: A History of Cuban Baseball*. New York: Oxford Univ. Press, 1999.

Evans, David. *The National Pastime 2002*. Lincoln: SABR/Univ. of Nebraska Press, 2002.

Foster, John B. Untitled column, Nov. 15, 1923.

Graham, Frank. "Graham's Corner," *New York Journal-American*, July 17, 1957.

Gutman, Dan. *Baseball Babylon*. New York: Penguin, 1992.

Holway, John B. *Blackball Stars: Negro League Pioneers*. Westport, Conn.: Meckler, 1988.

Holtzman, Jerome. *No Cheering in the Press Box*. New York: Holt, Rinehart and Winston, 1975.

Honig, Donald. *Baseball When the Grass Was Real*. New York: Coward, McCann & Geoghegan, 1975.

Indianapolis Freeman, Apr. 16, 1910

James, Bill, and Mary A. Wirth. *The Bill James Historical Baseball Abstract*. New York: Villard, 1988.

Kahn, Roger. *A Flame of Pure Fire: Jack Dempsey and the Roaring '20s.* New York: Harcourt Brace, 1999.

Kavanagh, Jack, and Norman Macht. *Uncle Robbie.* Cleveland/Lincoln: SABR/Univ. of Nebraska Press, 1999.

Kerrane, Kevin. *Dollar Sign on the Muscle: The World of Baseball Scouting.* New York: Beaufort, 1984.

Kirksey, George. United Press article, n.d., Luque file, HOF.

Klein, Alan M. *Sugarball: The American Game, the Dominican Dream.* New Haven: Yale Univ. Press, 1991.

Klem, William J. "My Last Big Game," *Collier's,* Apr. 21. 1951.

Lieb, Fred. *Baseball as I Have Known It.* Lincoln: Univ. of Nebraska Press. 1996. (Originally published New York: Coward, McCann & Geoghegan, 1977.)

_____. "Casual Comment" column, July 3, 1930.

Life, Oct. 1, 1956.

Leonard, Buck, with James A. Riley. *Buck Leonard, the Black Lou Gehrig: The Hall of Famer's Story in His Own Words.* New York, Carroll & Graf, 1995.

Maranville, Walter. *Run, Rabbit, Run: The Hilarious and Mostly True Tales of Rabbit Maranville.* Cleveland: Society for American Baseball Research (SABR), 1991.

Martínez, Martíno. Untitled newspaper column, author's collection.

Miñoso, Minnie, with Herb Fagen. *Just Call Me Minnie: My Six Decades in Baseball.* Champaign, Ill.: Sagamore, 1994.

Negro League Researchers/Authors Group, Society for American Baseball Research (SABR), Cooperstown, N.Y.

Negro Leagues Museum, Kansas City, Missouri.

The New York Sun, Mar. 16, 1917.

The New York Times, May 21, 1914; Sept. 25, 30, 1915; Oct. 5, 1916; July 19, 1917; Aug. 10, 11, 18, 1917; Feb 19, 21, 1920; Oct. 8, 1933; July 4, 1957.

Newsweek, May 29, 1944.

Okrent, Daniel, and Harris Lewine, eds. *The Ultimate Baseball Book.* Boston: Houghton Mifflin, 1991.

Oleksak, Michael M., and Mary Adams Oleksak. *Béisbol: Latin Americans and the Grand Old Game.* Grand Rapids, Mich.: Masters, 1991.

O'Neal, Bill. *The Texas League, 1888–1987: A Century of Baseball.* Austin, Texas: Eakin, 1987.

_____. *The International League: A Baseball History, 1884–1991.* Austin, Texas: Eakin, 1992.

Peary, Danny, ed. *We Played the Game: 65 Players Remember Baseball's Greatest Era, 1947–1964.* New York: Hyperion, 1994.

Peterson, Robert. *Only the Ball Was White: A History of the Legendary Black Players and All-Black Professional Teams.* New York: Oxford Univ. Press, 1992.

Philadelphia Inquirer, 1912.

Regelado, Samuel O. *Viva Baseball: The Latin Major Leaguers and Their Special Hunger.* Champaign: Univ. of Illinois Press, 1998.

Reidenbaugh, Lowell. *Baseball's Hall of Fame: Cooperstown, Where the Legends Live Forever.* New York: Arlington, 1986.

Riley, James A. *Biographical Encyclopedia of the Negro Baseball Leagues.* New York: Carroll & Graf, 1994.

Ring Magazine, Feb. 1928.

Ripley, Robert. Untitled article, Sept. 1912.

Ritter, Lawrence S. *East Side, West Side: Tales of New York Sporting Life, 1910–1960.* New York: Total Sports, 1998.

Rucker, Mark, and Peter C. Bjarkman. *Smoke: The Romance and Lore of Cuban Baseball.* New York: Total Sports, 1999.

Saturday Evening Post, Mar. 8, 1947.

Shatzkin, Mike, ed. *The Ballplayers: Baseball's Ultimate Biographical Reference.* New York: Arbor House/William Morrow, 1990.

Singletary, Wes. *Al Lopez: The Life of Baseball's El Señor.* Jefferson, N.C.: McFarland, 1999.

Sporting News, Mar. 8, 1917.

Sports Illustrated, Mar. 21, 1960; Aug. 9, 1965; Apr. 22, 1968.

Street & Smith's Baseball Pictorial Yearbook 1942. New York: Street & Smith, 1942.

Tarvin, A.H. Syndicated newspaper article, Aug. 9, 1923.

Thomas, Henry W. *Walter Johnson: Baseball's Big Train.* Lincoln: Univ. of Nebraska Press, 1998.

Thorn, John, and Pete Palmer, eds., with David Reuther. *Total Baseball.* New York: Warner, 1989.

Tiant, Luis, and Joe Fitzgerald. *El Tiante: The Luis Tiant Story.* Garden City: Doubleday, 1976.

Toot, Peter. *Armando Marsans: A Cuban Pioneer in the Major Leagues.* Jefferson, N.C.: McFarland, 2004.

Torres, Angel. *La História del Béisbol Cubano, 1878–1976.* Los Angeles(?): Torres, 1976.

Werber, Bill, and C. Paul Rogers III. *Memories of a Ballplayer: Bill Werber and Baseball in the 1930s.* Cleveland/Lincoln: SABR/Univ. of Nebraska Press, 2001.

Whelpley, James D., "The Cuban Census," *Harper's Weekly,* May 19, 1900.

Wilson, Lyle K. "Mr. Foster Comes to Washington," *The National Pastime 1998.* Cleveland/Lincoln: SABR/Univ. of Nebraska Press, 1998.

Archival Material, National Baseball Hall of Fame Library, Cooperstown, N.Y.

American Association League archive records.

Hiram Bithorn: Unidentified, undated, and/or unattributed clippings.

Louis Heilbroner: Memoranda to Garry Herrmann dated Dec. 30, 1910, and Jan. 4, 1911.

Adolfo Luque: Unidentified clippings dated July 1913, Mar. 13, 1915, Oct. 28, 1926, Nov. 1926, Nov. 29, 1928, July 31, 1930, May 4, 1933, Mar. 10, 1938, Mar. 28, 1940, July 8, 1957.

Unidentified, undated, and/or unattributed clippings.

Obituary, unidentified source, dated July 3, 1957.

Letters to Garry Herrmann dated Jan. 21, 1923, and Feb. 4. 1925.

Telegrams to Garry Herrmann dated Feb. 22, 1922, and Dec. 29, 1923.

Letter to Ford Frick dated Jun 7, 1949.

Armando Marsans: Unidentified clipping dated June 4, 1914.

Unidentified, undated, and/or unattributed clippings.

Letter to August Herrmann on *El Mundo* letterhead dated Mar. 2, 1913.

Telegram from W. G. Hirsig to August Herrmann dated July 18, 1913.

Telegram to Garry Herrmann dated Feb. 17, 1922.

Letter to Garry Herrmann dated Jan. 21, 1923.

José Méndez Unidentified newspaper clipping dated Nov. 6, 1915.

Emilio Palmero: Unidentified clippings dated Oct. 1913, Dec. 1913, Mar. 25, 1914, and Mar. 5, 1915.

Alex Pompez: Unidentified newspaper clipping, n.d.

Ramiro Seigle: Unidentified newspaper clipping dated Mar. 27, 1915.

Personal Interviews by the Author

Ruben Amaro Sr.: July 8, 2000, Oct. 10, 2003.
Santos Amaro: Dec. 10, 2000.
Julio Becquer: Dec. 5, 2001.
Dick Beverage: July 23, 2001, June 5, 2003.
Peter Bjarkman: Jan. 10, 1999.
Stewart Bower: Jan. 24, 2004.
José Cardenal: Dec. 12, 2001, Apr. 29, 2003.
Chico Carrasquel: July 18, 2001.
Phil Cavarretta: Nov. 6, 2003.
Orlando Cepeda: Apr. 9, 2001.
Joe Culinane: Dec. 14, 2003.
Harry Danning: Oct. 18, 2003.
Felix Delgado: Jan. 13, 2001.
Bobby Doerr: Nov. 11, 2003.
Bobby Estallela: July 3, 2001.
Rodolfo Fernández: Nov. 15, 1998, Dec. 6, 1998, Apr. 20, 2000.
Andres Galarraga: Sept. 7, 2001.
Dave Garcia: Sept. 3, 2000, Apr. 2, 2001.
Oscar Garmendia: Jan. 31, 1999, June 5, 2003.
Kid Gavilán (Gerardo Gonzalez): Aug. 21, 2002.
Preston Gómez: July 7, 2001, Dec. 8, 2001, Oct. 31, 2003.
Greg Gross: July 6, 2003.
Don Gutteridge: Nov. 8, 2003.
Ray Hayworth: June 6, 1998, Mar. 27, 1999, Apr. 20, 2000.
Myron "Red" Hayworth: Nov. 2, 1998, Apr. 30, 2000, July 23, 2003.
Willis Hudlin: May 29, 1998, June 6, 1998, Oct. 15, 1998, Dec. 14, 1998, Mar. 31, 1999.
Sid Hudson: July 7, 2001.
Max Lanier: Jan. 23, 2004.
Walter Masterson: July 7, 2001.
Jack McKeon: Aug. 19, 2003.
Charlie Metro: Dec. 10, 2000, Aug. 25, 2003.
Minnie Miñoso: June 27, 2000, Jan. 14, 2001.
Fausto Miranda: Feb. 1, 1999, July 22, 2000, June 5, 2003.
José Montiel: July 21, 22, 2000.
Manny Mota: May 21, 2001.
Emilio Navarro: Dec. 16, 1999, Mar. 22, 2000, Aug. 11, 2001.
Joe Nuxhall: Aug. 7, 2002.
Tony Oliva: Dec. 20, 2001.
Buck O'Neil: Nov. 4, 1998, June 2, 2000.
Camilo Pascual: Aug. 31, 2000.

Carlos Pascual: Aug. 12, 2000, Oct. 30, 2003.
Tony Pérez: Aug. 17, 2001.
Herb Plews: Dec. 10, 2001.
Ted "Double Duty" Radcliffe: Oct. 5, 1998, Nov. 6, 1998, Dec. 6, 1998.
Felo Ramírez: Aug. 18, 2000, Sept. 22, 2000, Aug. 19, 2003.
Ultiminio "Sugar" Ramos: Dec. 18, 2003.
Bobby Robinson: Oct. 18, 1998.
Lester Rodney: July 10, 1999, Mar. 6, 2001.
Billy Rogell: June 2, 1998, Oct. 22, 1998.
Harold Rosenthal: Oct. 23, 1998, Nov. 8, 1998, Dec. 17, 1998, Feb. 23, 1999.

Carlos Santiago: Apr. 18, 2000, May 21, 2001, Aug. 26, 2001.
Clyde Sukeforth: Sept. 25, 1998.
Tony Taylor: Aug. 18, 2001.
Eduardo Valero: June 5, 2003.
Armando Vasquez: Feb. 2, 2001.
Mickey Vernon: June 30, 2001, Oct. 30, 2003.
Bill Werber: July 9, 1999, May 12, 2001.
Adrian Zabala: Nov. 29, 1998, Feb. 1, 1999, Apr. 17, 1999, June 13, 1999, Aug 8, 2001.
Don Zimmer: June 19, 2002.

Index